THE

MISMEASURE

OF

PROGRESS

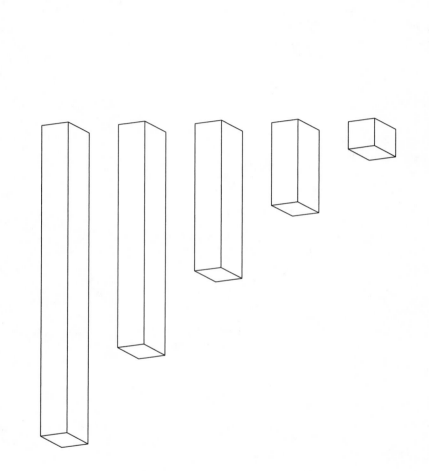

the

Mismeasure

of

Progress

Economic Growth and Its Critics

STEPHEN J. MACEKURA

The University of Chicago Press   *Chicago and London*

The University of Chicago Press, Chicago 60637
The University of Chicago Press, Ltd., London
© 2020 by The University of Chicago
Published 2020
Printed in the United States of America

29 28 27 26 25 24 23 22 21 20   1 2 3 4 5

ISBN-13: 978-0-226-73630-3 (cloth)
ISBN-13: 978-0-226-73644-0 (e-book)
DOI: https://doi.org/10.7208/chicago/9780226736440.001.0001

Library of Congress Cataloging-in-Publication Data

Names: Macekura, Stephen J., author.
Title: The mismeasure of progress : economic growth and
its critics / Stephen J. Macekura.
Description: Chicago : University of Chicago Press, 2020. | Includes
bibliographical references and index.
Identifiers: LCCN 2020024735 | ISBN 9780226736303 (cloth) |
ISBN 9780226736440 (ebook)
Subjects: LCSH: Economic development—Evaluation—
Methodology—History—20th century. | Economic development—
Evaluation—History—20th century. | Economic indicators—
History—20th century.
Classification: LCC HD75.M33 2020 | DDC 338.9—dc23
LC record available at https://lccn.loc.gov/2020024735

♾ This paper meets the requirements
of ANSI/NISO Z39.48-1992 (Permanence of Paper).

Contents

The Meaning
and Measurement
of Economic Growth

In 1969, British economist Dudley Seers was perplexed. Since the end of World War II, countries worldwide had experienced high rates of economic growth. In Western Europe, North America, and Japan, people were living longer, earning more money, and purchasing more consumer goods. In the Soviet Union, Eastern Europe, and China, high growth rates also reflected dramatic increases in economic production. Across the rest of the world, poorer countries were pursuing rapid growth to overcome centuries of exploitation and catch up with their wealthy counterparts.

Yet Seers felt that the world was in chaos. Despite the prosperity and peace that world leaders had said would come with "increases in national income," there were now "social crises and political upheavals" everywhere. Student activists, anti–Vietnam War protestors, and movements for civil rights, women's rights, and environmentalism all challenged the status quo. Seers also noted that growth rates had concealed troubling trends: persistent poverty in the United States and the United Kingdom, for instance, and high unemployment and political repression in what was then called the Third World. He wondered whether the belief that growth cured all ills was "rather naïve." He claimed not only that "economic growth ... may fail to solve social and political problems" but that "types of growth can actually cause them."[1]

To his fellow economists, Seers posed a simple but profound question: "What are we trying to measure?" The usual measure of growth in the West was gross national product (GNP). But perhaps, he suggested,

GNP was not a reliable or useful indicator of well-being. And even more than that, perhaps the pursuit of growth itself was misguided. By placing so much emphasis on growth as measured by GNP, Seers suggested, countries had neglected important aspects of governing: supporting civic life, encouraging the spiritual well-being of populations, promoting equality, protecting the natural world, and ensuring ample leisure time. The ongoing "addiction to the use of a single aggregative indicator" looked to Seers like "a preference for avoiding the real problems of development." Seers argued that countries needed new priorities—reducing inequality, eliminating poverty, providing more meaningful employment—and new metrics.[2]

Seers was not alone in making such arguments. In the pages that follow, I examine many like-minded thinkers: the growth critics. These were intellectuals and activists who along with Seers criticized economic growth as a policy goal and GNP as a measure of progress.[3] While many scholars and journalists have written about how growth became such a powerful concept during the twentieth century, far fewer have focused on dissenters who challenged the priority given to growth and GNP from the outset. This story is not the familiar one of GNP's architects and enthusiasts but the long history of critics who pursued alternative ways of measuring the world. For scholars, activists, and policy makers such as Seers, Phyllis Deane, Mahbub ul Haq, Morris David Morris, Nicholas Georgescu-Roegen, Herman Daly, and Marilyn Waring, questioning the meaning and measurement of growth was a necessary first step to creating a more just, equal, and sustainable world.

We need to know the history of the growth critics today, as a new generation echoes many of their arguments. Dozens of books and articles in the last decade have lamented the ongoing use of GNP and the continued faith that so many place in growth to solve political, social, or environmental problems.[4] The situation has become increasingly critical in light of the peril posed by global climate change and the increasing inequality within many countries. Today's critics hold that even though the global pursuit of economic growth has brought material prosperity to many, it now threatens to deepen wealth disparities and undermine the ecological basis for human civilization. While these arguments reflect contemporary concerns, they are not new. As we will see, the growth critics were here first. They struggled to bring about reforms on the necessary scale, but the traces of their efforts to imagine and build a world defined by something other than growth remain with us. The quest to redefine national economic aspirations and the measurement of economic life goes on.

The Growth Paradigm in Retrospect

What are the origins of economic growth as an idea? We can answer that question by studying economic growth not as a description of material changes (which is how the term is often used), but as a historical artifact of the twentieth century. The phrase "economic growth" is ubiquitous today, to the point that it seems universal and reflects an eternal desire for human beings to seek ever more production and consumption. Yet the concept is actually quite new.[5] Over the last couple of decades, scholars have demonstrated that the very notion of the coherent, calculable entity we call "the national economy" emerged only during the late nineteenth and early twentieth centuries. Statistical innovations made possible this new way of describing economic life. During the 1910s, 1920s, and 1930s, national income and product statistics gave meaning and numerical expression to the idea of discreet national economies. In turn, these statistical constructs formed the object—"the national economy"—that policy makers then sought to make grow.[6]

These new statistics did not produce the *desire* for growth, however. Economic growth became an explicit policy goal for national governments during the late 1930s and 1940s at the confluence of global depression, colonial upheaval, and war. Economists and statisticians devised national income and product accounts to help policy makers manage the Great Depression, plan strategies for colonial development, and mobilize for World War II, three major undertakings that called for new forms of economic knowledge to help manage new policy challenges. Economists also provided models of national economic activity. Policy makers working in important institutions (such as central banks and planning agencies) implemented fiscal and monetary policies based on those figures and models.[7]

In the postwar years, leaders worldwide adopted national economic growth—measured most often by GNP—as their foremost goal, promising that a rising tide of prosperity would lift all boats. They hoped that that future material abundance would create a world free from the class conflicts, social unrest, and political disorder that had characterized the recent past. Leaders believed that rapid economic growth was not merely desirable but necessary to meet the material needs of the postwar world. Growth also served as a symbol of national vitality. In countries as different as the United States, Sudan, and Japan, policy makers embraced economic growth measured by GNP as central to national purpose.[8] Growth became a "keyword," like "modernization" or "development," with wide impact.[9] By the 1950s and early 1960s, countries of all ideological stripes depicted their economic life in statistical aggregates, whether GNP or, as in the Soviet bloc, NMP (net material product). The Cold War between the United States and the Soviet Union was in large part a competition over which country could best generate growth at home and abroad. Both countries defined their goals for foreign aid and measured the success of their economies by using aggregate growth rates.[10]

The concept of sustained economic growth enabled leaders and citizens to imagine a world of nearly limitless prosperity. The pursuit of GNP growth, made possible by cheap fossil fuels, reshaped livelihoods and landscapes worldwide. It forever altered the nature of life on the planet. In historian John McNeill's words, "the overarching priority of economic growth was easily the most important idea of the twentieth century," but it was an idea that was defined by the twentieth century, too.[11]

In talking about "economic growth" as a historical construct, scholars have characterized it in a number of ways. It is an "ideology" of postwar capitalism, influencing leaders and citizens alike.[12] It is an "imperative" and powerful discourse used to define national purpose in the postwar international order.[13] Or, for Marxists, it is another way to characterize the accumulation of capital.[14]

Most usefully, historian Matthias Schmelzer has described economic growth as a "paradigm." The growth paradigm is a "particular ensemble of societal, political, and academic discourses, theories and statistical standards" that together produced a powerful and widely shared notion that growth, measured by GNP and the like, was "desirable, imperative, and essentially limitless."[15] This definition points to the significance of both ideas and practices. The desire for material improvement long predates the twentieth century, after all, but the specific national pursuit of economic growth measured by aggregate metrics was a feature the twentieth century.[16] From the 1940s onward, economic growth was both a powerful way to describe economic life and a social scientific concept defined by calculations that required data collection and measurement choices by experts. Many of the growth critics understood growth as a paradigm, too. Herman Daly, for example, first detailed growth as a "paradigm" in 1972 to criticize economists' faith in limitless growth and their use of GNP as an indicator of welfare.[17]

Ever since its emergence during the 1930s and 1940s, the growth paradigm has been powerful, flexible, and resilient. It has shaped the terms of economic debate and delimited the range of policy choices. Growth transcended the ideological and political divisions of the twentieth-century world. Countries capitalist and communist pursued growth as a goal, as did countries rich and poor. As Matthias Schmelzer has demonstrated, the growth paradigm rested on a set of assumptions often told as stories: that growth measured in aggregate statistics is necessary for progress; that growth is limitless; that it reflects overall well-being; that it should be the premier goal of national economic policy; that it acts as a solvent to defuse political and social conflict. These assumptions have been expressed, reinforced, and revived many times over in the previous eight decades.

The Growth Critics and the Limits of the Growth Paradigm

The growth paradigm, however, has never been that stable or universal. One major theme of this book is that there is a long history of conflict and disagreement over how to construct national income and product statistics—the numbers that give meaning to the concept of economic growth. These numbers are not just numbers: they are the basis of powerful quantitative claims about the world. National statistical offices collect specific kinds of data and calculate GNP, which then becomes an authoritative representation of "the economy." Citizens and leaders use those figures to argue for how to use the resources of the state and to justify various policy choices that do or do not grow the economy.[18] During the twentieth century, economists became especially important figures in this process. The discipline of economics supplied influential frameworks and concepts that leaders and everyday citizens alike used to make sense of the world. Economic statistics such as GNP have assumed a privileged role in public life and have defined popular expectations of what governments can and should do.[19] Yet acts of data collection and calculation are not neutral. Rather, they involve individuals making choices about what to count and exclude, how to acquire necessary data, and how to impute or assign value to activities in the world. We will see just how difficult it was to divine and manage these numbers.

We can recognize the tensions involved by looking at something as mundane as accounting practices. For instance, Simon Kuznets, an economist and statistician often credited with creating GNP, argued with his colleagues in the 1930s that spending on armaments should not count toward the national aggregates because it would give governments the perverse incentive to increase military spending to boost overall output. Economist Phyllis Deane tried to quantify unwaged work carried out by women in the British colonies during the early 1940s because she believed doing so would make their valuable labor visible in a way that conventional accounts did not. Economists Anwar Shaikh and Ahmet Tonak have recently claimed that many financial services are not productive because they simply move capital around. In all three instances, these arguments lost out, which had significant real-world effects. Recovering these efforts, though, exposes official statistics as objects of contestation. Studying such cases also reveals the value judgments inherent in statistical claims and shows why alternative ways of measuring fell short.[20]

The second major theme of this book is that many critics have also challenged the pursuit of growth itself as a worthwhile goal. Experts from around the world joined Dudley Seers in attacking the growth paradigm during the 1950s and 1960s, frustrated that, as happens today, the pursuit of GNP growth leads policy makers to neglect environmental degradation, social dislocation, and inequality. Likewise, during the 1970s reformers from the countries of the Global South, environmentalists, and feminist activists criticized the ways in which leaders used the growth paradigm to legitimate existing power relations—between countries, within countries, and even between individuals. Highlighting the close connection between ultimate goals and the metrics used to assess them, growth critics proposed other ways of defining social value and well-being that would prioritize not growth but concerns such as poverty alleviation, environmental sustainability, and social equality. Though they mostly fell into obscurity, those growth critics tried to craft an important counternarrative to the growth paradigm and its hegemony. By extension, contemporary growth critics join a history of dissent that is much longer and richer than often appreciated. But we can recover that history—and analyzing it will give us a valuable foundation for assessing future alternatives to the growth paradigm.

Focusing on debates over the meaning and measurement of economic growth allows us to see the history of twentieth-century governance in terms of conflicts among experts over the nature and limits of technocracy in modern life. The growth critics were all experts of varying kinds: many economists, but also sociologists, historians, and anthropologists. Most were from the wealthy capitalist countries of North America and Western Europe, though by the 1970s there were many scholars, activists, and political leaders from the Global South and from the Soviet Union and Eastern Europe who also critiqued the growth paradigm. Many growth critics were fundamentally transnational in their thinking, making connections across political and ideological borders in order to better assess the strength and flaws of the growth paradigm. They drew on their scholarly training and their ability to travel and communicate with like-minded thinkers from other places. They used their relatively strong positions of social influence within the academy, within national governments, and within international organizations to advocate for change. The growth critics often envisioned their primary audiences as both policy makers and the general public, although their activism tended to give priority to the former.

Dudley Seers illustrates this well. Seers studied at Pembroke College of the University of Cambridge in the 1930s and worked at Oxford University in the early 1950s. He also traveled extensively throughout the British Empire and visited many postcolonial countries throughout his professional life. As a development economist seeking to change policy, he networked extensively at international conferences and workshops, built an important think tank with the support of the UK government and multiple international organizations, and worked for the UK's Ministry of Overseas Development. His advanced training in statistics, experience advising on growth plans, and proximity to the halls of power all shaped his thinking and afforded him multiple ways to promote his ideas about how best to study and conceptualize social change.[21] He was a technocrat whose experiences led him to criticize technocracy. And as was the case for so many other growth critics, his initial participation in forging the growth paradigm shaped his subsequent criticisms of it.

Mismeasuring the World, Past and Present

Today's growth critics have built on this history as they continue to illuminate the limits and downsides of growth. Humanity as a whole is far richer than ever before, but a handful of individuals from a few countries possess an ever-greater proportion of that wealth. GNP was designed for a world of manufactured goods and capital flows managed by nation-states, yet the world today is one of digital exchanges, tax havens, globalized supply chains, extensive capital flows, and poorly regulated financial institutions. At the same time, the pursuit of growth, based on fossil fuels, has imperiled our planet and undermined the material basis of future abundance. Global climate change alone impels a reconsideration of the growth paradigm.

To challenge the growth paradigm does not demand rejecting quantification or expertise. In a technocratic world, statistical arguments advance ideological positions with greater efficacy than do appeals to morality alone. The divide between statistics and stories, between quantitative and qualitative depictions of the world, is often overstated. Statistics *are* a form of storytelling; quantitative evidence *needs* qualitative expressions of moral purpose to gain wide purchase. Put differently, new ways of measuring economic life can lead us to design new paradigms that promise a more equal and ecologically sustainable world. In the United States today, for instance, national economic growth rates conceal ominous social and economic trends, such as the maldistribution of income, the dramatic decline in life expectancy for middle-aged white people, and the racial wealth gap exacerbated by the great recession of 2007–9.[22] Employing measures that expose these trends, which aggregates such as GNP do not, can promote narratives that can galvanize public attention and guide policy changes. They also serve as a reminder that statistics are not beyond or above politics. Reformers must embrace the "frank politics of numbers" by using different kinds of statistics to promote new moral commitments about the most important issues of our time.[23]

There is an added urgency to this project. The economic expansion of the twentieth century may well have been an outlier—growth was exceptional, not typical.[24] This reality should spur new ways of living as well as provide new narratives and paradigms to make sense of our world. Economic growth long appealed to many political leaders because it allowed them to avoid addressing political trade-offs and class conflict. It sustained the fiction that human beings are somehow separate from a nonhuman "nature," ignoring the intimate and dense connections between the two. In order to create a more just and equal society, we must have a clear understanding of our collective needs beyond growth.

Reformers today, however, should be wary of replacing one set of numbers with another. As we will see, attempts to promote alternative indicators outside the growth paradigm have too often attested to the limits of technocratic innovation—in large part because they have not been engaged with a broader politics that could mobilize people to envision and desire change. As activists and policy makers seek to find new ways of measuring well-being, they should view these stories as cautionary tales and sources of inspiration. They must find ways to measure and value the lives of people and the health of the planet. They must produce information about how people live in relation to one another, recognizing that such knowledge is the foundation for effective and accountable politics. They must design metrics and nurture a political culture that exposes inequality and deprivation and that offers targeted interventions to redress such ills. They must build political movements and coalitions that make use of this information and present it through compelling narratives. In short, rethinking the pursuit of economic growth today requires more than just new numbers. As Dudley Seers recognized in 1969, asking what we are trying to measure is political. We measure what we value, and we value what we measure. To envision the world anew requires new tools, but also a clear articulation of the ethical commitments and politics that give them force.

But first, to understand the options that were foreclosed in the past and the origins of our current predicament, we begin with the history of social measurement before the growth paradigm. Before policy makers and leaders embraced economic growth as their preeminent policy goal, social scientists and social reformers had developed many other ways of measuring and valuing the world. Although the growth paradigm obscured these endeavors, they offer an important starting point to understand the history of debates over the meaning and measurement of economic growth.

ONE

Standard of Living, GNP, and the Narrowing of National Statistics

Statistics reflect objects in the real world, but they also give meaning to abstract concepts that come to have practical power. For example, ask a simple question: what is a country? Answers could include descriptions of landscapes or histories of the people who live there. Or they could refer to quantities: the number of the people residing within defined borders, the total territory under its control, and so forth. These statistics—total population, total area—refer to actual parts of a country. They are produced by counting and measuring and adding. What may seem like a simple process, though, is rife with complications. Errors in data collection and calculation are possible. So too are disputes over categories of citizenship that define who belongs to a particular country. Producing those statistics is less straightforward than it appears at first glance.

When we try to measure abstract concepts, the challenges are even greater. Take the notion of a national economy. To give a statistical representation of the economy requires many value judgments and exclusions. Defining a national economy requires creating a category called the "economic" and grouping together all the things we decide qualify as economic activity, such as building a factory, paying workers, selling shoes, or buying a bus ticket. All these activities are priced, paid for with money that marks their value. Relying on monetary exchange as an indicator of value, however, excludes those aspects of the social world deemed to be "noneconomic," such as taking a walk or participating in a protest. After deciding what is or is not "economic," the statistician must then decide on a methodology for imputing value to all those activities. Perhaps this comes from reviewing data of sales and purchases from governments and private businesses, and then using those figures to approximate the total goods and services in a nation. But even that leads to more questions. For example, if the owners of a factory in country A actually live in country B (and take profits to country B), how should statisticians in country A account for that factory? Or suppose country A has excellent data collection services, but country B does not. Country B also features a large population of subsistence-level producers—people who grow their own food, for example—so there are no prices associated with much of their economic activity. To what extent are country A and country B even comparable? Reaching a consensus on how to calculate something called "the national economy" is not an easy task. It is fraught with many value-laden decisions and depends on trustworthy information.

Next, deciding what to do with such statistics also raises important questions. For instance, how should leaders use these metrics when they have them? Should they make decisions about how to spend money based on a number that represents the entire economy, hoping that doing so would make that figure grow? One benefit of doing so is the possibility of clear public accountability. Accounting and accountability are closely intertwined. If a politician promises to make an economy grow, and then fails to do so, the public can hold that person accountable by voting for another one. But why should a leader emphasize economic statistics over alternative indicators, such as social or environmental ones? For the historian, there are even more questions to consider. What do the choices about which statistics to use reveal about cultural and political context in a given time? And why have some statistics received greater attention than others in the past?

This chapter explores these questions by analyzing statistics and state building during the late nineteenth and early twentieth centuries. It reveals how a transnational movement to depict workers' "standard of living" won widespread acclaim. Progressive reformers in the United States and Western Europe and social scientists and labor advocates in global organizations such as the International Labour

Organization (ILO) and the League of Nations produced standard-of-living statistics with the hope that such numbers would inspire governments to make targeted interventions that would improve the well-being of the most downtrodden and precarious groups in society.[1] Over time, however, experts and policy makers came to prefer national income and product metrics. Though both ways of measuring and depicting economic life attracted widespread intellectual and policy interest in the 1920s and 1930s, policy makers ultimately embraced aggregate national income and product statistics in the face of global depression and world war.

A Brief History of Measuring Society

Social measurement has a long history. Societies have used statistics to measure and track economic activity for millennia. The earliest form of measurement was single-entry accounting, which tracks direct transactions of goods exchanged. The Sumerians used clay tokens for this kind of accounting as far back as 3500 BCE. The famed Babylonian legal code of Hammurabi established simple accounting rules, too. In ancient Athens, accounting became a crucial foundation for democratic self-government. Official record keeping allowed for comptrollers and auditors to oversee public accounts. Corruption still existed, of course, but the Athenians imbued single-entry bookkeeping with moral and political authority.[2] During the Qin dynasty, Chinese administrators standardized units of weight and measurement and used standardized script to organize tax collection.[3] Financial accounting served as the bedrock of political accountability. With these early economic accounts, states could organize and manage basic information on their populations and territory.

Economic accounting practices remained largely static until Italian merchants and statesmen established the first double-entry accounting practices around 1300. Double-entry accounting allowed for more complex measurement of economic transactions, since it captured both debt and credit in a given exchange. It also incorporated time. If a debtor paid back some money in installments, double-entry ledgers could show how much was owed at any given moment. As trade activity increased and covered longer distances, merchants tracked debts as goods left storehouses and accounted for the income from sales once exchange had taken place. Double-entry accounting also served a broader public purpose. Balanced books implied responsible governance. When ruling classes of the Italian republics made public their economic transactions, they could claim their rule was responsible and prudent. Over the next few centuries, the political valence of such accounting waned as monarchies replaced republican governments across the world. Though monarchs were often far less interested in public accountability, double-entry accounting continued to be used in private realms.[4]

European imperial elites revived interest in economic accounting as empires seized territory beyond their borders. To both prepare for eventual war and count the productive potential of territories they aimed to exploit, the English crown began to experiment in measuring national economic activity. One of the earliest attempts to measure total national wealth came in the 1640s, when English doctor William Petty counted land in Ireland that the English state could tax. During the remaining century, officials argued over the best ways to measure and thus define what counted as a vital component of economic activity. For Petty, land and labor determined output, thus they demanded priority. For others, calculating the balance of trade provided better insight into national prosperity.[5] British elites continued to debate how to measure many aspects of economic life well into the eighteenth century, as quantitative analysis entered partisan politics.[6]

During the eighteenth and nineteenth centuries, governments expanded their collection and use of statistics. As nationalism surged during the nineteenth century, government statistics became an important part of national self-definition. Emerging experiments in government—as in the United States and France—that embraced representative democracy required regular censuses to determine the number of eligible voters.[7] Census data, moreover, often defined the boundaries of national belonging and social difference by enumerating who counted—literally—as members of the nation.[8]

Economic statistics became central to national commerce, too. Between 1840 and 1880, twenty-four countries established reliable trade figures.[9] By the late nineteenth century, political economists and statisticians in France, Germany, and the United Kingdom experimented with rudimentary calculations of the "national income," which described the annual flow of material goods and capital across a country's borders.[10] Large companies and governments adopted statistics to guide policies that were based on the effects that shifts in labor and consumption would have on capital accumulation and market activity.[11] Quantification pervaded everyday life, including new measures for the energy content of food (the calorie) that elites used to visualize, track, and manage food supplies across cultural and political borders.[12]

There were three important aspects of these changes that warrant mention here. First, in much of Europe and the United States statistics emerged as a field of study and a way of thinking through complex social problems.[13] The use of statistical reasoning took hold through the work of a handful of scientists who linked the emerging study of probability, error theory, and the measurement of mass phenomena. French scientist Pierre-Simon Laplace pioneered a mechanical explanation of the solar system based on probabilistic statistical calculations. Laplace's innovation was to note that statistics offered a way to move toward "precise measurement of a phenomenon that eludes precision."[14] When tracking either the orbit of a comet or the mortality rate of a population, one could never completely measure the object. But with a large enough sample size and a few calculations, a distribution would emerge that would show, probabilistically, how the comet would travel and what the mortality rate would be for a given population. Statistical thinking offered a way for leaders and lay citizens alike to understand large-scale changes in a world defined by nationalism, imperial rivalry, social revolution, population growth, industrialization, and migration. With these statistics, it "seemed to be possible to uncover general truths about mass phenomena even though the causes of each individual action were unknown and might be wholly inaccessible."[15]

Second, the use of statistics sparked larger debates about what nation-states needed to know about their subjects and how to use numbers in governance. Collecting data about population size, trade volume and balance, and mortality became part and parcel of how nation-states rendered their subjects "legible," in James Scott's terminology.[16] This was not a smooth process. Experts debated—as they had in seventeenth-century England—what should be emphasized in determining the size of a country's wealth. The act of placing a numerical value on the total economic stock within a nation's borders, though, transformed economic life into a measurable, calculable reality that could be used to describe and explain changes in a nation-state's overall economic health.[17]

Finally, it is important to recognize that, until the mathematization of economic knowledge in the 1920s and 1930s, most economists believed the factors of production were labor, capital, and land. This framework led to many debates about how the factors interacted and which were most significant. For instance, the French physiocrats of the eighteenth century believed that only agriculture was able to generate a net surplus year after year, so they defined both land and manufacturing—the other two key sectors of the economy—as sterile.[18] There were also great debates during the nineteenth century over whether natural resources were finite and thus economic life would eventually reach a "stationary state," in John Stuart Mill's term, or whether, *pace* David Ricardo, endless technological innovation and trade would circumvent natural limits. Popular statistical studies pointed in both directions, especially focusing on vital resources such as coal for industrializing economies. Thus optimists about rising future wealth and material abundance ran up against concern about the finitude of the natural world, in a contentious debate that would greatly intensify in the middle of the twentieth century.[19] Besides these occasional intellectual quarrels, though, nature was rarely counted as anything other than a stock of resources that could be transformed into commodities.

Thinking of a country's economic life in statistical terms related to its productive capabilities, and quantifying it in monetary ways allowed leaders to define their identity and compare themselves to others in numerical terms. Imperial powers used such numbers to compare themselves against their adversaries and assess one another's war-making capabilities. For example, in 1900 the Imperial Statistical Office of the Wilhelmine Empire produced a major tome that downplayed internal tensions to emphasize instead the "unity of the national economy" as a source of potential strength while revealing vulnerabilities relative to rivals such as France.[20] Policy makers and experts also deployed statistics to justify racial and ethnic exclusion. Sir Robert Giffen, former president of the United Kingdom's Royal Statistical Society, for instance, used statistics to show that rapid European population growth would "make European preponderance more secure" and thus could allay "the nightmares of yellow or black perils arising from the supposed overwhelming mass of yellow or black races."[21] Racial fears pervaded the writing of many early twentieth-century economists and social scientists, and eugenicists bolstered their beliefs with advanced statistical methods.[22] Experts also presented aggregate figures such as national income to heighten cultural and racial fears about shifts in national power. Japan, in particular, provoked racial and cultural anxieties among American observers because economic statistics suggested the country was poised for future prosperity and possible expansion.[23]

As industrialization took off in the late nineteenth century, the total size of a country's economy also revealed the total wealth available to be divided among competing classes. Thus, aggregate economic statistics also appealed to reformers who saw them as a first step in pursuing redistributive policies.[24] The Industrial Revolution and recurrent boom-bust economic cycles of the mid-to-late nineteenth century spawned myriad political and social upheavals in the United States and Europe. This was a core paradox at the heart of industrial capitalism. It brought tremendous wealth to some individuals and increased productive capacity, but it also generated widespread poverty and inequality. In response, militant labor activists and growing radical political movements from communism to anarchism fought for more equitable societies. Concerned about these trends, social scientific reformers collected data on the social and economic aspects of everyday life for workers.

Social Statistics, Social Reform, and the Standard of Living, 1850–1930

Social statistics became a topic of great interest to experts across the United States and Western Europe during the middle and late nineteenth century as industrialization reshaped societies. By 1881, nearly 44 percent of British workers, 26 percent of American workers, and 36 percent of German workers labored in industrial enterprises. By 1885, Great Britain, the United States, Germany, and France together accounted nearly 70 percent of world's total industrial production. In countries that had been largely agrarian or mercantile for generations, many reformers, intellectuals, and policy makers explored how these economic transformations had reshaped the social order.[25]

Social surveys and direct observations became the chief way to collect this data. French engineer-turned-statistician Frédéric Le Play was a pioneer of social research. He mixed direct participant observation with detailed quantitative studies of family budgets to depict the state of workers' families across Europe in his 1855 collection *Les Ouvriers Européens*. He saw such research as a tool to "furnish statesmen with a solid basis for resolving social questions."[26] In the United States, "moral statistics" on topics such as alcohol use, school attendance, and literacy helped elites to govern and track rapidly growing populations and also helped reformers to identify social ills and direct public attention to them.[27] The incipient labor movement likewise collected data to illuminate inequalities and poor living conditions of industrial workers.[28]

By the turn of the twentieth century, experts widened their scope to render rich and detailed portraits of poverty. British merchant and statistician Charles Booth's monumental *Life and Labour of the People in London*, published in seventeen volumes between 1889 and 1903, presented an array of charts and tables that quantified the depth of poverty in London.[29] In the early twentieth century, American progressives linked family well-being with the conditions of the built and natural environment, under the assumption that urban environments were "affecting injuriously large numbers" of residents.[30] Since progressive reformers often viewed the family as a microcosm of society, they believed that collecting statistics on "changes and disorders" within the family could provide policy makers with sufficient information to redress inequalities or the more grievous aspects of industrial life. Studies of family consumption habits and living patterns proliferated.[31]

Many of these social scientists sought to construct supposedly "objective" measures of poverty that balanced comprehensive data collection with concern for local differences. Objectivity, however, was elusive. The surveys often reflected the ingrained racial, cultural, gender, and class biases of the researchers. Nevertheless, this research provided "a framework within which poverty could be investigated as a problem of political or social economy . . . and of the policies and practices governing the distribution of income and wealth." Survey data gave reformers the empirical grounds to argue for understanding poverty less as a cultural or behavioral failing—as older notions of "pauperism" or "dependency" did—and instead as a policy failure that could be rectified through collective action.[32] Both grassroots activists and paternalistic elites used social statistics to make scientifically grounded claims about how best to reshape workers' lives.

Yet there was little consensus among reformers and policy makers about which statistics to emphasize. For instance, many labor leaders focused on workers' wages in order to argue for a minimum or "fair" wage.[33] Other reformers emphasized rising prices for consumer goods, especially as concern over the new concept of "inflation" found statistical expression. Economists began to construct "cost of living" indexes to capture such changes.[34] In their early years, creating the indexes was especially difficult in large countries such as the United States, where prices varied widely by region. Because of this regional variation, these metrics served a broader national project, for "the cost of living furnished a way of talking" about the national economy and "whether most people benefited from it."[35] Such indexes had the benefit of down-

playing distributional or quality-of-life concerns in favor of emphasizing the virtues of mass production by implying more goods would
decrease prices for all.[36] By the end of the nineteenth century, social
reformers had quantified many aspects of everyday life—including
unemployment levels, wages, suicides, crime rates, literacy rates, and
commodity prices—to track the effects of corporate practice and government policy on workers' lives.

This desire to measure and define social life found its most ambitious expression in a transatlantic movement to quantify the notion
of a "standard of living" for the "average" worker.[37] The notion that
experts could divine a widely comparable set of living standards
emerged as the United States and European countries grappled with
the disruptive and transformational effects of rapid industrialization, migration, and mass consumption.[38] In the United States, where
the concept was most widely embraced, standard of living generally
referred to the consumptive habits of American workers. It differed
from cost-of-living statistics, which tracked how much goods costs and
whether an abstract individual or family had the capacity to purchase
them. Standard-of-living advocates sought a more comprehensive
depiction of how people lived. For instance, a pioneering 1890 study
took a sample of American families and graded their standard of living based on the ratio of "paupers" to the general population; average
consumption of meat, wheat, oats, rye, and tropical fruits; per capita
use of cotton, wool, and silk for clothing; quality of housing; education;
wages compared to Europe; and land ownership.[39] Other studies took
a similar smattering of consumer goods and included basic income, as
well, implying directly that higher wages were necessary for a higher
standard of living.[40] Measuring workers' daily lives placed "notions of
the standard of living at almost the center of current economic thinking" by the 1920s.[41]

Social scientists in the United States and Europe linked the phrase
with a set of numbers that policy makers could use to compare classes
of workers within a country or across borders. They did so at a time
of tremendous unrest. World War I brought most of the industrial
world into direct conflict, reshaping state-society relations and gen-

erating a massive increase in economic activity. The 1917 revolution in Russia represented a radical challenge to the liberal capitalist order. Strife between labor and capital remained intense and widespread. Labor activism roiled major cities across the capitalist world. In 1919 alone millions of workers in many industries went on strike across the United States and Western Europe, and general strikes gripped urban areas from Seattle to the Ruhr to Barcelona.[42]

In this context, beginning in 1920 the International Labour Organisation (ILO) and the League of Nations sought to standardize the definition and collection of standard-of-living statistics. The ILO did so with a particular focus on "the very marked unrest among the workers" in countries deteriorating after the war (especially Germany), "in order to throw light upon the situation and to ascertain the means already adopted or contemplated in such countries for securing to the workers an adequate living wage." The ILO carried out social surveys to amass data on workers' income, wages, cost of living, and access to food and shelter.[43]

In 1929, the ILO began a more ambitious inquiry to compare living standards between Europe and North America. It did so with the backing of two corporate titans: American retail magnate Edward Filene and American industrialist Henry Ford. The Ford Motor Company hoped to use the study to figure out how much (or rather, how little) it could pay European workers as it expanded production in the continent, to "provide the individual worker, with or without dependents, with the necessary standard of living for maximum efficiency."[44] Long a fan of Ford, Filene contributed $25,000 to the effort. These wealthy benefactors made the study possible, but their support created concerns for some within the ILO, as well. ILO director Albert Thomas, a prominent French socialist politician and journalist, "complained about the terms and timetable set by his sponsors that jeopardized the ILO's claim to scientific impartiality and his mission to promote workers' rights," but he nonetheless believed the inquiry worth pursuing because he thought "living standards held the key to employment and international peace."[45] In the end, their project better exposed methodological difficulties than provided clear solutions. But it was

(1) Director-General Albert Thomas, under whose leadership the ILO sponsored studies into workers' standard of living across the world during the late 1920s and 1930s. Photograph courtesy of the ILO.

a starting point. Between 1920 and 1939, the ILO carried out studies of workers' income and cost of living in all European countries, the United States, Japan, China, India, and South America, all of which reflected a widespread desire to map out measurements of workers' basic wages and ability to purchase goods such as food, heating, electric light, and clothing.[46]

For all the interest in standard-of-living statistics, there was seldom much agreement on a definition for standard of living within the United States, and even less so when attempting to make comparisons to Europe.[47] Americans held a much more consumerist definition of standard of living than their European counterparts, who stressed the hard-to-define qualities of a good life. French labor economist François Simiand, for instance, distinguished between standards of a "manner of living" (*train de vie*) based on consumer choices and a "style of living" (*genre de vie*) based on noneconomic conditions such as social standing, the quality of a physical environment, and religious affiliation. He believed American scholars' focus on calorie intake or dollars spent on clothing were misguided at best and dehumanizing—turning human beings into consuming automatons existing outside cultural context—at worst. The distinctions between the diverse approaches touched on all aspects of life. At a discussion organized and hosted by the French Institute of Sociology to debate the Ford-ILO inquiry, French experts mocked American habits as poor imitations of the good life. Renowned sociologist Marcel Mauss quipped that American workers "don't even know what good cooking means" because "even women on the farms serve pork and beans from a can."[48]

Mauss's remark revealed important truths lurking beneath the inquiry. The research endeavor encapsulated the desire to transcend class conflict by raising standards of living, defined in consumerist terms. It also raised the important question of the purpose of such statistical investigations. The ILO-Ford inquiry was not primarily dedicated to dispassionate study of how people in European cities lived. As ILO officials explained to Edward Filene, the study did not "involve enquiries into wages and standards of living in European towns, but merely into the cost of giving European workers an American standard."[49] But for some the good life meant being able to buy cans of pork and beans; for others it signified the capacity to live without relying on canned goods. It remained unclear how meaningful any "standard" definition of standard of living could be and whether such a definition should be applied to different places and social groups in distinct cultural contexts.

Furthermore, effective standard-of-living statistics required reliable and extensive data, yet few countries had the capacity to collect and update such information. Writing to Royal Meeker, an American economist and head of the Scientific Division of the ILO, British economist and statistician Alfred Flux noted that reliable and comparable index numbers for cost-of-living statistics for most countries were inconceivable. "We can count on the fingers of one hand the countries which obtain information even approximately adequate" to such a task, he wrote.[50] Absent reliable data, a meaningful metric of standard of living would be elusive.

There was also debate among experts over the ultimate purpose that standard-of-living statistics should serve. For some, a high standard of living represented the need for hard work and was a tool for disciplining workers for their lack of productivity. Early experiments demonstrated that overall well-being depended on "the industry of the producing classes," wrote the American social scientist J. Richards Dodge in 1890. Firmly within a producerist ethos, he claimed such statistics revealed the need to encourage the "largest variety of production" across the country.[51] They could also be used to serve nationalist aims. American social worker Maurice Hexter, for instance, suggested that standard-of-living statistics revealed the superiority of American factory life. "Compare the sodden and slovenly population of India and China with the progressive workmen of a New England town. Compare the efficiency of the Ford automobile shops with a $5.00 minimum daily wage and any other similar factory. With this as a basic fact we can readily deduce the importance of a rising standard of living," he wrote.[52] For others, standard-of-living statistics called on policy makers and leaders to pay close attention to the distribution of wealth and opportunity. French sociologist Maurice Halbwachs argued that social statistics—especially those about consumption habits—clearly revealed class distinctions in industrial society. Although he believed that different cultures defined wants and needs differently, such as whether one preferred fresh pork and beans to canned, he argued that social statistics could express the more invidious differences that arose between classes. Consumption habits, whether a family relied on cheap beans or regularly ate more expensive foodstuffs, reflected class divisions.[53] With a keen understanding of such differences, states could then level out opportunities and access to goods by increasing social insurance and welfare, by more progressive taxation, or by other redistributive policies.

Standard-of-living metrics in particular and social statistics more broadly piqued policy makers' interest in the 1920s. National governments increasingly sought social profiles of everyday life. The United

States under Herbert Hoover was a leader in this regard. During his time as secretary of commerce from 1921 to 1929, Hoover oversaw a vast expansion of the department's data collection and statistical analysis, culminating in the publication of a massive report, which buoyed Hoover's optimism about American prosperity. As president, in his first year Hoover created the Research Committee on Social Trends to produce more related research. Led by University of Chicago sociologist William Ogburn, the committee produced a major study of social life in multiple American communities that mixed participant observation, social surveys, and statistical analysis. It marked the high tide of the technocratic embrace of standard-of-living and social statistics as tools for policy making.[54]

As various organizations studied the standard of living and social lives of citizens all across the world, the economic context shifted rapidly. What began with a stock market crash in the United States in the fall of 1929 quickly turned into a global calamity. The Great Depression generated deep suffering around the world. Global trade waned, international monetary cooperation collapsed, and faith in liberal capitalism eroded. Policy makers yearned for solutions to redress a crisis of unparalleled enormity. And as they searched for answers, they also demanded new ways of measuring economic life to understand the scope of the problems around them.

The Great Depression and National Income Studies

The Great Depression struck amid two important trends in statistical research. Standard-of-living and social statistics were one. The other built on earlier research on national wealth to calculate the total economic activity within a country's borders. This research—on economic activity loosely fitting under the umbrella term "national income"— also featured fractious debates over what to count and how best to use the information. Attempting to measure the national income of a territory was a very minor endeavor involving only a few economists and statisticians working with limited data during the late nineteenth and early twentieth centuries.[55] As late as 1916, Irving Fisher, one of the leading American economists, could justifiably lament, "Unfortunately, there are no available statistics for income in the United States. We can only guess as to what the amount of it may be."[56] Social statistics had received far more interest from both reformers and experts during the early decades of the twentieth century.

During the interwar years, however, scholarly and public interest in national income statistics increased. Economics became more formalized and increasingly mathematical, with the introduction of abstract models.[57] Likewise, the necessity of mobilizing industrial resources and raising taxes to fight World War I impelled government officials and statisticians to seek new ways of measuring economic activity, a trend that continued into the late 1910s and 1920s to help countries track payment of war reparations.[58] The American economist Wesley Mitchell expanded on these efforts with a rigorous mathematical analysis of what he called "the money economy" premised on "the fact that economic activity takes the form of making and spending money incomes." Mitchell used this definition to calculate the movement of "business cycles" to make sense of the evolving boom-bust cycles under capitalism.[59] Mitchell's research provided an empirical basis for describing economic activity through the flow of money in a given space. Over the following years, Mitchell and like-minded researchers developed schematic models of a social space called "the national economy" that pictured the economic life of a nation-state as a "circular flow of production, income, and expenditure."[60] Mitchell's work as director of the National Bureau of Economic Research (NBER), a Boston think tank designed by labor and business leaders to use economic research for social improvement, generated more elaborate and detailed income measurements.[61]

The NBER and its statistical research reflected similar Progressive Era paternalism as Henry Ford and Edward Filene's support for data on worker consumption habits. The organization originated as an endeavor of John D. Rockefeller Jr., who faced widespread condemnation for his company's role in the violent suppression of labor unrest in Colorado coal mines in 1914. The objective of the NBER, the Rockefeller Foundation argued, would be "to create a saner attitude on economic and social problems" given that "unrest [was] widespread."[62] Over the 1920s, the NBER produced multiple studies of the US national income with social objectives in mind. Oswald Knauth, one of Mitchell's close collaborators, said that the goal was to know if the national income was "so large as to make its proper distribution the primary source of public interest, or . . . so insufficient that its increase is the question of prime importance."[63] Fear of labor uprisings led the early NBER income studies to estimate distribution of the national income, but it did so in a way that blurred the distinction between industrial laborers and their far better paid managers.[64]

The experience of the Great Depression jolted government leaders to take greater interest in such research. Initially, President Hoover tasked the Research Committee on Social Trends to produce a sprawling multivolume report on various aspects of social life during the early stages of the Depression.[65] As the economic situation worsened during the spring of 1932, progressive senator Robert La Follette Jr. demanded that the government produce national income statistics. Aspects of the Depression had become painfully clear. Thousands of banks had failed; millions of Americans had lost their jobs and were now struggling to feed themselves and their families; hundreds of shantytowns—soon dubbed "Hoovervilles"—popped up across the country; destitute veterans marched on Washington, DC. Official economic data and statistics were so rudimentary that it was impossible to grasp the totality of the crisis. Without a lucid diagnosis of the depth and breadth of the Depression, La Follette believed, an effective prescription would be elusive and hard to evaluate.[66]

Responsibility for the task fell to a thirty-one-year-old Belarusian American economist named Simon Kuznets. A student of Wesley Mitchell's renowned for his statistical acumen, Kuznets had long supported moving economics away from its qualitative, philosophical past and toward a more scientific and mathematical future. He also believed that reliable statistics would offer a strong empirical base for crafting socially just policies. When Kuznets submitted his report to the Senate in 1934, he outlined two measures of national income: "National Income Produced," the net value of goods and services produced, and "National Income Paid Out," which calculated the income from current production received by individuals as owners of capital and as workers. The estimates were a hit. President Roosevelt used them to assess the speed of recovery during the campaign of 1936, and they provided policy makers with the means to define the scope and content of major spending initiatives thereafter. The report even became a best seller.[67]

All across the world, national income measures became associated with fighting the Depression, boosting national production, and assessing the distribution of income within a country. By the late 1920s, most European countries had formal estimates for national income, though the quality of the underlying data and measurement techniques varied considerably. This fact led the League of Nations to take on the task of standardizing national income estimates. Standardization efforts began in earnest in 1928 at a conference in Geneva. The meeting resulted in an agreement among all major industrialized countries to maintain a common repertoire of statistics (though it said little about national income metrics), though efforts to develop a "world-wide system of statistics" faltered because of the "inadequate development" of data collection in many countries and "obstacles of a purely political character" such as whether to require countries to collect and publish statistics on munitions production.[68] The League of Nations Economic and Financial Organisation expanded these efforts, as it sought to collate worldwide statistics on national income and business cycles.[69]

By the mid-1930s, the growing interest in aggregate economic statistics rivaled the public interest in social statistics. Both sets of numbers offered tools for governments to make sense of the messiness and complexities of a world in tremendous flux. Both provided policy makers with ways of seeing how the Great Depression played out in quantitative terms. One could view a decrease in national income or a slowing rate of its expansion. Alternatively, one could trace a decline in the standard of living for different groups as individuals lost jobs, income, and access to basic goods.

Yet the two sets of numbers represented two very different ways of telling stories of economic life. National income figures encouraged policy makers to think of an abstract concept representing an entire country: the national economy. Standard of living invited policy makers to view their society in terms of social classes, or in other words, of how people lived *within* the national economy. The two metrics reflected distinct values and priorities. For national income, policy makers would turn to the notion of abstract growth as a goal to uplift all, whereas standard-of-living advocates alerted policy makers to the importance of distributional questions and the use of state power to make direct and calibrated policy changes to help particular groups.

The fate of these two ways of seeing and describing the world became intertwined during the 1930s as the League of Nations and ILO tried to make sense of how to raise living standards in a world wracked by economic and political turmoil. As the Great Depression wore on, the League of Nations embarked on three major research initiatives related to economic and social policy. One line of research focused on business cycles and depressions, culminating in the 1938 Delegation on Economic Depressions. A second revived earlier Progressive Era concerns about hunger and poverty through the Mixed Committee on Nutrition, which studied the relationship between nutrition, public health, social context, and economic policy. Finally, the league also continued earlier ILO work through its Sub-committee on Standard of Living of 1938 under the direction of Australian diplomat Frank MacDougall and British economist Noel Hall.[70]

The initiatives shared a set of concerns. On the one hand, these initiatives reflected concerns among leading countries—chiefly the United States, Great Britain, and France—about the connection between hunger, poverty, low wages, unemployment, and social unrest. The Great Depression threatened to upend social order and exacerbate class conflict. In the wake of Bolshevik communism in the Soviet Union and the popularity of fascism in Germany, Italy, and Japan, leaders of liberal capitalist countries sought strategies to redress the conditions that gave rise to radicalism without courting radical politics.[71] As an extension, the initiatives also reflected a crisis of the imperial order; the Depression undermined the capacity of imperial powers to maintain order at home and abroad in their vast territorial empires. There was great faith that better knowledge and statistics related to economic and social life could enable policy makers to see the best way out of the crisis. When the United States, Great Britain, and France announced an agreement to stabilize and coordinate monetary policy in September 1936, they did so, in US secretary of the treasury Henry Morgenthau Jr.'s words, to support "the restoration of order in international economics relations and to pursue a policy which will tend to promote prosperity in the world and improve the standard of living of peoples."[72]

Many experts shared a belief that underconsumption was the root cause of the ills afflicting the liberal capitalist world. People were hungry because they were unable to consume enough food; standards of living were low because people lacked capacity to buy goods; economic fluctuations and depressions reflected a crisis of consumer demand. This view was especially evident in the League of Nations' work on standard of living. The subcommittee attempted to standardize data collection and statistical presentation, reconciling old divisions between "style" and "standard" of living by broadening the latter to include physiological well-being and incorporate more people—chiefly agricultural workers and the unemployed.[73] The key, though, was consumption. The group focused on "how consumption might be facilitated, sustained, and managed to fight depression" through higher living standards, in contrast to the more aggressively production-focused war machines of Nazi Germany and the Soviet Union.[74]

Focusing on consumption also helped to circumvent long-standing debates over the indeterminacy of the meaning of "standard of living" and differences in cultural context. It was "difficult to say whether the standard of living . . . of a Belgian 'worker' is higher than that of a French 'worker' since the question of what is a 'representative' or 'average' worker arises and even when answered the data are not available to fit it," wrote an ILO official in 1937. "When the scope of enquiry is extended to countries so dissimilar as Eastern and Western countries, the difficulties of defining the question and then obtaining the data are insurmountable." Thus the ILO believed that measures of wages, real income, and consumption of key goods per head would be the most appropriate statistics, even though they required "interpretation with great caution."[75] By 1939, the League of Nations' Sub-committee on Standard of Living focused its research on "reliable and scientific standards" of consumption and the "physiological needs of different classes of the population" of various countries.[76]

These debates were not arcane or unimportant. Policy makers looked at statistics as valuable tools for desperate times. The Great Depression led to upheaval and dislocation; radical ideologies took hold across Europe and East Asia; anticolonial uprisings challenged the imperial order. Living standards provided the conceptual foundation for understanding the perils of the Great Depression and the future of liberal capitalism. The league's efforts, as with the collection of social statistics in general, reflected a deep faith that such information could resolve class conflict, poverty, and social strife through empirically based social policies. "The social factor must take precedence over the economic factor," ILO director Albert Thomas claimed in 1931, and standard-of-living statistics would help policy makers measure and identify social inequalities laid bare by economic calamity.[77] According to Noel Hall, in a world where leaders had become so preoccupied with "internal stability" amid the global depression and the rising influence of fascism and communism, the capitalist world needed better social information to improve overall welfare.[78] Debates hit close to home for the League of Nations' experts. Discussions over standard of living took place as the Economic Committee itself was split between "free" (liberal capitalist) and "controlled" countries (under Nazi and fascist rule) riven by ideological conflict, a contraction in world trade, and weakened monetary cooperation.[79]

There were political implications to collecting this information. The League of Nations' efforts focused on how well-being of all citizen-consumers might be improved to redress deprivation and to counter the political radicalism they feared would follow from it. This data would allow heads of states to direct their energy and resources to aid the neediest groups, ensure widespread abundance was evenly shared, and strengthen liberal capitalism in a world where communism and fascism had gained many adherents. In this sense, standard of living held tremendous power. It enabled reformers and policy makers to see inequality and chart its growth in numbers laid out like a balance sheet, revealing groups of people in need of aid. Acquiring such information was all the more important because policy makers feared totalitarian systems might be better suited to deliver rapid improvements in living standards. As Swiss diplomat William Rappard said, "the strength of the totalitarian systems lay largely in this claim to represent the interests of the whole population," whereas liberal capitalist democracies bogged down in battles between competing interest groups. Only through cooperative international study and coordinated international action could the liberal world compete effectively.[80]

By the end of the 1930s, policy makers linked standard-of-living research and national income statistics by suggesting that aggregate growth would raise standards of living through a trickle-down process. The League of Nations' work revealed as much. Noel Hall's 1938 report of the league's Sub-committee on Standard of Living argued that governments worldwide "should be focussed [sic] on a single objective, the raising of the several national standards of living."[81] League experts argued over whether freer trade, incentivizing competition, improving transportation and public works, direct state intervention through antipoverty programs, or some other mixture of measures would best do this. The discussions rarely produced consensus, and the league ultimately studied how increases in government spending, rearmament, and high tariffs and exchange controls affected standard-of-living indicators.[82] Hall stressed the improvement of workers' consumption habits through a "redistribution of productive resources," but also the need for "well-designed policies to stimulate production, particularly if they are international."[83] By 1937, the League of Nations Secretariat determined that the subcommittee should "give first place to methods of increasing the national income itself and to the consideration of methods likely to increase the efficiency of national production and distribution."[84] By 1938, the ILO, in their ongoing studies, had decided to stress "without minimising the importance of subjective well-being . . . such objective elements of welfare as income, consumption, social services and working conditions."[85] By 1939, the League of Nations Secretariat claimed that the standard of living "depends in the last analysis on the size of the income of the community or group, the distribution of that income and the uses to which it is put."[86] Standard of living, put more simply, was a function of monetary wealth, and it could be divined through aggregate income statistics. The result of these international research initiatives was to blur the lines between a set of consumerist statistics and economic aggregates while playing down qualitative depictions of well-being.

In 1945, the League of Nations' final report on economic matters placed even greater emphasis on aggregate economic production for standard of living. Countries rich and poor needed to substitute "positive for negative aims—not the relief of unemployment when it develops, but the attainment of high and stable levels of output and employment in keeping with the capacity of industry and agriculture; not the protection of particular interests against foreign competition, but the encouragement of general expansion." The report noted that "policy must be concerned not only with the size of the national income, but also with its distribution," though the focus was squarely on "expansion" of national income to achieve it.[87] Discussions of standard-of-living statistics, so rich during the 1920s and 1930s, narrowed as economists increasingly argued for growing aggregate income as the best way to lift standards of living. By this time, too, many economists had begun to use national income per capita as shorthand for expressing the standard of living.[88]

Gross National Product and the Rise of Economic Growth

War solidified the place of national income statistics in government. By the late 1930s, especially as Nazi expansionism in Europe intensified in 1938 and 1939, the exigencies of war mobilization reshaped national economic policy. In the United States, the United Kingdom, France, and the other allied countries, the management of underconsumption shifted toward recognition of a need to plan for dramatic increases in a country's capacity to produce armaments, forestall price inflation, and manage a factory labor force while millions of men prepared to move to the fighting fields.[89]

Economists played important roles in the war effort. In the United Kingdom, economist John Maynard Keynes had during the 1930s offered a compelling picture of how the aggregate economy functioned, and many others built on Keynes's insights to study how changes in investment, consumption, and production could generate increases in national income levels.[90] During World War II, Keynes rejoined the British Treasury, where had worked after World War I. He also published, in 1940, a pamphlet entitled *How to Pay for the War*. Drawing on British national income estimates by statistician Colin Clark, Keynes suggested the British could fund the war effort and avoid hyperinflation by reducing home-front demand through a combination of taxes and bond sales.[91] Austin Robinson, a close colleague of Keynes's from Cambridge who held multiple governmental positions during the war, agreed with Keynes. He directed two economists, James Meade from Oxford University and Richard Stone from Cambridge, to develop the country's first official set of national accounts and GNP estimates, which were published for the UK's government budget for the first time in 1941.[92] Thereafter such figures became central to British policy making.[93] They also portended important shifts in how governments functioned. "It is not yet on a big scale," Stone wrote to Clark as the UK government began regular collection of such statistics in early 1942, "but it certainly contains the seeds of something of great importance for the future."[94] Similar shifts in accounting and budgeting along Keynesian lines occurred in Canada, as well.[95]

In the United States, Kuznets and his colleague Robert Nathan worked with Roosevelt's War Production Board to help manage wartime budgeting.[96] Simon Kuznets explained in 1940 that national income estimates offered many political uses of "planning and prosecuting measures of economic policy," which at the time meant "calculations of what share of national income may be safely diverted for social insurance or war defense."[97] Kuznets and a team of economists put together a blueprint for expanding US national product to boost domestic production and enable the military to meet procurement needs. Kuznets also launched comparisons of Allied national incomes and GNP figures during the war. He wanted to study the United Kingdom in particular, since he viewed the numbers as crucial to "untangle and define relative financial responsibilities after the war" for expensive aid programs such as Lend-Lease.[98] National income had proven useful in peacetime; now, during war, economists' successful planning and budgetary analysis made such statistics central to national economic policy making.

As the war wound down in 1945, policy makers in the United States, in the United Kingdom, and elsewhere began to worry about prewar economic troubles returning. The scope of devastation around the globe was mind-boggling. Over fifty million people had perished during the war. Major cities—London, Berlin, Warsaw, Tokyo—had been devastated. Millions of refugees searched for succor across Europe and Asia. Diseases, from cholera to smallpox, threatened millions more. Growing food, heating homes, and all the other basic daily activities necessary for survival seemed perilously difficult with fuel shortages wracking the war-torn regions of the world. Many experts feared that wartime spending and mobilization would decline too rapidly amid demobilization, recovery, and reconstruction. What, then, were governments to do?[99]

Many leaders answered that question by promoting economic growth. The phrase "economic growth" was relatively new, entering public discourse in the English-speaking world only during the late 1930s and early 1940s. By the late 1940s, economic growth referred not to growth in resources or wealth or trade but to the national economy.[100] By this time, there was a new metric often used to define what constituted the national economy: gross national product (GNP). In the late 1930s and early 1940s, there was a subtle shift in national economic accounting practices. Economists began to tabulate not just the aggregate income of a country, but its final product. National income measured the *total income earned* by citizens in a given year that resulted from their ownership of resources used in the production of goods and services. By contrast, the national product was the total market value of goods and services *produced* within a national economy. The concepts were closely related: the national product generated the national income.[101] But during the war, GNP figures had become popular for planning procurement policy and production targets as well as assessing the productive capacity of adversaries.[102]

By the war's end, policy makers looked to GNP growth as a guiding indicator of overall economic health as they believed high growth rates would allow them to avoid the difficult questions associated with demobilization. Rapid growth enabled countries to achieve "full employment." In country after country, national governments stressed the need to create stable jobs for restive populations. Growth made this possible by allowing policy makers to maintain both low unemployment and increases in production.[103] More broadly, growth offered a political rhetoric to galvanize public spirit and defuse potential domestic conflict. In the United States, growth became a powerful buzzword during the Truman administration under the belief that future expansion was necessary to avoid difficult political trade-offs and potential class conflict.[104] Likewise, across Western Europe and Japan economic growth became the solution for all the challenges of postwar reconstruction, the key to mitigating distributional conflicts, and the key to strengthening liberal capitalism against the spread of Soviet communism. "Indices of production and growth allowed supposedly apolitical criteria for dealing with the rivalries among the postwar contenders in France, Italy, and elsewhere," according to historian Charles Maier. "They provided a justification for separating constructive growth-minded labor movements (Social-Democratic or Christian) from divisive and allegedly self-seeking Communist ones."[105] Measuring national economies "became the new basis of national self-consciousness" in post-1945 Europe.[106] In postwar Japan, growth discourse washed away anxieties about "surplus population," unemployment, and "backwardness" of economic culture as a "means at long last to achieve an internal reformation deferred by the errors of Japan's modern past" through wholesale transformation of society.[107]

In this way, the growth paradigm was forged after World War II. Economic growth measured in aggregate statistics became the preeminent goal for capitalist countries. Through the 1940s and 1950s, policy makers, leaders, and economists embraced the growth paradigm as a way to transcend the class conflicts of the past, spark recovery from the war, and direct public attention to the promise that future gains could alleviate any short-term concerns without radical political transformation.[108] Growth triumphed over many other possible economic agendas during the immediate postwar years. In the United States, for instance, growth trumped alternative objectives such as balance, stability, and redistribution, which might have pointed policy makers to priorities other than expansion of productive capacity and ever-increasing mass consumption.[109]

Because growth held such wide appeal for national governments, postwar leaders hoped to construct an international architecture that would facilitate national growth while limiting competition. Since many elites believed that declining trade and collapse of cooperation on monetary issues had exacerbated the depression, they viewed cooperation and coordination of economic policy as a key for postwar recovery.[110] The many international organizations and agreements established between 1944 and 1947—from the International Monetary Fund (IMF) and World Bank to the General Agreement on Tariffs and Trade (GATT) to UN's Economic and Social Council—stemmed from the assumption that national economic growth required international arrangements to minimize geopolitical conflict. The Bretton Woods regime of international monetary regulation, in particular, reinforced the primacy of domestic economic expansion within an international framework designed to mitigate the autarkic tendencies that had emerged during the interwar years. By linking the US dollar to gold at a fixed rate, countries could hold dollars as reserve assets on terms interchangeable with gold. Expanding beyond the old gold standard, this modified system allowed the world's money supply to expand far faster than it had before. The IMF also permitted countries to postpone currency convertibility and place restrictions on transnational finance. The result was that the Bretton Woods system prioritized "domestic economic stability and national economic growth" by relying on an institutionalization of American financial hegemony through international institutions and organizations.[111] More broadly, international economic cooperation "aimed to shelter nation-states from globalisation's disruptive effects" and empower national elites to make national economic growth a priority without engendering dangerous infighting among capitalist countries.[112]

The 1945 final report of the League of Nations' Committee on Depressions set the tone for this approach to international economic affairs. "So as long as national economic policies are based on fear and not on confidence and mutual aid they are bound to be essentially negative, restrictive, and self-destructive," it claimed. What was needed was "effective international economic collaboration" between countries and policies that would allow for "the encouragement of general expansion."[113] International cooperation and international institutions would ensure that countries could pursue growth as they saw fit.[114]

While impetus for these initiatives lay in the depression, by 1947 the desire for growth was intertwined with broader geopolitical concerns and great-power politics. The Soviet Union embraced the rhetoric of growth and the politics of productivity, too. Economists there had developed the Material Product System (MPS) to quantify aggregate production, and they subsequently crafted theories to grow socialist economies.[115] Vladimir Lenin had claimed that "socialism is accounting" because of the importance of tracking the flow of goods in a command economy.[116] Over the 1920s Soviet economists focused on the principles driving economic expansion and the rates of change in national income, and they linked development with rapid industrialization beginning in the first five-year plan of 1929.[117] As the vast agricultural country began to industrialize, Soviet leaders trumpeted high growth rates as a symbol of strength.[118] After the war, Soviet leaders saw rapid economic growth as a necessity for reconstruction but also a bulwark against capitalist foes. In February 1946, Soviet premier Joseph Stalin took the stage at Moscow's Bolshoi Theater to deliver a thunderous speech promising that the country's new five-year plan would "organize another powerful upswing of our national economy that will enable us to raise our industry to a level, say, three times as high as that of prewar industry." The war had validated the Soviet system, he claimed, and the postwar years would show that it was the superior form of political economy for generating widespread prosperity.[119]

The speech alarmed leaders in the major capitalist countries. Soviet economic growth depended on extracting resources from the countries on its immediate periphery, which was consistent with Stalin's desire to bolster his country's security against its capitalist adversaries.[120] When the Soviets rejected Marshall Plan aid, which Stalin deemed a deceptive ploy to rehabilitate German power, tensions increased. Policy makers in Washington viewed the battle between capitalist and communist economic growth as incompatible with global stability and peace. By 1948, the first objective of US foreign policy was to "reduce the power and influence of the USSR" while expanding and deepening the liberal capitalist world to ensure access to vital raw materials, promotion of "free" trade, and above all, the expanding production of national output.[121]

Growth, in other words, appeared to be a zero-sum game in the emerging Cold War. In the Soviet world, growth provided fuel for reconstruction and preparation for war. To many leaders in the capitalist world, Soviet aspirations portended a threat to their own emerging postwar order. US and European leaders' embrace of growth, in turn, reinforced Soviet concerns over the threat of capitalist expansionism. The growth paradigm took hold because it satisfied many countries' domestic needs. Yet capitalist and communist leaders alike worried that they would be secure only if they could shape the international environment in a way that promoted their own growth while undermining their adversaries' capacity to do the same. As a result, the pursuit of economic growth exacerbated tensions between the superpowers.

Conclusion

By the end of the 1940s, as leaders embraced national economic growth as their foremost priority, GNP became the dominant way of depicting national economic activity. The emerging growth paradigm, however, triumphed over alternative ways of narrating economic life. Discussions of living standards narrowed as the rich standard-of-living research in the early twentieth century gave way to the widespread use of GNP as a proxy for well-being.[122] Economists used GNP estimates to tell new and compelling stories about the past and future. In the mid-1940s, Kuznets won a series of grants from the Rockefeller Foundation to "establish how fruitful empirical study of economic growth can best be planned" using historical explorations of how national income and product statistics changed over time.[123] Colin Clark used the statistics similarly under the assumption that the "economist can sometimes help to analyze the causation of historical events hitherto obscure" that in turn could illuminate the "deep-seated forces," "factors," and "decisions of the human will" that explained how economies grew, shrunk, or achieved stasis.[124] Once these reconstructions were in place, countries could be understood in terms of their economies, and economists could set out to identify key "factors" that explained changes from year to year.

In this research, economic growth became a historical narrative—an all-encompassing one—to describe national changes. All narratives simplify and reduce, and the story told in Kuznets's and Clark's charts of national aggregates obscured labor violence and struggles for equity. Policy makers used such stories—the GNP was once this, it can be that—to legitimize their policies and power. These powerful stories presented nation-states as coherent and whole entities, in contrast to how standard-of-living researchers used their data to direct attention to various social groups and communities. For leaders, GNP growth was a process that minimized class conflict and social unrest, a narrative about the past and future trajectory of their countries, and a central point of comparison between different ideological systems.

The rise of the growth paradigm played out in only a few countries, those that would become known as the "First World" (industrialized capitalist countries) and "Second World" (communist countries). But there were larger international changes afoot, as well. The global depression, World War II, and the emerging Cold War created uncertainty about the future of colonial rule. Anticolonial movements demanded political liberation and the opportunity to overcome the poverty and exploitation that colonialism had produced. Imperial powers took note, and many promoted development in their territories in the hopes of limiting unrest and staving off demands for independence. As a result, the pursuit of rapid economic growth would not be confined to Europe, North America, and Northeast Asia; growth rates became symbols of progress for the emergent "Third World," as well. Colonial elites and nationalist leaders puzzled over a few basic questions, however. They needed national income and GNP estimates for growth plans and to assess progress, but would conventional accounting techniques and growth models transfer well beyond the industrial world? And what would happen if they did not?

TWO

Decolonization and the Limits of Economic Measurement

In the fall of 1941, as war raged across the globe, British economist Austin Robinson wondered if Britain's national income estimates "were capable of universal application" in countries both "advanced and primitive." World War II, after all, was a conflict between empires. The United Kingdom, like other major combatants, held a vast overseas empire from which it drew resources and subjugated local populations. Robinson asked, "What do we really know to-day about the standards of life of the millions in the Colonial Empire for whose welfare we are responsible?"[1] He believed that older, piecemeal studies of colonial living standards were insufficient. National income estimates had helped reshape how the UK and the United States managed their domestic economies by making legible aggregate national economic activity. Might such statistics offer the same value abroad? He reached out to the National Institute of Economic and Social Research (NIESR) to fund research into that question.

Over the following years, the NIESR sponsored the first extensive investigations into how to count, measure, and calculate economic life in the colonies. They were led by a young economist named Phyllis Deane, who began her research in the colonies of Northern Rhodesia and Nyasaland. The methods she honed there became a model to replicate elsewhere. In 1941 only a dozen or so countries produced national income estimates. Two and a half decades later, every single country in the world produced national income estimates and GNP figures, and all used them to some degree in national policy making. So how and why did this change occur?

The desire for "universal application" arose as imperial officials had begun to emphasize development in their colonies. Too often treated as a phenomenon of the Cold War era, international and intercolonial development predated it. Imperial authorities turned to aid for development—promising increasing prosperity and improved living conditions—to relegitimize imperial rule and forestall the possibilities of widespread unrest and radical demands for political change.[2] Colonial development was not new, as empires had for decades pursued forced schooling and acculturation programs, large-scale infrastructure construction, and technological improvements in agriculture. What changed in the early 1940s was the object of development. Similar to what was taking place within the United Kingdom, policy makers sought to develop the national economy, defined by aggregate economic statistics, of a colony as a whole. This shift meant that colonies needed to reform everyday governing practices to make their economic activity legible in this new way. The change also inscribed a territorial dimension onto economic life. By giving economic representation of the economy a geographical boundary, these statistics further yoked political independence to the nation-state form.[3]

The construction of national income statistics was far from a smooth process. Many economists struggled to find a "universal" method for measuring activity. In her initial estimates, Deane encountered multiple problems that stemmed from limited data, confounding value judgments, and difficult decisions over how to categorize putative economic activities. Though Deane estimated much of what she could, she and many other economists expressed great caution about their data's limitations. There was a thriving debate among experts in the late 1940s and 1950s about whether such statistics were at all useful for colonial policy making, and whether postcolonial leaders should make policy geared toward rapid economic growth as the industrialized countries had begun to do. In the history of international development, economists are often treated as naive and overly confident in their models. The history of constructing national accounts reveals instead a group of experts well aware of their epistemological limits.[4]

Deane's cautious approach, however, gradually fell out of favor during the 1940s and 1950s. As the need for European and Japanese recovery intensified after the war and as Cold War tensions deepened, measuring economies became a vital task for the United States, European powers, and the international institutions designed to manage the postwar order. At the same time, many anticolonial nationalist leaders embraced GNP growth rates as symbols of national power, prestige, and promise. The caution and calls for local specificity that Deane and others counseled lost out, and by the early 1960s the growth paradigm went global.

The History of International Development to 1940

The use of "development" to describe wholesale societal transformation, much like the phrase "economic growth," has a shorter history than many suspect. The word "development" first came into widespread use in English during the middle part of the nineteenth century to describe how officials could spur and manage the process of improvement in far-flung parts of the empire.[5] Development discourse became bound up with the challenges of managing and justifying imperial rule and maintaining racial and cultural superiority.[6] The United States experimented with development in its domestic and overseas territories through forced schooling, changing modes of dress, and language instruction alongside brutal land dispossession and violent displacement of communities into bounded reservations.[7] European empires also adopted a development focus. Both the French *mission civilisatrice* and the Dutch Ethical Policy, for instance, emphasized hygiene, irrigation schemes, local education, and public works as central to the expression of imperial legitimacy.[8] These schemes enriched the metropole, too. In French colonial policy, for instance, concepts such as *mise en valeur* and "constructive exploitation" linked social improvements in the colonial periphery to increasing wealth in the European core.[9]

Development efforts intensified during the interwar years and World War II. US government officials and US corporations worked to ensure the free flow of vital raw materials for the war effort, construct markets for US goods, and help build up good will among local populations—especially in Latin America—as a bulwark against radicalism.[10] European empires engaged in similar efforts. The United Kingdom, for example, expanded its policies "to develop the natural and human resources of the empire and manage the perceived problems and disorder generated by colonial rule" through top-down infrastructure programs, social engineering projects, and agricultural improvement schemes. British policy makers hoped development policy would alleviate social and political tensions while building markets for British goods and ensuring the postcolonial world would stay tethered to the metropole through aid and trade.[11]

To help manage development programs, imperial officials collected information about their colonial subjects. For example, British authorities in India compiled extensive census and trade statistics. A handful of economists even ventured national income estimates for India during the late nineteenth and early twentieth centuries. V. K. R. V. Rao—who studied with John Maynard Keynes, Richard Stone, and Colin Clark as one of the first economics PhD students at Cambridge—carried out a study of Indian national income during the early 1930s.[12] Data collection expanded as imperial authorities sought scientific approaches to colonial issues. The UK Colonial Office compiled basic economic information—mostly on tax revenue, imports, and exports.[13] The most extensive of these was a project that ran from 1929 to 1939 called the African Research Survey, which collected medical, social, and ecological information on life throughout the British holdings on the continent. Data collection, scientific research, and policy making were closely intertwined. Lord Malcolm Hailey, who oversaw the major report of the project published in 1938, used this research to help shift colonial research and reform efforts toward more top-down planning. In South Africa, social scientist Edward Batson carried out extensive social surveys of Cape Town to create a "poverty datum line" of minimum needs for households, which reformers used to advocate for the advancement of people from poverty, much as standard-of-living statistics had been intended to do.[14] Throughout this period, there were fierce debates over support for local and vernacular forms of knowledge and development inspired by scientists' on-the-ground experience.[15]

After the start of World War II, however, the pursuit of locally specific data and small-scale development initiatives fell from favor as
colonial developmental efforts became increasingly understood within
the framework of national income accounting. This shift derived in
part from a broader embrace of planning by colonial governments.
Great Britain's 1940 Colonial Welfare and Development Act rested
on the notion that development "was something that could be made to
happen" through expert guidance.[16] To generate development, authorities needed to envision possible futures and identify the policy interventions necessary to achieve them. Austin Robinson's desire to extend
national income accounting thus emerged just as the imperial state
had deemed this planning important to imperial practice, committing
foreign aid to "uplift" the colonies.[17] Having reliable estimates was necessary, too, to track the effects of extensive British capital investment
and foreign aid on the overall income of a colony.[18]

In addition, many imperial officials and economists argued that
increasing production was the best way to improve colonial standards
of living in a process similar to what played out in thinking about
standards of living in the United States and Europe during the 1930s
and 1940s. Assistant undersecretary of state for the Colonial Office
Gerard Clauson made this point clear in a paper in 1942 that circu-
lated to many experts, including Keynes. To "raise the general standard of living" in the colonies the UK needed to "level up" and thus "to
increase the aggregate consumption of mankind." Since the "aggregate consumption of mankind is roughly but not exactly equal to the
aggregate output," increasing output should be the policy priority, he
argued. He juxtaposed such a strategy against anything more out-
wardly redistributive. "Redistribution may be a wide, even essential,
measure of social justice," he wrote, "but it is a policy of second best."
Redistribution would, in his metaphor, "level down" and threaten the
aggregate consumption of "mankind."[19] Similar assumptions undergirded Austin Robinson's question of what was known about the "the
standards of life of the millions in the Colonial Empire." National
income and product calculations "provided the foundations of all clear
thinking about the economic problems" of the UK, he wrote to the

NIESR in 1941. He believed that having similar statistics for the colonies would unlock the key to effective national economic governance there, too.[20]

Phyllis Deane and the Northern Rhodesia Quandary

When Austin Robinson won support for the NIESR to study the national income of the colonies in 1941, the task of carrying out the research fell to twenty-three-year-old economist Phyllis Deane. The daughter of an admiralty engineer, Deane was born in Hong Kong just before World War I. Her family moved throughout the British Empire before they settled in Scotland. She enrolled at the University of Glasgow in the mid-1930s, where she studied with economist Alec Cairncross. Cairncross was, along with V. K. R. V. Rao, one of the first economics PhDs from Cambridge. Deane's connections to the larger Cambridge network led Robinson to task her with the data collection for his project. Deane reported to a team comprising Robinson, Richard Stone, and St. Lucian economist W. Arthur Lewis, who had recently received his PhD from the London School of Economics and would become one the most important experts on economic growth. The goal of Robinson's grant was to "experiment with the application of current English techniques of measurement to a primitive substance economy" (Northern Rhodesia and Nyasaland) and compare it to an "advanced Colonial economy" (Jamaica). Deane had a twofold task: to construct the measurements, but also to hone the techniques and where applicable advise on data collection methods.[21]

Deane's research design flowed from existing data and national income metrics. Much of the data available to her came from the African Survey or similar research endeavors, such as a 1937 nutrition survey of Nyasaland. In terms of accounting, she followed the methods developed by Stone and James Meade in 1941, calculating a nation's income, output, and expenditure ("triple-entry" accounting), which they presented in simple terms for the purposes of making international comparisons. Deane would be the first researcher to test out this method abroad, as she collected systematically all relevant

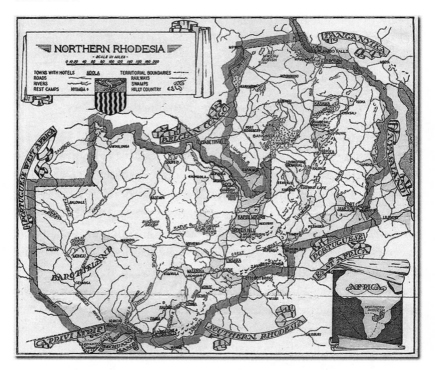

(2) Map of Northern Rhodesia, ca. 1950. Map courtesy of
Stephen Luscombe, https://www.britishempire.co.uk.

economic data and produced national income estimates for Northern
Rhodesia and Nyasaland.[22]

Deane went to Northern Rhodesia at an important moment in the
colony's history. Northern Rhodesia is modern-day Zambia, a land-
locked country in South Central Africa. Prior to 1929, it was a minor
part of the British Empire, best known as the site of imperial doctor-
turned-explorer David Livingstone's death. But in 1929 imperial officials discovered vast copper mines, the largest in the world outside
Chile. Population estimates showed that the white European population increased fivefold from 1925 to 1940, and the migrant labor population tripled between 1927 and 1930. As copper became critical for
wartime manufacturing and the burgeoning consumer electronics
industries, Northern Rhodesia appeared likely to be an important cog
in Britain's empire.[23]

As soon as Deane arrived, however, she encountered multiple unexpected challenges. The first was a conceptual problem. She noted two distinct forms of economic activity in Northern Rhodesia: a "highly capitalised" industry based on copper extraction and a "substantial proportion of subsistence production." The latter rarely included either money or clear prices. In the United States and the United Kingdom, items that did not get to market were simply excluded from calculations (including unpaid labor, such as women's housework). But this was "impracticable," Deane wrote, for Northern Rhodesia.[24] Deane characterized subsistence production as important yet problematic for the statistician. Using typical racist tropes to describe local agricultural practices, she characterized household farming as "backward" and lacking sophistication. She struggled to identify occupational categories (since many people, especially women, performed multiple work-related roles in the household) and had to rely on "guesswork" when calculating total output. She estimated prices for beer production and small-scale manufacturing (such as weaving rugs) but left out crucial women's work such as firewood collecting, which took varied amounts of labor and time.[25]

The subsistence quandary related to a second problem: there was no data on much of the population's production, consumption, and investment habits. This "great dearth of information," as she called it, was a "serious obstacle" to producing a "comprehensive picture of the economy." She admitted the limits of her empiricism. "Frequently there was no basis whatever for estimate and resort had to be made to pure guesswork," even for the more heavily capitalized economic activities, she wrote.[26] The only reliable data came from information on import and export statistics and the income tax department's returns (which she noted was a "small European population"). The 1931 census of the territory did not include the "native population" in rural areas, and there were no vital statistics involved on them.[27] The colony, in other words, could barely even see as a state should.

The very nature of colonialism itself prompted a third problem that led Deane to make a small but important methodological change. Official national income estimates in the United States and the United Kingdom included the income of residents and excluded the income arising from foreign capital employed in producing the output of the territory. But in Northern Rhodesia, as in most colonies, "foreign capital" (in this case, British capital) dominated. Thus it became apparent "that in Colonial territories a great deal of the value produced accrued to foreign capital and it was therefore necessary to have a concept which included the income of foreign companies."[28] Northern Rhodesia's overall national income thus increased by including income to foreigners who owned factories but did not live there.

In the end, Deane argued against Robinson's original goal: a clear comparable framework for accounting in postcolonial territories. Rather than synoptic plans laid down from London, Deane instead suggested the colonial national incomes "must be hammered out from the experience of local administrators and economists on the basis of a much closer knowledge of the economics concerned."[29] She emphasized the importance of local and "firsthand knowledge."[30] There was also a need to bring in other forms of expertise. "Gaps in quantitative information have had to be filled by deductions from the largely qualitative researches of anthropologists, agriculturalists, ecologists, and other experts."[31] She estimated what she could through surveys and observation. For instance, to calculate the monetary value of the work done by women milling the grain for a family at home, Deane sought out a few millers elsewhere in the colony who worked for wages. She used their prices and average working time to extrapolate figures for all millers across the territory. She recognized these guesses, while sound and based on extensive research, derived from a process that was "difficult, uncertain, and highly subjective."[32] Her estimates were bracketed by her careful, repetitive expressions of the limitations of her work.

Deane published her final report in 1948 as *The Measurement of Colonial National Incomes*. She generated three separate income listings based on loose racial categories: one for the European population; one for Africans; and one for Asian workers who had moved to the colony from the larger empire and Indian Ocean world. She then added these together to form the total income: 13.5 million pounds. Deane took the same methods and applied them to neighboring Nyasaland, although she encountered similar problems there. She also included an estimate of Jamaica's national income, which was less challenging to calculate because the greater presence of a cash economy and more reliable tax receipts made data collection less cumbersome. Northern Rhodesia ranked above Nyasaland (4.8 million pounds) and below the territorially smaller but more economically "advanced" Jamaica, which, at 19 million pounds, was the wealthiest of all colonies included in the initial surveys of the 1940s. Her comparisons also revealed how much each colony kept as income at home. She calculated that 42 percent of Northern Rhodesia's total taxable income went to foreigners, for instance, compared to only 4 percent in Jamaica.[33] But even these comparisons, she noted, were provisional at best. "The experiment in colonial national income measurement raised more problems than it solved," she reflected. "It has not paved the way to effective international or even intercolonial comparisons, although it reveals the bigger obstacles."[34] Even with estimates in hand, caution and uncertainty about the results reigned in Deane's writing.

Deane was convinced that the measurement difficulties she encountered were not insurmountable. She emphasized the importance of accounting for all forms of production, especially the unwaged work of women. "If the concept of national income is to have any meaning when applied to a colonial economy," she wrote, "it must include the self-subsistence output of the native farmer."[35] In 1953, she published a follow-up volume using a more capacious accounting framework. *Colonial Social Accounting* included attempts to estimate all putative economic activities, including ones, such as firewood collection, that she had sidestepped earlier. Deane believed that this was necessary to ensure not only that all activity was accounted for, but also that experts and policy makers could make legible inequalities in labor and wealth. Both an "increase in the volume of economic goods and services produced" and "an improvement in its distribution over time and among persons and groups," Deane wrote, "were important ends of economic policy."[36] To make such estimates effective, she called for "periodically comprehensive surveys and censuses" of agriculture, population, occupation, and budgets to build up local capacity for data collection.[37] She concluded that more reliable data, flexible definitions of production, and local knowledge were all key ingredients in effective accounting.

Dudley Seers, S. Herbert Frankel, and Critiques
of Economic Measurement

Deane's report received mixed reviews. Stanford University economist William Jones wrote of it, "If we expect the native society eventually to be remade in the image of the European, then, when that time comes, national income estimates of the kind made here will be just as valid as they are in Europe or the United States. In the meantime they may even serve as some sort of index of the extent to which the native economy has been Europeanized, although a better measure would seem to be that of national income originating in the money economy."[38] In this sense, collecting data and making national accounts could itself be a way to track development as more and more Africans entered into the "money economy." Others were less sanguine. Colin Clark called it a "qualified success." He argued that only in colonies such as Jamaica that could be classified as a "money economy" (and not those in Africa with what he called a "natural economy" without the large-scale use of money) was "the value of this technique apparent."[39]

Still, similar studies proliferated. Austin Robinson wrote that he was optimistic that by revealing conceptual challenges and data deficiencies, Deane's research might "spur the Colonial Governments to replace" the unreliable figures with "better and more authoritative estimates" and help local authorities "see the need for extending and improving their collection of statistics."[40] Convinced of the value of national income estimates, economists began calculating the size of other colonial economies. British Australian economist Frederic Benham produced formal income estimates for the British West Indies, where he was an adviser to the Development and Welfare Commission. In 1945, Benham took a position with the UK's Commissioner General for South East Asia, and he subsequently produced the first major estimate of Malaya's income in 1951.[41] There were new institutions built to support these endeavors, as well. In 1945, John Maynard Keynes and Richard Stone set up a new Department of Applied Economics at Cambridge University, which received commissions from the Colonial Office and the United Nations alike to carry out statistical research for the colonies. The first major income estimate for Nigeria, produced by affiliated economists A. R. Prest and I. G. Stewart, was one of many such studies.[42]

In all these estimates, researchers encountered similar problems to what Deane had identified in her initial experiments. In his study of the British West Indies, Benham lamented the small percentage of reliable income tax receipts, meaning that all estimates would have to come from the output side of the table. But that, too, was a challenge, because estimates for subsistence production, small-scale manufactures, and bartered goods amounted to "little more than guesses." Even survey questionnaires were "seldom much use," as many citizens simply refused to complete them without coercion.[43] Prest and Stewart noted similar problems in Nigeria, arguing that it was "impossible to say as the line between business-personal and intra-personal transfers is never sharp and clearly defined. Therefore we are confronted with difficulties of concept as well as those of measurement." As a result, the two took Deane's work even further by including *all* intrahousehold transfer payments in national income, a move that deviated far from Stone's preferred methods.[44] Subsequent research did not fare much better. One Nigerian researcher, Pius N. C. Okigbo, who updated Prest and Stewart's figures a few years later, wrote that it was "impossible to overstate the arbitrariness of the process of 'quantification'" in determining national product estimates.[45]

These ongoing data collection difficulties and conceptual debates sparked a wider discussion over the use, misuse, and nonuse of national accounts in colonial and postcolonial territories. One important early critic of such measurements and their use in policy was British economist Dudley Seers. Seers studied economics and statistics at Cambridge University in 1930s under the supervision of Joan Robinson and Maurice Dobbs. In the late 1940s, he took a position as an economic adviser for the UN, working closely with Polish economist Michał Kalecki (and later with the Economic Commission for Latin

America and the Caribbean). Widely respected for his statistical acumen, insightful economic analysis, and jovial manner, he established a promising career as both an economist and a civil servant. In 1951, the Colonial Office sent Seers and a colleague to assess the economic development strategy of the Gold Coast (modern-day Ghana). The resulting report featured the first instance of what would become the core feature of Seers's scholarship: critiquing the use of national income statistics in development economics and policy. Much like Deane, Seers noticed that most people he encountered lived on subsistence agricultural production, but there was not "adequate information" available to include it in the national accounts. Moreover, there was "no information" on important aspects of economic activity, which meant the national accounts were "rather rough estimates" with a "number of omissions."[46] Seers argued that the dearth of good data made economic indicators a shaky foundation for good policy. Policy makers needed to "look at the complete picture, including many economic but immeasurable considerations, and many non-economic considerations, before deciding on the scale and type of development," he claimed.[47]

Other economists wrote more forcefully against national income estimates for the colonies and argued that they should not be used in planning at all. The fiercest such critic was Oxford-trained South African economist Sally Herbert Frankel. Frankel produced a major survey of capital investment in African colonies in a project related to Lord Hailey's survey in 1938.[48] His foray sought to calculate national income estimates for the South African government.[49] Very quickly, though, he soured on the possibility of effectively measuring national income and using it for policy making. Keynesian concepts and measurement techniques were not transferable and misguided at best, he believed. He lambasted Deane's initial work by suggesting it was similar to asking "whether the system of accounting applicable to General Motors can throw light on the operations of a wayside petrol station run by a man whose main livelihood is obtained with the assistance of his wife and children from an agricultural allotment."[50] He criticized Deane's loose production boundary and the seeming difficulty of defining which activities should be estimated as productive and which should not.[51] He even challenged one of the most basic assumptions of emerging GNP calculations—that they were designed to show output within one year. Choosing a single year as the temporal boundary was "very artificial," he wrote.[52]

Frankel's critique of economic measurement derived from his cultural chauvinism, racism, and suspicion of economic planning. He doubted that elaborate accounting techniques should apply to the colonies because he disregarded most colonial subjects' "economic" activity as "backward," in writing shot through with racist assumptions and steeped in a sense of cultural chauvinism. He wrote, "In the economically 'backward' communities economic activity cannot possibly be regarded as governed by highly refined individual choices or abstract evaluations.... For the most part these peoples are engaged in narrow economic pursuits circumscribed by an environment from which they have, as yet, learned to wring only a precarious existence in accordance with the traditional social and economic precepts to which they still cling."[53] He was skeptical that any country should adopt such statistics as the basis for budgetary planning, however, because he believed planning was contrary to effective governance. An early member of the Mont Pelerin Society, he argued that governments should simply seek to promote private enterprise and avoid any coordinated planning or targeting. He stated, "development depends not on the abstract national goals of, and the more or less enforced decisions by, a cadre of planners, but on the piecemeal adaptation of individuals to goals which emerge but slowly and become clearer only as those individuals work with the means at their disposal."[54] For Frankel, national income statistics were flawed because they did not fit the reality of how most Africans lived and because he rejected the notion that national economies could be effectively planned or managed at all.

Frankel's thinking aligned with that of many like-minded Mont Pelerin Society members, including Friedrich Hayek, who doubted that sophisticated economic statistics, mathematically informed economic theory, or econometrics serve to help forestall economic crises or plan for prosperity. These economists placed "the economy beyond the space of representation." They argued that measuring national

economies was a foolhardy exercise because national economy activity was spontaneously formed, difficult if not impossible to capture
in numerical accounting, and best structured through laws to allow
market activity to flourish rather than to permit deliberate management by expert planners.[55]

While there were many critics of national economic accounting
by the late 1950s, there were important political differences among
them. For Frankel, trying to calculate national income or use it for
planning purposes was misguided because it would empower colonial
states and distort the functioning of supposedly free markets. Deane
and Seers, by contrast, believed national income and product accounts
were effective tools for estimating all relevant economic activity, difficult and fraught though calculating the figures was. When policy
makers understood the limitations of the data before them, they could
still make policy based on this empirical foundation. They believed
that state intervention was both possible and indeed often worthwhile.
What remained to be seen, of course, was how the critics' arguments
would fare amid growing pressures to homogenize how countries calculated and defined their economies.

Pressures to Standardize and Desires for Growth

Despite the growing chorus of criticisms about the suitability of
national income and product statistics for planning development in
the postcolonial world, there was an even more powerful set of arguments for using the numbers and standardizing data collection and
measurement practices. For one, many economists believed, as Austin
Robinson did, that aggregate indicators would help colonial authorities and postcolonial foreign aid agencies plan their way around social
crises and radical politics. For instance, the Gold Coast colony experienced a series of riots and labor unrest in 1947 and 1948. Of Deane's
book one fellow NIESR expert wrote that it, "gives us an excellent
piece of pioneer research. . . . It would be interesting for instance to see
these methods applied to the Gold Coast in 1947–8 before the riots. It
might help us to understand what was happening there better than

we do at present. It would be useful as well as interesting if the records were so up-to-date that where necessary understanding could come in time to prevent disturbances."[56] Just as growth enthusiasts argued the case for wealthy countries, adopting national aggregates as proxies for national economic well-being held promise for policy makers who hoped to abjure social and political conflicts in colonial territories by promising future abundance.

An emerging subfield of economics research bolstered this way of thinking. The work that Deane, Benham, and Seers carried out in the 1940s and 1950s resonated with a belief that the nature of economic life in the nonindustrialized world was qualitatively different than in the United States and the United Kingdom. As a result, these places needed distinct economic doctrines, theories, and statistics to engineer growth. This was the birth of "development economics." The first critical work in this vein came from an émigré economist, Paul Rosenstein-Rodan, who, while in exile in the UK during the war, studied why parts of southern and southeastern Europe had yet to industrialize. Rosenstein-Rodan argued that there was widespread "disguised unemployment"—surplus and underused labor throughout the countryside—that hampered productivity. Absent high levels of local capital investment or widespread entrepreneurship, rural areas stagnated. Rosenstein-Rodan diagnosed that in such areas of "underdevelopment," large-scale and short-term infusions of capital from the outside could spark new industry, open new employment opportunities, and in the process transform largely agrarian economies into prosperous industrial—and hence "modern"—ones.[57]

During the late 1940s, investigations in the seemingly particular circumstances of the non-Western world flourished. For instance, economists Raúl Prebisch and Hans Singer, working through the United Nations, identified a long-term tendency for the price of agricultural exports to decline relative to manufactured goods, thus producing and deepening systemic inequality between wealthy industrial countries and poorer agricultural ones.[58] Arthur Lewis, part of the team advising Deane for the NIESR, published an influential theory of development for largely rural areas in 1955 called simply *The Theory of Economic Growth.*[59] By the start of the 1950s, Singer, Rosenstein-Rodan, and other economists, such as Rangar Nurske, became convinced of the need for a "big push" of large-scale capital investment in the "Third World" to overcome the "gravitational pull of [their] ancient stagnant order" and make them into growing, modern economies.[60] National income provided a valuable shorthand tool to make comparisons across borders, and by the early 1950s, much as in the wealthy world, Hans Singer reported that there was a growing sense that changes in GNP growth would "trickle down" to reshape life for citizens taking part in the industrialization process.[61] Over the 1950s and 1960s, experts increasingly linked the study of how to generate aggregate growth with broader social and political studies about how to create social and cultural change under the umbrella of "modernization theory." Modernization theory held a powerful place in midcentury social science. Experts such as American Walt Whitman Rostow, whose 1960 book *The Stages of Economic Growth: A Non-Communist Manifesto* encapsulated the link between the growth paradigm and international politics, became important players justifying wealthy country foreign aid programs to Third World governments eager for rapid change.[62]

After all, anticolonial movements worldwide demanded not only political independence, but also a reordering of economic power to combat colonialism and the unequal world order it bequeathed. Measuring national economies became important for many reasons. Reconstructions of past income levels would reveal just how much colonial rule had shaped the current sad state of affairs. Lord Hailey, the author of the British Colonial Office's monumental statistical survey of its African colonies in the 1930s, worried that low national income figures would serve as powerful "propaganda" for anticolonial sentiment by revealing in stark terms how poor the colonies were compared to the metropole.[63] For many anticolonial leaders, economic growth supplied both a language for describing aspirational change and a revolutionary break with the colonial past. In India, Prasanta Mahalanobis, an eminent statistician and head of the country's powerful planning commission, adopted GNP as the metric for his five-year plans. Jawaharlal Nehru, the country's first postindependence prime minister, embraced GNP growth as the "means to build a modern nation."[64] In Kenya, Tom Mboya, the country's minister of justice and leading figure in its development efforts, argued that the first objective of Kenya's planning was to "attain higher growth rates of our national income and, therefore, achieve higher living standards for all people."[65] In postcolonial Sudan, "the rate of economic growth became the measure of a successful government."[66] Low or insufficient growth could imperil those whose legitimacy rested on major economic transformation. In Indonesia, Sukarno's revolutionary postcolonial government struggled and ultimately lost power as the country experienced high inflation and low production by the mid-1960s. Subsequently, General Suharto staked his New Order regime's legitimacy on its capacity to improve the situation through a "commitment to modernization and the promise of stability and rapid economic growth."[67] For these leaders, measuring GNP and making it the cornerstone of growth plans amounted to "an act of sovereignty."[68]

Policy makers in Washington and London embraced this new research as the Cold War and decolonization drew superpower competition to the colonial and postcolonial world. Looming global decolonization presented policy makers with a pressing question: When colonial territories became independent states, which system would they seek to emulate? To make their respective cases, countries offered foreign aid to spark economic growth. Development soon became a widespread term to describe the goals of economic and social policy. US, European, and Japanese officials linked European and Japanese recovery to the construction of new markets abroad, thus tying prosperity in the core to economic growth in the periphery. Moreover, US officials came to understand communism as a response to conditions of material scarcity and inequality. Promoting growth became a tool to halt the spread of radical ideologies in decolonizing areas. The United States' Point Four program, announced in President Truman's 1949 inaugural address, marked the elevation of development to a primary feature of international politics.[69] A new array of international organizations also provided development aid, such as the Food and Agriculture Organization, several UN commissions, and the International Bank for Reconstruction and Development (the World Bank).[70]

These new organizations reinforced the centrality of national income figures in describing national economic life. They did so in a number of ways. The United Nations required its members to pay dues, which it calculated as a percentage of national income. The Committee on Contributions determined these figures by requesting information from the member states. When these numbers were incomplete or unreliable, UN staff collected various statistics from published and unpublished research. In many cases, this process was extensive, even if it left much to interpretation by a few statisticians in New York and Geneva. National income estimates for the "Near East" countries of southwest Asia were derived from "relevant economic statistics" available through published materials "plus general information and opinion about these countries" collected by experts.[71] In addition, the World Bank calculated loan repayment rates from national income figures.[72] To help countries meet the demand for economic statistics, a network of statisticians and economists helped them develop the capacity to produce such statistics. The UN Statistical Commission, the US Point Four program, and the US Bureau of the Census all sent statisticians abroad.[73] By the 1950s, then, there was an international infrastructure that made possible the adoption and standardization of national economic statistics.

As national income estimates became the norm, Richard Stone, one of Deane's principal advisers, sought to promote their standardization across borders. Stone worked with a variety of international organizations during the 1940s—the League of Nations, the Organisation for European Economic Cooperation (OEEC), and, ultimately, the United Nations' Statistical Commission—to develop common national accounting rules and procedures.[74] His work for the UN culminated in a major 1953 report, published as *A System of National Accounts and Supporting Tables* (SNA), which set the global standard.[75] Stone emphasized easy comparability over the local specificity that Deane had championed. He sought standards that could accommodate the wide range in local statistical capacities and cultural differences, so he defined the production boundary narrowly. He included all waged legal activities (prostitution was thus excluded) as well as "primary production" defined as "agriculture, forestry, hunting, fishing, mining and quarrying" that remained for household consumption. But unlike Deane, he excluded "all non-primary production performed by producers outside of their own trades and consumed by themselves"; thus everything from homemade beer production to small-scale manufacturing and weaving to gathering firewood were left out.[76] Stone and the five-person expert group—no women among them—excluded most unwaged household labor. Stone later acknowledged the problems in making such a choice but noted the lack of information on these activities was too great to overcome; he hoped that at some point in the future clever researchers would figure out how to value them.[77]

Although Stone's work became the basis for national accounting standardization, it did not end expert debate over the suitability and reliability of national income and product statistics. As Stone neared completion of his study, the UN General Assembly voted in January 1952 to have the Secretariat compile annual reports on "changes in absolute levels of living conditions in all countries."[78] The first report, published in 1954, harkened back to the ILO and League of Nations' early work on standard of living. It stated that "the problem of levels of living must be approached in a pluralistic manner," including study of health and educational indicators. Despite this emphasis on nonmonetary valuations of well-being, though, the report did not recommend any single reliable set of indexes for "standards" or "level" of living because there was no consensus on which numbers to use.[79] A similar story played out elsewhere. The World Bank, for example, explored the possibility of using similar "standard of living" statistics in its early missions but concluded that the many indicators of high standards of living could best be achieved through increases in "the size of the national product in relation to population."[80] Dudley Seers argued that rather than constructing national accounts according to international standards, countries should "concentrate on improving specific rather than aggregate data" and develop statistical policy "designed for the problems of the territory and the statistical resources available."[81] While in these instances experts argued against clear standardization or reliance on GNP as a proxy for well-being, the international and national trends continued to move toward standardization and the widespread adoption of "macroeconomic abstractions" among national planners.[82]

Local capacity issues persisted through the 1950s and 1960s, despite the international standardization efforts. In Ghana, for instance, efforts to survey local production and consumption habits ran up against confusion and hostility. Researchers contracted to carry out basic data collection for Kwame Nkrumah's government's early household surveys encountered a wide range of challenges, from local people being "reticent" to give information to inaccurate answers. "A large amount of the data," one surveyor wrote, "was obviously incorrect."[83] Similar stories appeared elsewhere. In Egypt, the category of "farm" income obscured the country's myriad agricultural arrangements, and the standardization demanded by international estimates reproduced "a process of homogenization and averaging" that skirted local distinctions.[84] British economists attempting an early product account for Tanganyika encountered "a good deal of suspicion of government statistical collection" because officials did not effectively explain "the purpose of economic statistics." Not only did villagers distrust the roving researchers; some Tanganyikan government officials mistook the traveling economists for calculator salesmen.[85] During the independence era, some postcolonial governments tried to override Stone's international standards to include subsistence activities in their national accounts, but the lack of reliable survey data continued to make such estimates difficult. Zambia, the successor state to the colony of Northern Rhodesia, sought such estimates in its national accounts but had to rely on limited data from the Food and Agriculture Organization (FAO) well into the late 1960s. In much of sub-Saharan Africa regular surveys did not appear until the early 1970s.[86]

Yet for all the persistent problems of concept and measurement, the urge for international standardization won out. World Bank loans; UN dues payments; the power of growth rates as symbols of progress; the widespread push for increased production in a Cold War world all trumped experts' calls for local specificity and warnings over the flattening effects of standardized income across different regions. V. K. R. V. Rao wrote in 1953 that even as statisticians warned against the use of national income for comparing countries' well-being, "nevertheless, such comparisons are daily being made."[87] Moreover, economist and UN statistical commission official Harry Oshima stated in 1957, "the need for national income and expenditure statistics in underdeveloped countries will not diminish, but grow, because a measurement of the economy as a whole in value units and the quantification of each and all of the structural parts in a common unit are indispensable."[88] The cultural power and political valence of growth measured in GNP trumped expert concerns.

The Cold War, Decolonization, and the Globalization of the Growth Paradigm

There was a final and important reason why the criticisms of national income accounting had little impact: across the world leaders and citizens had embraced economic growth with enthusiasm. The growth paradigm seemed to be working well, as the scarcities of the depression and the sacrifices of wartime mobilization faded into memory. In the United States, GNP doubled from 1950 to 1965. New goods—television sets, a wide range of automobiles—flooded the domestic market, which US consumers bought en masse as millions settled into new suburban homes, shopped in vast new suburban malls, and consumed new forms of mass entertainment.[89] Though unevenly distributed, in public discourse and national policy, US elites promoted growth as a solution for social problems and as a way to undercut possible labor radicalism.[90] The focus on economic growth at home was matched by a similar desire to pursue growth abroad. An influential National Security Council report (NSC-68) of 1950 claimed, "The United States could achieve a substantial absolute increase in output and could thereby increase the allocation of resources to a build-up of the economic and military strength of itself and its allies without suffering a decline in its real standard of living" as long as GNP increased long into the future.[91]

Such thinking became commonplace among national security elites. "Not only the world position of the United States, but the security of the whole free world, is dependent on the avoidance of recession and on the long-term expansion of the US economy," the Eisenhower administration noted in the summer of 1953. "Threats to its stability or growth, therefore, constitute a danger to the security of the United States and of the coalition which it leads."[92]

Western European countries and Japan also made national economic growth the foremost goal of economic policy and centerpiece of national consciousness. The resulting changes were remarkable. The immediate postwar emphasis on full employment and increasing production and productivity dovetailed into nationally distinct but equally growth-oriented economies that linked low unemployment with expanding tax bases, generous social welfare policies, and high levels of production and consumption. Unemployment, as a proportion of the labor force, reached historically unprecedented lows during the 1950–69 period. In Western Europe, for those two decades only Italy averaged an unemployment rate over 5 percent annually (5.6 percent). The United Kingdom (1.4 percent), France (1.4 percent), and West Germany (2.5 percent) all vanquished the high unemployment of the interwar years.[93] High GNP growth rates symbolized recovery and transformation. For the 1950s, West Germany (6.5 percent average GNP growth rate), Italy (5.3 percent), and France (3.5 percent) stood out as remarkable successes of the growth moment.[94] Japan was the most remarkable of these states, averaging nearly 11 percent annual GNP growth from 1955 to 1970.[95]

All throughout the wealthy capitalist world, this rapid economic growth made possible robust social welfare programs that further defused class tensions and provided for social stability. There was wide variety in social policy and the forms that welfare took. West Germany's conservative leaders celebrated its "social market economy," which though based on competition, free trade, and the market also included important public investments in areas such as housing. By contrast, the British government established a universal "cradle to grave" system financed largely through national taxation that made important social services, such as health care, free at the point of service. Scandinavian countries' welfare policies included robust public provisions and steep progressive taxation to minimize income inequality.[96] Japan constructed a welfare state with typical health and social security provisions, though the country's social spending was consistently lower compared to Western European countries.[97] The United States built a federalized and racially blinkered welfare state that often served to reinforce racial and gender inequalities, one in which many benefits were "hidden" and "submerged" through an elaborate set of tax deductions most accessible to those with higher incomes and that often obscured federal payments to private companies.[98] There were, in other words, multiple "worlds of welfare capitalism" constructed during the postwar boom.[99]

In all these countries, the provision of social welfare services and social security policies strengthened the commitment to the growth paradigm among leaders and citizens alike. From 1950 to 1973, the average industrial country's public sector rose from 27 to 43 percent of GDP, while social transfers increased from an average of 7 to 15 percent of GDP.[100] Alongside the welfare states, governments invested in research and development, higher education, and major infrastructure (especially for automobile and air travel) that further stimulated high GNP growth rates.[101] While countries differed in the extent and form of state intervention in national economic life during this period, all mainstream political parties in the capitalist world were committed to a vision of political economy oriented to short- and long-term expansion. In the short term, the growth paradigm generally served to defuse violent conflicts between capital and labor under the promise of future shared gains, while the "funds needed to pay for the expansion of welfare states were in turn provided by stable politics." The "promise of eternal growth," in the words of Matthias Schmelzer, made possible the "consensual politics of welfare capitalism."[102] Welfare programs and public investments further served to "build and sustain consensus" in the growth paradigm as a framework through which citizens could make claims on state finances and through which states could make manifest the fruits of an expanding economy.[103]

International organizations within the capitalist world reinforced the growth paradigm. Nation-states maintained their commitments to the postwar international economic architecture through organizations such as OEEC, which was later reformed in 1960 as the Organisation for Economic Cooperation and Development (OECD). The OECD reinforced an international order that promoted national economic growth while minimizing international conflict.[104] Likewise, the desire for Western European integration stemmed from a hope among its architects that "increased trade within an integrated European market would accelerate the growth of per capita national incomes" and inculcate social values "akin to liberal capitalism" that would undermine support for communist tendencies and further militate against class conflict.[105] Embracing the growth paradigm both continued to serve national interests and formed the basis of international economic cooperation among capitalist countries into the 1960s.

The socialist and communist countries also pursued rapid growth during this period. Mao Zedong viewed economic growth as necessary for China's national development, consolidation of his party's control over the country, and waging Cold War. Mao believed his Great Leap Forward would spark a major "boost in the agricultural and industrial production in China," which would be "beneficial for all the countries of the socialist camp, for all of global communism, for everyone, who fights against colonialism and imperialism."[106] Mao's large-scale development initiatives also required a vast expansion of the country's statistical capacity to measure and report on its economic growth targets.[107] In the Soviet Union, Nikita Khrushchev, Stalin's successor, continued to pursue growth even as he moved away from shock industrialization toward a more consumer-oriented system. He also oversaw a series of major development projects designed to boost agricultural production such as the Virgin Lands campaign. Like Mao, Khrushchev viewed national economic growth as part of a geopolitical strategy. He engineered his domestic reforms in order to "beat postwar capitalism at its own game—mass prosperity."[108] As he told the Soviet presidium in late 1959, "Our ideological debates with capitalism will be resolved not through war, but through economic competition."[109] Soviet statisticians calculated at the end of the 1960s that the Soviet GNP increased by a factor of 7.5 between 1950 and 1968.[110] The Soviet Union presented its dramatic increase in industrial production as symbolic of the power of central planning.[111]

During this high tide of the growth paradigm, issues about measuring growth did not fade away entirely. One interesting set of questions surrounded how to assess the validity of Soviet growth and properly calculate aggregate figures for socialist economies. In the United States, for instance, the Rockefeller Foundation supported a series of attempts by economists, working through the National Bureau of Economic Research (NBER), to assess the validity of Soviet growth claims.[112] It was a challenging intellectual task that stemmed from dubious official reports and technical difficulties in measuring economic change absent a market-based system of valuation long discussed in the "socialist calculation debate."[113] Researchers found high growth rates for the Soviet Union (though ones that often fell short of the Soviets' professed totals), but they noted ongoing challenges in measurement such as "selectivity of published data," "ambiguity" of definitions and concepts, and "the general overstatement of absolute levels of output."[114] Yet Soviet claims of rapid growth so alarmed US officials that the State Department Bureau of Intelligence and Research covertly estimated Soviet growth in approximations of GNP throughout the decade.[115] Even with these methodological and conceptual challenges, GNP set the terms of the Cold War economic rivalry.

The pursuit of national economic growth for geopolitical ends shaped the ways in which the superpowers interpreted the politics of decolonization. The United States expanded on the Point Four program throughout the 1950s.[116] In 1961, the Kennedy administration deepened the US commitment to foreign aid by creating the Agency for International Development (USAID) to organize development efforts and by establishing the Alliance for Progress for Latin America in the wake of the Cuban revolution of 1959. "Economic development assistance can no longer be subordinated to, or viewed simply as a convenient tool for meeting, short-run political objectives," the president proclaimed. "Long-range, self-sustained economic growth of less developed nations is our goal."[117] Growth at home and growth in the Third World were mutually constitutive. "A generous foreign aid program is a long-term investment in the free world, and it is also easier to maintain out of a growing national product," Kennedy adviser and economist Walter Heller explained. "In addition, a strong and growing American economy provides a dependable market for the exports of the underdeveloped countries and permits them to help themselves."[118]

The communist powers responded in kind. Stalin had shown little interest in Third World politics, but Khrushchev adopted a more aggressive policy of providing material support to help position the Soviets as the leader of global revolution over their Chinese (and later, Cuban) counterparts. The Soviets sent experts and aid abroad throughout the late 1950s and early 1960s to countries such as India, Egypt, and Ghana. The Soviet Union also nurtured its own field of development economics, with scholars drawing often on experiences in Central Asia and emphasizing central planning, mechanization of agriculture, and industrialization (for some, though not all, countries). In all cases, the "state was to be the only engine of growth."[119] On January 6, 1961, Khrushchev announced that the Soviet Union would support wars of "national liberation" across the globe, a siren call placing it in the vanguard of anticolonial and Marxist revolutions. By the early 1960s, Mao's China joined the competition, jostling for support among fledgling minority communist parties throughout the Third World, often inciting conflicts with Soviet-backed communist and nationalist regimes, as in India and Algeria.[120]

By the early 1960s, the growth paradigm had truly gone global. In late 1961, the UN General Assembly proclaimed the 1960s as the "United Nations Development Decade" (on President Kennedy's urging). To give the phrase meaning, the General Assembly encouraged all developing countries to set GNP growth rate targets of at least 5 percent per year. Economic experts still recognized the many flaws with the reliance on GNP figures. Their value as analytic shorthand and symbolic marker of development, however, was too great. As the OECD explained, "The test of national product or income is particularly crude because of the inadequacy and unreliability of the information about the less-developed countries which is available to us. . . . Nevertheless, this is the only short-hand measure available to us."[121] National politics and geopolitical concerns made growth seem imperative. "The present interest in growth is not accidental," economist Evsey Domar wrote in 1957. "It comes on the one side from a belated awareness that in our economy full employment without growth is impossible and, on the other, from the present international conflict which makes growth a condition of survival."[122] The Cold War and decolonization provided the intellectual and strategic justification for economic growth, while the pursuit of rapid economic growth exacerbated Cold War conflict. "The cold war will last a very long time," British economist Peter Wiles wrote in 1956. "Only by outgrowing the enemy can we keep on winning it."[123]

To help win that war, economists played important roles as producers of new research and as policy advisers. By the early 1960s, growth theory moved to the center of mainstream economic research. In 1956, American economist Robert Solow and Australian economist Trevor Swan developed separate models that became known as the neoclassical growth model or the Solow model. It showed that over the short term the rate of growth was independent of the rate of saving (which challenged established thinking) and that over the longer term, technological innovation drove growth.[124] Solow and a rising generation of growth theorists caught the eye of President Kennedy, who hired or appointed "growthmen" such as Solow, Walter Heller, James Tobin, and Leon Keyserling. By 1961, economists and policy makers alike were living in the "kingdom of Solovia," where Solow's growth model reigned supreme as the administration adopted, in Solow's words, a major "growth-oriented program."[125] These economists epitomized a widespread technocratic liberal triumphalism that promised stable growth, the smooth management of social and political conflict, and national power.[126]

A parallel and related group of development economists built on the work of Paul Rosenstein-Rodan and Arthur Lewis to bring the latest research to bear on the Third World. Development economists and growth experts traveled the world to share their expertise. Indian development became an object of particular fascination among economists and statisticians: Simon Kuznets, Jan Tinbergen, Nicholas Kaldor, Leon Keyserling, Ragnar Frisch, Milton Friedman, Wassily Leontief, Michał Kalecki, and M. I. Rubinshtein among many others visited India for research and consulting purposes during the late 1940s and 1950s.[127] Arthur Lewis was a key adviser to Kwame Nkrumah's government in Ghana.[128] The Ford Foundation and Rockefeller Foundation supported the spread of growth experts and centers dedicated to the study of economic growth in countries such as Pakistan.[129] By the early 1960s, development economists who proposed ways to achieve rapid growth had become important figures in policy making, as policy makers sought ways to spark and sustain growth. Far removed from the cautiousness of Phyllis Deane or the skepticism of Dudley Seers, growth theorists and modernization experts acted as engineers for the growth paradigm, suggesting that their models and analysis could be used to guide countries through stages toward a prosperous future.

Conclusion

During the two decades after Austin Robinson pondered what the British knew about the economic well-being of their colonial subjects, measuring and valuing economic life in terms of GNP and defining economic purpose in terms of growth went global. The effects of this transformation were many. The global diffusion of national statistical agencies and the standardization of national income accounting further linked political independence to the nation-state form. In this process, GNP became the dominant metric of national economic policy making and a stand-in for national vitality. GNP growth also provided a conceptual framework for understanding the tectonic shifts in international politics, such as those caused by the erosion or erasure of territorial empires. The fixed hierarchies that structured colonialism—a world of rulers and the ruled—gave way to a more fluid hierarchy of developmental phases. GNP defined these phases, conveying how countries related to one another. India was "poor" compared to the United Kingdom because GNP figures suggested it; Argentina was richer than Ghana, because GNP figures suggested it. Yet all these countries could, by growing their GNP, move up in the developmental hierarchy. GNP growth performed a narrative role, explaining one country's future in terms of another's past—to imagine that India's economy was equivalent to the United States' in an earlier era, for instance—which enabled anxious Cold War policy makers and restive anticolonial elites to measure economic life and define national goals with easily comparable aggregates.

Powerful though this growth paradigm was, its diffusion betrayed the myriad logistical and conceptual difficulties that statisticians and economists encountered. Looking back, it can be tempting to view the critiques of experts such as Phyllis Deane, Dudley Seers, and S. Herbert Frankel as irrelevant. But to do so would be overlook the range and extent of the debate over the meaning and measurement of economic growth across the colonial and postcolonial world. And, as we will see, the concerns voiced by the critics in the 1940s resurfaced over the coming decades. The downsides and flaws of the growth paradigm were not evident just in hindsight. Intellectuals and activists identified a range of problems associated with the growth paradigm even as it pervaded the postwar world. For leaders, growth may have appeared a necessary "condition of survival," as Evsey Domar claimed. But for a growing chorus of critics, the global pursuit of growth seemed far less necessary—and far more dangerous—than most believed.

THREE

The Growth Critics

They had diverse backgrounds, but they shared similar frustrations. The pursuit of growth in the United States had created "voracious, wasteful, compulsive consumers," wrote the American journalist Vance Packard in 1960.[1] Economic growth governed by a technocratic elite rendered social life in the wealthy, industrialized countries alienating and aimless. "Everything has become function and object of the economy," argued French social critic Jacques Ellul in 1964, with little space for ways of living that did not contribute to increasing output.[2] The growth paradigm produced societies whose "productivity is destructive of the free development of human needs and faculties," argued the German social theorist Herbert Marcuse in the same year.[3] These critics found common cause with many who worried that all the promises of growth had not materialized as planned. In a searing speech in 1968, Pakistani economist and planner Mahbub ul Haq lamented that despite enviable GNP growth rates, "most people remained unaffected by the forces of economic change since the development had fast become warped in favour of a privileged minority."[4] Where rapid growth had occurred, it did so in uneven, unexpected, and often deleterious ways.

Few articulated the growing frustrations with the growth paradigm as fully as British economist Dudley Seers. As one of the world's foremost experts on economic measurement, Seers had spent much of the 1940s and 1950s traveling to set up statistical offices in developing countries and to teach young statisticians how to model national

(3) Dudley Seers (1920–83). Photograph courtesy of
the Institute of Development Studies.

income. By the mid-1960s, however, Seers began to rethink the basic assumptions of his work. He argued that experts, policy makers, and leaders had mistakenly believed that high GNP growth rates would generate widely shared prosperity, build social cohesion, and minimize political conflicts. Two decades of contrary experience, however, led Seers to argue that growth enthusiasts too often had conflated economic expansion with social transformation. "Why do we confuse development with economic growth?," he asked in 1969.[5] To Seers, asking what economists were trying to measure was a way to pose even more basic questions: who development benefited, how it was pursued, what developers could do, and most of all, what development *should* do and what it should mean.

The group that I call the growth critics included activists, intellectuals, and policy makers who criticized different aspects of the growth paradigm. Some, such as Packard and many environmentalists, highlighted the harmful ecological consequences of growth. Others, such as Ellul and Marcuse, linked the pursuit of material abundance with the growing technocratic and alienating nature of contemporary society. Growth critics in the Second World challenged various aspects of the Soviet bloc countries' pursuit of rapid expansion, as well. At the same time, international development experts and Third World intellectuals echoed Haq's and Seers's concerns that the focus on GNP growth led policy makers to overlook vast social and political problems, from inequality to authoritarianism to poverty. Many of these thinkers attacked growth as a policy goal and the use of economic metrics such as GNP as indicators of well-being. All these critics emerged during the high tide of the growth paradigm during the 1950s and 1960s. There was no single event or moment that gave rise to the growth critics. Rather, it is important to understand that growth enthusiasts and critics coexisted in the same time and space, in tension and conflict over the meaning and promise of the growth paradigm.

The growth critics often shared a broader critique of modernity voiced by leftist student activists, protest movements, and counterculture thinkers. They decried growth and its metrics (such as GNP) as the root cause behind environmental decline, social dislocation and alienation, mass culture and loss of tradition, and growing inequalities of power and wealth. But it is fruitful to read the upheavals of the "global 1960s" alongside the growth critics. So much of what animated protests and unrest stemmed from the fact that what growth enthusiasts had promised—widespread and widely shared wealth, the dissolution of social conflicts—did not come to fruition. In other words, disappointment with the unexpected aspects of what growth did generate (pollution, distant elite governance) and what it did not (equality, democracy) informed widespread dissent and activism. Similarly, growth critics often associated the problems of modernity with the pursuit of rapid economic growth. While they often drew their conclusions from specific cases—be it Packard's reporting on American cities or Haq's work for the Pakistani government—the growth critics depicted the problems of growth as global and universal, affecting all societies.

Moreover, it is important to note that the growth critics were not just activists and intellectuals; many were also experts who had once been growth enthusiasts. Dudley Seers and Mahbub ul Haq were two of many experts who had previously supported the propagation of national income accounting methods and growth-oriented national planning yet had come to doubt the virtues of doing so. Widely respected economists such as Hans Singer, Albert Hirschman, Colin Clark, and Simon Kuznets grappled with the realization that they had not been accounting for environmental destruction, the social dislocation that stemmed from industrialization and mechanization, and persistent poverty. The growth critics embodied this irony, as they confronted the downsides of technocratic governance to which they had contributed.

Environmental Critiques

As leaders worldwide pursued rapid economic growth during and after World War II, environmental thinkers raised concerns about the new orthodoxy. Conservationists Fairfield Osborn and William Vogt both published best-selling books in 1948 that warned of the environmental consequences of economic growth.[6] The ecologist and wildlife enthusiast Aldo Leopold's *A Sand County Almanac* (1949), called for a new "land ethic" and "ecological conscience" to balance the economic drive that shaped postwar American life.[7] Other environmentalists saw similar problems abroad. British scientist Julian Huxley, German zoologist Bernhard Grzimek, Swedish scientist Kai Curry-Lindahl, and many former colonial game wardens and national park officials, such as Belgian Jean-Paul Harroy, worried similarly about the loss of protected spaces in the colonial and postcolonial world and created a new international nongovernmental organization (NGO), the International Union for the Conservation of Nature (IUCN) to promote the protection of natural spaces and conservation practices.[8] The early environmental critics of growth revealed that many experts were well aware that the pursuit of growth was significant not only for what it promised but for what its enthusiasts overlooked or ignored.

During the 1950s and 1960s, environmental growth critics focused on how growth had reshaped the wealthy industrial world and on looming fears that it would do so across the so-called developing world. Growth theories, be they capitalist or communist, left little space for the natural world. The material fact of increasing production and consumption required vast inputs of fossil fuel energy. Industrialization, urbanization, and agricultural mechanization all imperiled the nonhuman world and human health. Concerns over the implications of global economic growth—resource exhaustion, the erosion of protected spaces, pollution, and much else—shaped the thinking of many mid-twentieth-century environmental thinkers, such as Osborn, Vogt, Leopold, Huxley, Max Nicholson, and Russell Train.[9] For them, the ideological divisions of the Cold War world were less significant than the fact that both systems aspired to a vision of industrial modernity that threatened planetary well-being.

In one major set of arguments, environmental growth critics claimed there were ecological limits to economic growth. Already by the early 1950s, there were growing fears among the wealthy countries about resource scarcity limiting future abundance. Many postwar US officials worried about shortages of critical materials and hoped that conservation practices, organized and guided by scientists working through the United Nations, could help manage their development according to progressive era notions of wise use."[10] These concerns became acute during the Korean War. President Harry S. Truman convened the President's Materials Policy Commission (or Paley Commission) in 1951 to examine potential global resource scarcities. The report acknowledged the prospect of future shortages, but it also dismissed any need to rein in economic production and recommended continued "growth and high consumption." The commission also called for the creation of Resources for the Future, an organization to study future resource needs; it was established in 1952 with grants from the Ford Foundation.[11]

Over the 1960s, more critics raised alarms about limits to growth.

Kenneth Boulding was a leading figure on this front. Born in Liverpool, England, in 1910, in the late 1930s Boulding migrated to the United States, where he earned a reputation as a promising young Keynesian economist. During the following decades, however, he worried about the environmental consequences of the growth paradigm and became a well-known and popular critic of conventional economic analysis. A clever writer who relied on unusual metaphors to convey his ideas, in 1966 he published what became an oft-repeated critique of growth economics. He contrasted the "cowboy economy"—an economy focused on growth and a mistaken belief in "infinite reservoirs from which material can be obtained and into which effluvia can be deposited"—with an idealized "spaceship economy" based on restraint and recycling. Boulding's emphasis on creating economic systems that respected the inherent biophysical limits imposed by "spaceship earth" set the stage for similar widely publicized research.[12] Garrett Hardin's influential study of the "tragedy of the commons" was based on the assumption that "it is clear that we will greatly increase human misery if we do not, during the immediate future, assume that the world available to the terrestrial human population is finite."[13] A related critique focused on the use of industrial technologies that used large quantities of natural resources. German British economist E. F. Schumacher was the most prominent figure to argue instead for small-scale, contextually "appropriate" technologies to reduce resource use, waste, and pollution.[14]

By the end of the decade, the concern about ecological limits found its most forceful expression among those who linked population growth with environmental decline and resource exhaustion. Stanford biologist Paul Ehrlich's 1968 book *The Population Bomb* epitomized the growing chorus of critics who believed that absent coercive (and often forcible) population control measures, conflict would arise as growing numbers of people competed for increasingly scarce resources.[15] Research by a small but well-funded NGO called the Club of Rome amplified these fears. Led by a transnational network of businessmen, bureaucrats, and scholars, and supported by the OECD and Rockefeller Foundation, the Club of Rome brought in experts in technological forecasting, whose models suggested that resource use, population growth, pollution, and technological change would inter-act to curtail future economic expansion. At one of the group's first meetings in Bellagio, Italy, in October 1968 the discussion coalesced into a "blunt critique of unbridled economic growth and its social and ecological consequences."[16] Over the next few years, the group sup-ported computer-based systems analysis produced at MIT, led by Donella and Dennis Meadows. The result, the 1972 *Limits to Growth* report, predicted that planetary limits to growth would be reached "within the next one hundred years," causing a "sudden and uncon-trollable decline in both population and industrial capacity."[17] As we'll see, the report drew widespread attention to the ecological downsides of growth.[18] With Boulding, Hardin, Schumacher, and Ehrlich, the *Limits to Growth* team's arguments shared a depiction of economic growth as a process that required limitless resources, an assumption that growth enthusiasts had foolishly embraced frameworks of techni-cal progress and substitutions as solutions for ecological limits, and a fear that future growth would threaten the well-being of all.

In addition, a second and related set of environmental growth criti-cisms concerned the untallied "costs" of economic growth. Environ-mental growth critics also feared that the growth process generated extensive pollution and waste that imperiled human health and eco-systems alike. Such worries were nothing new, of course. Some of the earliest conservation efforts of the eighteenth and nineteenth centu-ries focused on scientific concerns over wasteful resource depletion and excessive pollution.[19] What became apparent to many growth crit-ics over the 1950s and 1960s was that generating economic growth *required* harmful chemical inputs into the production process that left as dangerous outputs. Rachel Carson's 1962 book *Silent Spring* revealed how thoroughly Americans had been exposed to dangerous pesticides. The book ignited widespread controversy and debate over the extent of chemical pollution.[20] Subsequent environmental writ-ers treated pollution as a threat to human and wildlife health and a symbol of values gone awry. Vance Packard's study of the wastefulness of American society tied waste to social and moral degradation. The national "emphasis on ever-greater productivity and consumption" raised the possibility of developing the economy "within the confines of a psychologically sick and psychologically impoverished society."[21] Social critics Murray Bookchin and Herbert Marcuse linked growth and its profligacy with a broader ideology of domination. In Marcuse's words, the "perfection of waste" and the "quantification of nature" led humankind to a flawed view of nature as a holding tank of resources waiting to be exploited for ever-greater production and consumption.[22]

In general, many of the environmental movements that swept the world focused in part on such "costs" of growth to human well-being: air pollution, water pollution, industrial and household waste, deforestation, and erosion all loomed large. In addition to the well-known crusaders for pollution control, over the 1960s a number of economists argued that the root cause of pollution was that the numbers used to give growth meaning—aggregates such as GNP—obscured these costs to policy makers and markets alike. Pollution, critics often pointed out, was literally not counted in assessing the size of a country's income and product. British economist Ezra Mishan's widely heralded 1967 book *The Costs of Economic Growth* captured this line of argument: growth produced "disamenities"—ranging from industrial pollution to noise—for which economists did not properly account.[23] Mishan suggested that the continued pursuit of growth would reduce rather than increase social welfare. Even the *Economist* acknowledged that Mishan's book revealed "real and growing defects in western society."[24] Kenneth Boulding put the issue in plain terms in 1970: "When somebody pollutes something and somebody else cleans it up, the cleanup is added to the national product and the pollution is not subtracted; that, of course, is ridiculous."[25] GNP obscured environmental degradation and incorporated many undesirable costs associated with pollution.

Building on these arguments, a number of economists drew on older economic traditions in resource economics and agricultural economics to highlight the costs of growth. Robert U. Ayres and Allen Kneese, two economists working with Resources for the Future, the think tank that emerged out of the Paley Commission report, laid out the case that modern economic growth and the economic thinking on which it rested was fundamentally flawed because it could not account for aspects of production and consumption—pollution, waste—that existed outside the closed economic models that had shaped national policy. They called these "externalities," a concept developed by British economist Arthur Pigou to describe a cost not priced into a given activity. The core problem was "viewing the production and consumption processes in a manner that is somewhat at variance with the fundamental law of conservation of mass." They argued, "water and air are traditionally examples of free goods in economics," yet allocation problems loomed "larger as increased population and industrial production put more pressure on the environment's ability to dilute and chemically degrade waste products. Only the crudest estimates of present external costs associated with residuals discharge exist but it would not be surprising if these costs were in the tens of billions of dollars annually."[26] In this line of thinking, growth generated problems that could outweigh its benefits, and the absence in existing economic models of effective information (prices) for these costs rendered their consequences effectively invisible. Along with concerns about ecological limits to growth, arguments about the costs of growth pervaded environmental critiques of the growth paradigm during the 1950s and 1960s.

Social Critics in an Age of Affluence

As environmental growth critics raised alarms about growth, many others found common cause, drawing connections between the pursuit of material abundance and its immaterial consequences. One of the core assumptions of growth enthusiasts was that economic expansion would establish the conditions for a world of leisure and social harmony. Yet beginning in the mid-1950s there was a growing sense in wealthy countries that such a world was not in the offing. Growth had produced tremendous material abundance, but it did not redound to psychological or spiritual fulfillment. The growth paradigm had produced prosperity, but it was unevenly distributed. The pursuit of growth had refashioned economic life, but it also created undesirable social changes.

Across the wealthy world, intellectuals and activists critiqued the ways in which growth and the modernity it promised had left many feeling frustrated, constrained, and disappointed. French social critic Jacques Ellul provided an early outline of many such concerns in *The Technological Society* (1954). Ellul linked the focus on economic growth with the growing power of technocrats and administrative planning that left humanity with "nothing more to lose, and nothing to win."[27] Herbert Marcuse and his Frankfurt School colleagues shared similar concerns. Marcuse drew connections between Cold War militarism and rapid economic growth—dual threats to social well-being—in his 1964 book *One-Dimensional Man.* "The union of growing productivity and growing destruction; the brinkmanship of annihilation; the surrender of thought, hope, and fear to the decisions of the powers that be; the preservation of misery in the face of unprecedented wealth constitute the most impartial indictment," he claimed, "even if they are not the raison d'être of this society but only its by product: its sweeping rationality, which propels efficiency and growth, is itself irrational."[28] Growth produced a society defined by a preoccupation with productivity and consumerism that undermined meaningful freedom. "The enchained possibilities of advanced industrial societies are: development of the productive forces on an enlarged scale, extension of the conquest of nature, growing satisfaction of new needs and faculties. But these possibilities are gradually being realized through means and institutions which cancel their liberating potential, and this process affects not only the means but also the ends."[29] Growth generated new forms of domination and despair rather than greater human freedom or social harmony.

Marcuse and Ellul's criticisms resonated with intellectuals who depicted the increase of aggregate product and mass consumerism as misguided social priorities. Alvin Hansen, American economist and prominent Keynesian during the New Deal, warned that "quality [as opposed to sheer quantitative measures of output] and social priorities at long last must concern us or we perish in the midst of plenty."[30] Renowned poet Archibald MacLeish sounded what would become a recurrent alarm of the growth critics: growth produced existential

hollowness and despair. He wrote, "We are prosperous, lively, successful, inventive, diligent—but, nevertheless and notwithstanding, something is wrong and we know it."[31] Paragon of the US liberal establishment Arthur Schlesinger enjoined his compatriots to move beyond the
economic growth "creed" to a new focus on "enlarging the individual's
opportunity for moral growth and self-fulfillment." Canadian economist John Kenneth Galbraith lamented US policy makers' preoccupation with "the production of private goods" rather than a more careful
and bespoke focus on "public needs" and the "distribution" of aggregate
output.[32] French social theorist Jean Baudrillard linked the "mystique
of GNP" with an increasingly misguided cult of consumerism and
materialism in his 1970 book *The Consumer Society*.[33] Concerns about
equality and distribution grew in prominence across the world. For
instance, in 1965 eminent French sociologist Pierre Bourdieu debated
government statisticians and economists about the effects of quantitative growth and social equality, helping to raise the salience of such
issues at the OECD.[34]

Fears over the social consequences of growth became especially
acute in the United States during the late 1950s and early 1960s.
American intellectuals lamented how the pursuit of growth encouraged crass consumerism, spiritual aimlessness, and social anxieties.
Sociologist David Riesman commented in 1958, "It is extraordinary
how little we have anticipated the problems of the bountiful future,
other than to fall back on remedies which did not work in the less bountiful past, such as individualism, thrift, hard work, and enterprise on
the one side, or harmony, togetherness, and friendliness on the other."[35]
Social critic Robert Nisbet echoed these themes, arguing that growth
did not mean that the United States had become "free of social problems." Rather, in studying the persistence of social problems such as
poverty, violence, and bigotry, he relied on philosophers from "Hesiod
to Schweitzer" who argued that when "developing wealth and power
a society must draw upon personal qualities—avarice, ambition, ego-
ism, and others—which are the very antithesis of the qualities upon
which social harmony and moral consensus rest."[36] The pressures of
social mobility, an aggressive work ethos, and a preoccupation with

productivity contributed to the rise of medical concern with "stress," a term that first entered public consciousness following the publication of physiologist Hans Selye's 1956 best-selling book *The Stress of Life*.[37] Economist Robert Heilbroner's 1956 study on the "quest for wealth" reflected how thoroughly the growth paradigm shaped how social scientists came to understand historical change. Heilbroner argued that acquisitiveness was a driving force behind all humanity. He placed the contemporary United States as the logical end point of the deep-seated, universal drive to generate more economic growth.[38]

These social critics of growth grew in prominence as social conflicts gripped much of the First World. In the United States, the civil rights movement laid bare the persistent inequalities that the growth paradigm had not eradicated—and in many cases, had exacerbated. Discriminatory policies and practices had consistently excluded communities of color from the shared abundance. Early civil rights activism often focused on sites of consumption—bus boycotts, sit-ins at lunch counters—where African Americans had been denied free and equal access.[39] Racial wealth and income inequality was an important theme of the civil rights movement. As Martin Luther King Jr. famously declared more than once, "the Negro lives on a lonely island of poverty in the midst of a vast ocean of material prosperity."[40] Subsequent US government studies affirmed what King and many activists had long known: that aggregate economic indicators had inadequately revealed the scope of racial inequalities, especially as urban rioting over the course of the 1960s had drawn together the concerns for civil and political rights with the realities of economic injustice. A federal commission designed to study social unrest noted the "paradoxical situation" of "economic indicators" that were "generally registering continued progress" while "the streets and the newspapers" were "full of evidence of growing discontent—burning and looting in the ghetto, strife on the campus, crime in the street, alienation and defiance among the young."[41]

The feminist movement likewise exposed the invisibility of women's contribution to society and how a political economy focused on male breadwinners had repressed women. Feminist writer Betty Friedan, for instance, articulated these themes in many popular essays and her breakthrough 1963 book *The Feminine Mystique*. So much of the prosperity generated in the postwar years, she argued, had either excluded women or been structured around social norms that locked women within the domestic sphere. The "feminine mystique" masked what she called "occupation: housewife," where women's household labor went unremunerated and left the role "housewife-mothers" as the "model for all women."[42] Women's self-fulfillment, Friedan claimed in a popular 1960 essay for *Good Housekeeping*, would come only when "women begin to *use* the education, the freedom, the labor-saving appliances, the added years of life which have become available to them in recent decade."[43] Feminist activists often highlighted the ways in which women's work, especially domestic labor, was excluded from conventional accounts. In one of the earliest expositions of such research, social scientist Lisa Leghorn used a survey by Chase Manhattan to find out "what a wife was worth" to highlight all the ways in which women's activities had been elided in official statistics.[44] Leghorn built on the same thinking that had guided Phyllis Deane's pioneering research from the early 1940s but with a powerful contemporary valence amid a rising tide of feminist activism.

Concerns about the growth paradigm percolated up to policy makers. In February 1960, President Dwight Eisenhower convened a commission on "national goals" to invite leading scholars, businessmen, journalists, and politicians to discuss the country's moral purpose amid its economic boom. Presidential candidate Robert F. Kennedy spoke about many of the flaws of the growth paradigm in a March 1968 speech. Kennedy pointed out that although US GNP was over $800 billion, it counted "air pollution and cigarette advertising, and ambulances to clear our highways of carnage . . . special locks for our doors and the jails for the people who break them . . . the destruction of the redwood and the loss of our natural wonder in chaotic sprawl . . . nuclear warheads and armored cars for the police to fight the riots in our cities." GNP—and by extension, those who relied on it as a measure of welfare—did not account for "the health of our children, the quality of their education or the joy of their play . . . the beauty of our poetry or the strength of our marriages, the intelligence of our public debate or the integrity of our public officials." In short, it measured everything "except that which makes life worthwhile."[45]

By the end of the 1960s, the criticisms against growth and its attendant components—materialism, consumerism, pollution—were widespread. Student and worker protests swept the world in the 1960s, roiling cities such as Washington, Paris, Berlin, Rome, Mexico City, Tokyo, and Toronto. Critiquing many aspects of modern life, from the Cold War and militarism (exemplified by the US war in Vietnam) to the spiritual vacuity of consumerism, student protestors sought to imagine a world of new values and a new politics beyond the growth-fueled postwar technocracy.[46] At the height of activism in 1968, student protestors in Rome and Paris held up placards with the names "Marx, Mao, and Marcuse," merging revolutionary socialism with critical theory to argue against the capitalist status quo.[47] Protestors linked GNP growth to a variety of ills, as in Japan where activists rallied round the slogan "Kutabare GNP" (or, "to hell with GNP") because high GNP growth seemed responsible for widespread pollution, inequality, and inflation.[48] Activists challenged their leaders' pursuit of rapid national economic growth and even the "legitimacy and prestige" of the nation-state itself.[49]

That the protests and social unrest occurred during a period of relative growth was especially troubling to leaders. An extensive 1970 survey by the *Financial Times* of Australia revealed an "underlying uneasiness" among leaders as they acknowledged high poverty and growing social and labor unrest despite strong GNP growth rates.[50] NATO formed a special committee dedicated to the social and environmental "challenges of modern society" because to many elites, in the words of West German sociologist and committee member Ralf Dahrendorf, the very "vitality" of their domestic societies was in question amid the unrest and unanticipated ecological problems they faced.[51] Business leaders also recognized the scale of the unrest. "There is no question that youth has been the catalyst for widespread public attention" to all the "dislocations" and "negative aspects" of economic growth, claimed a contributor to IBM's in-house magazine, *Think*.[52]

In all these cases, elites struggled to make sense of the growing dissatisfaction and frustration.

Social critics of growth and modernity were not limited to the capitalist world. There was growing discontent within the Soviet Union and Eastern Europe, too. Official concern in the Soviet Union focused on the country's economic troubles. Soviet statistics suggested that the country's growth rate had declined over the 1960s (7 percent NMP for the decade compared to over 10 percent for the 1950s). Subsequent analyses revealed that the authorities had greatly exaggerated growth, with the CIA estimating a growth rate of only 4.9 percent on average for the 1965–70 period and subsequent independent investigations showing it to be only about 4.1 percent. Soviet economists and central planners struggled to manage the complex economic system they had created.[53] The few top-down attempts to boost performance floundered. For instance, Premier Alexei Kosygin launched a series of reforms in 1965 to increase the output of consumer goods to respond to the growing discontent over the patterns of Soviet growth, but to little avail.[54] Eastern European leaders fared little better. Czechoslovakian officials experimented with piecemeal reforms during the 1960s, which contributed to a brief increase in national income growth but also led to "disarray and confusion throughout economic policymaking circles" with little consensus on how far to promote liberalization.[55]

Reformers argued that the Soviet political system hamstrung its ability to make economic changes. Dissidents such as the physicist Andrei Sakharov railed against the Soviet leadership for its inability to adapt to new technologies and worried that past growth had contributed to an antidemocratic and inflexible political structure. Sakharov and two fellow critics wrote in 1970, "We surpass America in the mining of coal, but we lag behind in oil drilling, lag very much behind in gas drilling and in the production of electrical power, hopelessly lag behind in chemistry and infinitely lag behind in computer technology." Only by political reforms to change the "antidemocratic traditions and norms of public life that appeared during Stalin's period and have not been completely liquidated" could the country even begin to adapt to the electronic and informational technological changes in capitalist economies.[56]

Yet for many others, especially young people, lagging growth was not the only problem. Youth and worker discontent simmered amid growing anomie and frustration with repressive state authorities. A 1964 survey in the Soviet Union revealed that four out of every five students refused to heed the leadership's call to take part in Khrushchev's Virgin Lands campaign, which led leaders to worry about the regime's domestic vulnerabilities.[57] A socialist counterculture and protest movements also emerged in the 1960s, though at a much smaller scale than that which swept across Western campuses and cities. Intellectuals and artists explored the world beyond social realism, and students confronted what they saw as the rise of technocratic elites and a stifling and ossified government bureaucracy that had deviated from the revolutionary era and corrupted socialism's emancipatory possibilities. Future leader Mikhail Gorbachev and his wife, Raisa, were members of the new subculture. They and their friends spent the 1960s pondering the future of socialism and reading Western philosophers popular with their counterparts across the Iron Curtain, such as Jean-Paul Sartre, Martin Heidegger, and Marcuse.[58]

Students and intellectuals challenged orthodoxy in the Eastern bloc but faced considerable repression from authorities. In Leipzig in October 1965, young music fans protested the East German state's crackdown on rock-and-roll music. East German authorities responded with water cannons, truncheons, and attack dogs, an "assault that that established a pattern in the state's relationship with nonconformist youth culture."[59] In East Germany and the Soviet Union, authorities launched periodic campaigns against youthful consumers and intellectuals—"degenerates" in Khrushchev's words and "do-nothings" in East German slang—who bucked cultural orthodoxy and flaunted their frustrations with the state.[60] A Polish woman who participated in the early 1968 protests in Warsaw recalled that she and her fellow students rebelled because they felt that "something had gone wrong both in Poland and the entire socialist camp. We were surrounded by poverty, fear, depression, stupefying propaganda, suspicion and mutual distrust." Students joined workers' demonstrations, held furtive seminars, and participated in protest marches in the hopes of bringing about a more humane and effective form of socialism.

Authorities responded aggressively, suppressing the dissident movements through violence, widespread arrests, and a campaign of "psychological terror."[61] The Soviet response to the Prague Spring in 1968
encapsulated the growing sense that Moscow would not countenance
mass protest or major liberalization campaigns.[62] Dissidents and protestors persisted in their efforts to critique Soviet modernity, despite
the state repression, into the 1970s.[63]

Social scientists in the Eastern bloc grappled with these develop-
ments much as their Western counterparts did. In 1965, for instance,
the Czech Academy of the Sciences brought together leading experts
to search for "new, humanist variants of a technologically advanced
civilization."[64] Given rapid technological change and "rapid development of the material basis of human life," the report's main author,
philosopher Radovan Richta, argued that the socialist governments
needed to redress the widespread social dislocation caused by technological innovation and rapid economic growth. The report called
for increasing investment in science and research and shifting labor
from industrial sectors to "science and research, technological preparation, highly skilled occupations, and to public welfare." The report
also included demands for a more socially conscious work and life balance, one not at odds with twenty-first-century workplace wellness
culture. Planners needed to address "air and water purity, nature preservation, healthy modes of life, [and] mental health" to help citizens
adapt to modern life.[65]

What linked all these disparate protestors and scholars together
was a shared sense that modern societies faced serious social issues
that could not be resolved through greater economic growth alone.
Though there were "diverse goals" among those who protested the status quo, there were also many "entanglements" between activists in
the United States, Western Europe, and Eastern Europe. The "relative affluence, along with democratization in Western Europe and the
post-Stalinist thaw in the East opened spaces for youth to develop distinctive identities and interests and for students, workers, and intellectuals alike to articulate sharp critiques of both communism and
capitalist democracies."[66] Despite the limited political space avail-

able within Eastern European countries, youthful counterculture protestors nonetheless drew connections across borders. As one East German protestor recalled, "The protest forms of the 68ers and their models for an alternative way of life made a great impression" on him and his friends.[67] The many hopes invested in the growth paradigm had instead transformed into a wide-ranging set of disappointments and frustrations as dissidents searched for ways to protest and methods to build an "alternative way of life." Across the First and Second Worlds, by the 1960s, growth critics questioned why a world of plenty that promised to be so prosperous had become rife with so many social problems.

Poverty, Inequality, and Unemployment: Growth Critics during the Development Decade

As such critiques of growth in the wealthy countries intensified in the 1960s, international development experts questioned the pursuit of economic growth measured by GNP in the Third World, too. At the forefront was Dudley Seers. Beginning in the mid-1960s, Seers argued that existing development plans and foreign aid projects directed resources away from projects that would address the "needs of the people" and toward initiatives that enriched local elites and fueled unsustainable consumption patterns in the rich countries.[68] Moreover, despite high GNP growth rates, deep poverty, inequality, and unemployment persisted. World Bank president Robert McNamara told international development experts in 1970 that the "equivalent of approximately 20% of the entire male labor force" was unemployed in the Third World. Population growth rates meant that per capita income was diverging between wealthy and poorer countries, and unequal distribution of land ownership had deepened inequalities (McNamara suggested that in India 12 percent of families controlled half of all cultivated land and in Brazil less than 10 percent of families controlled 75 percent of the land).[69] In the face of such statistics, Seers argued that using national economic growth as the object of development had stunted development economists' and developing countries' leadership by equating aggregate growth totals with true development.[70] The high levels of poverty and unemployment were serious problems. "The noses of the social scientist and the statistician should be rubbed into such social realities during the decades that lie ahead," Seers wrote in 1969.[71]

Over the 1960s, many other experts from the Global North and Global South voiced related criticisms. Seers's longtime friend and colleague Hans Singer derided those with a "tendency to think of development as an economic process" and instead sought to promote research and policy that treated development as a holistic process.[72] Economists had just begun to realize in the 1960s, he said, that "those queer fish and lesser breeds—sociologists, anthropologists, psychologists, etc.— had after all a lot to contribute to the problems of economic development."[73] Singer aimed his ire on those development economists who believed that "the test of development performance was the increase in GNP . . . that the increase in GNP would be more or less evenly spread, or at any rate would quickly 'percolate' to the poor."[74] Malawian economist Thandika Mkandawire likewise lamented the "development decade" the 1960s because of development economists' "complicity in the mythmaking" of the wonders of GNP growth and planning.[75]

Critics also challenged the core assumptions, concepts, and theories that undergirded Third World growth politics. Arthur Lewis suggested in 1965 that high growth rates had not led to lower unemployment and that new strategies were necessary to curtail persistent unemployment.[76] By the late 1960s key experts from Latin America, such as Raúl Prebisch and Osvaldo Sunkel, worked with the UN Council on Trade and Development (UNCTAD) and the Economic Commission for Latin America (ECLA) to expose the persistent divergence between the wealthy and poor countries and enrich the body of critical development research that became known as dependency theory.[77] Albert Hirschman noted that in Latin America the urge for rapid growth had contributed to a continent-wide turn toward militaristic authoritarianism, as "economic growth entailed not infrequently a sequence of events involving serious retrogression in those other areas, including the whole-scale loss of civil and human rights."[78] Modernization theory came under fire, too. Conservative scholars such as Robert Nisbet and Samuel Huntington decried the modernization theorists' reliance on abstract, static categories to explain historical change and their faith in universal progress. Marxist-inflected critics such as Sunkel and Andre Gunder Frank built on insights from dependency theory to argue that "underdevelopment" in the Global South did not result from "tradition," but rather from the imperialism that had relegated much of the world to the fringes of a rapacious capitalist economy.[79]

Development experts also attacked many key elements of development economics. Swedish economist Gunnar Myrdal criticized the use of Western economic categories such as "unemployment" that were "inappropriate to the conditions on the ground" that left "mountains of figures" that had "either no meaning or a meaning other than that imputed to them."[80] Indian economist Amartya Sen questioned the place of welfare economics in development, critiquing the utilitarian assumptions undergirding the field as a "particularly unsuitable approach to use for measuring or judging inequality" and calling for the consideration of philosophy, ethics, and political decision making in economic inquiry.[81] British economist Douglas Rimmer levied antistatist arguments against the preoccupation with GNP growth that mirrored S. Herbert Frankel's earlier critiques. He argued that many flaws in development planning stemmed from the "artificial" nature of African central governments that did not hold meaningful control or effectively track the daily lives and economic activity of their populations. "The national accounts," he argued, "relate to the fortunes of an entity whose status, save in the eyes of a handful of administrators and expert advisers, is wholly fictitious," and thus plans based on them were doomed to fail.[82] As a measure of development experts' struggles, both Dudley Seers and Albert Hirschman detected a dramatic decline in the relevance of development economists' theories for the Third World.[83]

Mahbub ul Haq captured the growing sense that the focus on national economic growth measured in GNP no longer carried the promise for the Third World it once did. Haq had studied economics as an undergraduate at Cambridge University (alongside Amartya Sen).

(4) Mahbub ul Haq (1934–98). Photograph by G. Franchini,
courtesy of the World Bank Archives.

He earned a PhD at Yale University before returning home to Pakistan. Much like Seers, Singer, and others of his generation, Haq was initially a growth enthusiast. He worked as the chief economist in Pakistan's Planning Commission, serving as the "architect and writer" of the country's second five-year growth plan in 1960. Yet over the 1960s, he became wary of the focus on growth. He wondered whether national economic growth should remain a top developmental priority given that it had led to vast domestic income inequality and "failed to translate into improvements in the lives of Pakistan's masses."[84] In a speech in Karachi in April 1968, Haq criticized the consolidation of wealth to the country's richest twenty-two rich families and "tried to focus national attention on justice in the distribution of wealth in the midst of celebration over a rapid rate of growth."[85]

Haq soon left Pakistan to work in the World Bank, where he continued to critique the development community's preoccupation with GNP growth. "The hot pursuit of GNP growth," he told the Society for International Development conference in 1971, had "blurred our vision."[86] He was especially focused on the persistent poverty and inequality within countries. For Haq, Third World governments, foreign aid programs, and development experts needed to shift their focus from national GNP growth to directly alleviating the suffering of the most impoverished populations. Haq's arguments contributed to a larger rethinking of international development priorities away from national economic growth and toward reducing poverty, minimizing inequality, and satisfying the basic needs of the poor.

These new goals for international development came into focus through a series of transnational research projects, reform projects funded by international organizations, and expert deliberation at conferences and academic meetings. Dudley Seers played an important role in connecting the concerns of such discussions with quality of life, poverty, and social indicators. In 1964, Seers set up a think tank funded by the British government at the University of Sussex called the Institute of Development Studies (IDS) to broaden the study of development and seek new approaches to contend with the many criticisms of the growth paradigm.[87] Along with his colleagues Hans Singer and Richard Jolly, Seers steered the IDS to study issues of poverty, unemployment, and well-being in Third World countries. A partnership with the International Labour Organization (ILO), which had, nearly five decades prior, pioneered much of the transnational research into workers' standard of living, supported their work. In 1969, to celebrate its fiftieth anniversary, the ILO announced the World Employment Programme. Economic growth, ILO director-general David Morse said, had not "fulfilled the promises and expectations that were placed in it in terms of better living standards for the masses," and the ILO planned to shift from a "G.N.P.-oriented" strategy to an "employment-oriented" strategy and improving living conditions across the Third World.[88]

The partnership between the ILO and the IDS derived from a

shared sense that growth plans had neglected meaningful employment as a goal, an oversight that had deepened poverty and social frustrations. In many Third World countries, Mahbub ul Haq noted, employment was "an afterthought to the growth target in gross national product" and "poorly integrated in the framework of planning."[89] Noting that high unemployment and rising population growth had deprived "many of the world's underprivileged people of the benefits of economic progress" and worried that this might "lead to widespread unrest," the ILO program hoped to assist Third World governments by combating poverty through increases in income-generating employment.[90] The organization began by carrying out a series of pilot studies of distribution and employment problems. In 1970, Seers led the first research team to Colombia; in 1971 he led the second to Sri Lanka (then Ceylon); and in 1972 Hans Singer and Richard Jolly led the third mission to Kenya.[91] The resulting reports from the three missions challenged the nature of growth theory, the purpose of foreign aid, and the object of development interventions. The reports detailed how income inequality, social alienation, and poverty afflicting the three countries hampered social well-being, revealed the need for noneconomic indicators of development, and called for new priorities beyond growth.[92]

The mission reports inspired important changes in development lending practices. World Bank president Robert McNamara and vice president Hollis Chenery, for instance, lauded the work as a persuasive articulation of a "pro-poor" agenda that comported with McNamara's evolving thinking about development.[93] In a famous 1973 speech, McNamara echoed the report's major themes and oversaw a dramatic reorientation of bank lending away from capital-intensive projects designed with a "big push" in mind in favor of localized projects designed to ameliorate community-level poverty. World Bank lending to the Third World rose from an annual average of $1.01 billion in first half of the 1970s to $4.2 billion in 1980. Spending on projects in poverty-oriented programs of rural development, education, population, nutrition, health, sewerage, and small-scale industry tripled from a total of $6.62 billion in the period 1971–75 to $18.84 billion in the period 1976–80, while assistance for growth-oriented infrastructure declined from 60 percent of the bank's portfolio to just one-third.[94] Mahbub ul Haq, who served as the bank's director of policy planning for much of the decade, estimated that small-scale, poverty-oriented projects rose from only 8 percent of the bank's overall lending in 1970 to over 30 percent by 1980.[95]

Development experts termed this new way of pursuing development the "basic human needs" approach. Seers had begun using the phrase "basic needs" to describe the goal of providing the most fundamental requirements of physical well-being to poor populations as early as 1969, but by the early 1970s the ILO missions and the bank's new policies made the phrase a popular and widespread antipoverty "slogan" and "program" in the development community.[96] Development experts such as Haq and British economist Paul Streeten used the phrase to refer to policies needed to provide the elemental aspects of human existence—access to quality food and clean water, adequate shelter, good health care—and relieve poverty through targeted, localized projects rather than the major national interventions geared at generating growth.[97] GNP alone could not adequately capture the extent to which poor populations had their basic needs met. Development was "not merely a question of how much is produced, but what is produced and how it is distributed," Haq said. "The GNP measurements, unfortunately, do not register social satisfaction."[98] Seers, Haq, and many others saw that studying the effectiveness of poverty-oriented interventions required new measurement tools.

A global network of heterodox development experts helped to sustain the new thinking on development and the shift in lending priorities. In addition to the IDS, similar organizations brought together like-minded thinkers to share research and discuss strategy for reshaping policy, such as the African Institute for Economic Development and Planning, an UN-funded think tank led by Egyptian French Marxian economist Samir Amin, and the Third World Forum, a network of researchers that met at workshops and conferences featuring critical development scholars such as Haq, Seers, Amin, and Sri Lankan economist Gamani Corea who likewise embraced elements of the basic human needs approach. These centers often empowered intellectuals from the Third World, such as Haq, Amin, and Corea, to participate on equal footing alongside their counterparts from the North Atlantic. Participants in this global civil society shared a sense that economic growth was no longer a catch-all solution for the problems plaguing the Third World. Corea wrote in 1971, "There is now a widespread realization that high growth rates by themselves will not ensure" the achievement of "urgent social goals" such as "the reduction of unemployment, of income inequalities, of mass poverty, illiteracy, bad housing and poor nutrition."[99] A major transformation was afoot, and the institutions and associations forged between diverse development scholars helped to lay the groundwork for a rethinking of the growth paradigm in international development circles.

Economists against Economic Growth

Development economists such as Seers, Singer, Myrdal, and Haq were not the only economists who questioned the virtues of growth theory and growth policies during the 1960s and 1970s. During this era, many other economists who had been pioneers in early constructions of GNP figures and growth theories became outspoken growth critics, too. For instance, Colin Clark decried the preoccupation with growth worldwide, which he termed "growthmanship."[100] He was especially frustrated with policy makers who relied on "careful choice of statistics to prove that countries with a political and economic system" that they favored had "made exceptionally good economic growth" while pointing out that the countries administered by "political opponents" had "made exceptionally poor economic growth," treating flawed statistics as gospel. He claimed that the experience of the depression and early postwar years—when capital was scarce—had led economists to put too much faith in capital investment as the driver of economic expansion. "Too much of our economic thinking however still appears to take an oversimplified view of the problem, based upon the conditions of those times, that are not likely to recur," he wrote.[101] Given the historical disconnection, in the 1960s he wanted governments to "avoid attempting to force accelerated growth."[102]

Simon Kuznets harbored similar misgivings. In a confidential report to economists working in the White House written in 1955, Kuznets acknowledged, "there seems to me to lie an opportunity for rather critical examination and for consideration whether . . . we may want to give up some part of economic growth for the sake of reducing damage to other, non-economic values." He cited many reasons, such as the "the claim that our intoxication with economic success makes us both too generous and too arrogant . . . in dealing with other nations" and that "we have minimized in our domestic life the value of spiritual and intellectual achievement, and hence are failing to satisfy the higher wants of human beings."[103] In the same year, Kuznets published an essay on growth and inequality that "challenged many sacred cows of growth theory and hazarded speculations that found empirical support over the ensuing decade."[104] He showed that inequality had increased in many of the Third World countries. He acknowledged such inequalities might diminish in the long run, but in the short term alleviating poverty required a deeper consideration of political, social, and demographic changes beyond "the province of economics proper."[105] In his 1971 Nobel Prize lecture, Kuznets argued, "the most distinctive feature of modern economic growth is the combination of a high rate of aggregate growth with disrupting effects and new 'problems.'" He noted that growth had produced greater aggregate wealth and innovation, yet he also claimed that it brought "unexpected negative results" such as increased pollution in the wealthy countries and a loss of stable social structures and uneven patterns of expansion in the Third Word.[106]

More broadly, many economists called into question foundational elements of growth economics during the postwar years. Keynesian economics faced a series of critiques from thinkers such as Milton Friedman and Robert Lucas who called for unleashing the power of market-based mechanisms in the wake of low growth, high inflation, and rising unemployment in the United States.[107] Friedman, Lucas, and similarly minded economists attacked the sociological assumptions that had structured Keynesian thinking, arguing that a society could be "analytically dissolved altogether into its individual, utility-maximizing parts" less through studies of aggregate wholes than by applying microlevel economistic analysis of individual choices, incentives, and costs across a range of human behaviors.[108] With the relationship between social science and policy making in turmoil, the OECD even proposed setting a "social science policy" to improve scholarly research by commissioning country analyses of the social sciences in France, Norway, Finland, and Japan to "detect deficiencies and to enhance their efficiency" in each nation.[109]

Amid this tumult, economists began to search for new concepts and frameworks for studying economic life that responded to the problems associated with growth. One small but impassioned group of heterodox economists explored how their field might move past its focus on understanding and promoting growth to instead support a more ecologically minded approach. Prior to the late nineteenth century, economic analysis had often incorporated studies of the land and natural environment. Early twentieth-century mainstream economics largely dropped consideration of natural processes from its theories and models.[110] By the 1960s, however, a transatlantic group of economists were taking up Kenneth Boulding's suggestion to imagine how economics might take stock of "spaceship earth" by rethinking the metaphors and models used to describe economic and natural processes.[111]

Mid-twentieth-century social scientists described the human and nonhuman world in terms of systems.[112] In turn, abstract models depicted the systems in terms of discreet components (often described as variables) that were often separate from one another. Most growth theories rested on models of the national economy conceived as a closed system of monetary flows, shaped by component parts of production, consumption, and investment, with little consideration of how they related to, say, models of particular ecosystems or natural systems such as the nitrogen cycle. By the late 1960s and 1970s, a strand of growth theorists argued that the dominant models for growth and depiction of the economy as a system were flawed, and thus new models and new systems were necessary.

The key figures in this work were Romanian economist Nicholas Georgescu-Roegen and one of his doctoral students, American economist Herman Daly. Georgescu-Roegen was a polymath who studied mathematics, statistics, and economics at universities in Bucharest, London, Paris, and Boston during the 1920s, 1930s, and 1940s before returning to his native Romania, where he lived during World War II. After the war he moved to the United States, where he accepted a permanent position in the economics department at Vanderbilt University and established a reputation, in Paul Samuelson's words, as a "topnotch innovator" in economics despite an "intense" personality and often "haughty" demeanor.[113] In a series of articles over the 1960s that were dense and filled with extensive discussions of advances in physics and biology, Georgescu-Roegen argued that the pursuit of economic growth and existing economic theory were misguided because both economists and policy makers neglected to incorporate the biophysical dimensions of human life in their understanding of the world. He lamented the disjuncture between how economists defined economic systems and how natural scientists understood ecological processes.

Georgescu-Roegen believed that economics rested on flawed mechanistic models, and in their place he advocated for the use of the second law of thermodynamics and the concept of entropy as the guiding metaphor for the discipline. He argued that it was the "entropic transformation of valuable natural resources (low entropy) into valueless waste (high entropy)" that signaled an economic system out of whack with natural processes. Drawing on the entropy concept, he called for a new "bioeconomics" that took the flow of energy as its guiding principle to suture together economic and ecological insights into a new way of depicting and theorizing the organization of the material world.[114] Rather than treating value narrowly in terms of market prices, he hoped to encourage economists to a broader view that recognized that "the earth's supply of available matter and energy is humankind's dowry and should be conserved to the greatest extent possible for future generations."[115]

Many other like-minded thinkers drew on Georgescu-Roegen's research to fashion what would become the field of "ecological economics." Kenneth Boulding argued for more "evolutionary" models of change that broke free from economics' "essentially Netwonian type models of equilibrium or very simply dynamics" that dominated the discipline.[116] In 1971, American ecologist Howard T. Odum published *Environment, Power, and Society*, in which he proposed new models that linked energy flows with monetary flows, integrating natural systems into the production and consumption of goods and services. The book was a landmark that applied insights from systems theory and ecology to social and economic issues.[117] Ecological anthropologists studied how societies and territories together formed unified, stable ecosystems and argued that rituals served as regulating mechanisms for the system.[118] Humanist scholars in this era began to critique prevailing descriptions and reductive narratives of nature at the same time, as well. For example, pioneering ecological literature critics and environmental historians such as Carolyn Merchant searched for the origins and consequences of the mechanical models of economies and depictions of natural systems.[119] Ecological economists would build on this research—especially from the natural sciences—to challenge many core assumptions of growth theories and indeed of economics as a whole by placing human-environmental interactions at the center of their inquiry. They also offered a distinct way of conceptualizing economic life. Instead of describing the national economy as a machine to be engineered, as many economists did, ecological economists often viewed it as a living organism that needed to be nurtured.

The most important earlier contribution to ecological economics came from Herman Daly. Born and raised in Houston, Texas, Daly studied for his PhD in economics under Georgescu-Roegen at Vanderbilt University during the 1960s as Georgescu-Roegen worked on his "bioeconomics" approach. Daly expanded on that research (and related scholarship by Kenneth Boulding) to argue that economic growth amounted to a scientific and policy paradigm that needed to be replaced with a new one premised on the "steady state," a system in equilibrium.[120] Daly drew on earlier writing by John Stuart Mill, who back in the 1840s famously contrasted those political economists who envisioned a "progressive state" of ever-increasing economic activity against an ideal "stationary state" that featured far lower population growth, less cultivation of wild land, and less exorbitant resource use.[121] He also built on the work of ecologist Eugene Odum, who characterized mature ecosystems based on "protection, stability, and quality" as the basis of his new model.[122] Daly defined the steady-state economy as a "physical concept" defined by "constant stocks of people and physical wealth (artifacts) maintained at some chosen, desirable level by a low rate of throughput. The throughput flow begins with depletion (followed by production and consumption) and ends with an equal amount of waste effluent or pollution."[123]

For Daly, GNP growth in the wealthy countries meant "the satisfaction of ever more trivial wants, while simultaneously creating ever more powerful externalities which destroy ever more important environmental amenities." He wrote, "a policy of maximizing GNP" was "practically equivalent to a policy of maximizing depletion and pollution."[124] Economists, Daly argued, needed to "awake from the dogmatic slumber of growthmania induced by the soporific doctrines of relative scarcity and absolute wants" and build theories based on the recognition of finite physical limits and desires that form within the limits of social relations.[125] By adopting a steady-state model, countries could still achieve basic needs while averting ecological catastrophe and creating more equal and sustainable patterns of living. Daly was one of the most blunt and tireless growth critics during the 1970s.

Daly's research on the steady-state concept was an important organizing point for larger critiques of growth economics. Daly's phrase resonated with similar arguments from the Club of Rome, which had called for an "equilibrium" economy in the *Limits to Growth* report.[126] The steady-state concept also became a point of contention among like-minded growth critics. Georgescu-Roegen preferred his formulation of "bioeconomics" to Daly's because he believed the steady-state economy could not last indefinitely because of the finite nature of resources available in the earth's crust and the planet's carrying capacity. Thus the only "desirable" state was "not a stationary but declining one."[127] Kenneth Boulding also appreciated Daly's work but quibbled with its conclusions, as he argued that "equilibrium" was "unknown in the real world," and instead ecologically minded economists needed to conceive of a research program and policies geared to what he called "sustainability of the first degree" that was "evolutionary and developmental" rather than stationary.[128] For these differences, though, they all shared a desire to link studies of energy, ecology, and resource use as a way to revise conventional economics. They remained on the margins of the economics profession, but ecological economists made a powerful set of rejoinders to the optimism of growth enthusiasts.[129]

Conclusion

Although the 1960s are often described as glorious years of robust economic growth, this triumphalism elides the myriad growth critics who engaged in scholarly and public debate throughout the decade. Some growth critics argued that growth has biophysical limits. Others suggested that the focus on GNP growth contributed to a crass and hollow materialism that robbed the wealthy world of more meaningful work and spiritual fulfillment. In the Second World, fears of weak growth among leaders were matched by grassroots activists' consternation that increases in production had not generated any political liberalization or embrace of democratization. For the Third World, high growth rates swept across all countries but also created persistent social dislocation, poverty, and unemployment. Growth did not alleviate inequality, either. Indeed, it seemed that rapid growth could actually increase it, as Mahbub ul Haq argued. What, then, was growth good for?

For the growth critics, the answer to that question was not simple or straightforward. Over the course of the late 1960s and 1970s, growth critics diverged and debated among themselves over the root problems with the growth paradigm and the proper solutions. Some suggested that inviolable ecological limits meant that growth needed to be abandoned, that all people, especially those in the wealthy world, needed new lifestyles premised on far lower energy and resource use. Others homed in on capitalism as the core source of the growth paradigm's flaws, with Western radicals and many socialist thinkers beginning to imagine new roles for planning around growth's downsides. Still others, especially many leaders from Third World countries, argued that growth was not in and of itself a problem, but rather that the international system of rules and regulations that structured unequal and uneven patterns and forms of growth was. As the next two chapters show, growth critics began to imagine alternative ways of organizing power and measuring the social world.

FOUR

The Growth Paradigm in Crisis

In October 1975, hundreds of people from around the world attended a conference in Houston, Texas, called "Alternatives to Growth." American millionaire oil tycoon and real estate developer George Mitchell sponsored the gathering as a response to the *Limits to Growth* report. He invited a range of people with diverse intellectual backgrounds and interests: members of the *Limits to Growth* team and the Club of Rome; Carl Madden, the chief economist for the US Chamber of Commerce; Sicco Mansholt, the former president of the European Common Market; multiple sitting US senators; policy makers from countries ranging from Japan to Switzerland to Iran; and growth critics such as Mahbub ul Haq and E. F. Schumacher. Mitchell even sponsored cash prizes for most the promising research proposals on transitions to a steady-state economy.[1] The wide-ranging conversations about the future of growth at the conference suggested to participants that the growth critics' arguments resonated widely. This breakthrough had serious consequences. Two officials from the Ford Foundation who attended the conference reported that it indicated to them that "the limits-to-growth phenomenon is not principally a technical or analytical one—it is a social movement with non-trivial political implications."[2]

Observers left the meeting with a clear sense that the growth paradigm was in crisis. "The social movement surrounding the 'limits' idea is a real one," the Ford Foundation officials wrote. "There is adequate history to suggest that political movements of this sort can be effective, even when initially based on no more than a vague sense that the policy being pursued by the powers, although endorsed by all the right experts, is fundamentally wrong for ethical or historical reasons."[3] An official from the CIA, who had been tasked with observing the conference, agreed that the meeting offered "worthwhile and stimulating" discussions of the "perplexing and significant problems" exposed by the growth critics.[4] While in retrospect it was an exaggeration to call the growth critics a coherent "movement," they had nonetheless sparked feelings of concern, anxiety, and uncertainty about the future of the growth paradigm across the world. During the 1970s, growth critics became important players in framing major debates of international politics. Activists, political leaders, and policy makers all wrestled with the possibility that limitless growth was neither possible nor desirable. They also pondered how to reorganize economic and political power accordingly.

Whereas over the 1950s and 1960s the growth critics raised many issued related to the natural environment, social dislocation, inequality, global poverty, and the limits of conventional economic analysis, during the late 1960s and 1970s these topics gained more widespread attention as important and urgent matters among leaders, policy makers, and the global public. The growth critics resonated because of important material changes that made the notion of limits to growth visible to many citizens, especially in the wealthy countries. The geopolitics of energy created a sense of crisis, which peaked in the 1973 oil embargo. So too did a rise in Malthusian fears of runaway population growth. The politics of energy and population revealed in stark material and ecological terms how the growth paradigm had reshaped the natural world and humankind's relationship to it. Once it became clear to many that growth might have fundamental limits, the growth critics' arguments garnered broader support.

The growth critics also participated in related debates about the nature of political economy and international relations. Growth critics stressed that there were ecological limits to growth and moral reasons to resist the growth paradigm in ways that paralleled broader debates over the long-term viability of both capitalism and communism. By the 1970s in the United States and Western Europe, ongoing social unrest, the unpopularity of the Vietnam War, rising inflation and unemployment, and the breakdown of the Bretton Woods system fueled a growing sense that there was something amiss within the capitalist world. Whether capitalism was itself beyond redemption divided many growth critics. Growth critics argued over the extent to which capitalism could exist without the high growth rates many had come to expect. In the Soviet Union and within many Eastern European countries, critics also considered whether their own economic system required reform in the face of sluggish production and social upheaval.

The crisis of the growth paradigm was also clear in wide-ranging discussions over the future of international order. While experts in the East and West contemplated the future of the growth paradigm, activists and leaders from the Global South aspired to refashion global governance and alter the rules and organizations that had structured the growth paradigm. The New International Economic Order (NIEO), for instance, marked an effort by the so-called Third World countries to reshape the rules of the global economy in order to prioritize growth of the Global South over that of the Global North. While the NIEO proposed rules that its advocates hoped would produce growth for everyone over the long term, others, such as reformist development experts including Mahbub ul Haq, wondered if lifestyle changes were also needed within the wealthy countries to limit consumption and energy use while allowing the poorer countries to develop without similar restrictions. These proposals suggested that the configuration of international power was in flux as the institutions that had sustained the pursuit of national economic growth underwent rapid changes and faced fierce critiques.

Altogether, these debates, proposals, and proclamations left growth critics in an odd position. Elements of their critiques—social, environmental, moral—achieved greater popularity and pushed figures from the margins of expertise and political power in the 1960s toward the center of international politics a decade later. Critics' arguments imbued the myriad crises of the 1970s with an added urgency.

And yet, few endeavors to imagine alternatives to growth generated much consensus. The broader sense of crisis opened up political and intellectual space for a range of efforts over the coming decades. Growth critics advocated for new goals that societies might pursue and an array of new measurements to give them meaning.

Energy and the Materiality of Growth

Nowhere were the flaws of the growth paradigm more evident than in the dramatic increase in energy use and the realization that economic prosperity depended on fossil fuels. Economic growth was a profound material undertaking. The global emphasis on increasing production during and after the 1940s required vast stores of energy. US petroleum demand alone jumped from just over 1.1 billion barrels in 1939 to almost 1.76 billion in 1945 to 2.35 billion in 1950.[5] During World War II, coal and oil use skyrocketed, as they were sources for the electricity that surged through wartime factories and fueled military technologies (submarines, tanks, airplanes, and much else). In the postwar years, fossil fuels made possible the production and consumption of the consumer goods that so many citizens took as the everyday outcomes of growth. The shift within the United States in the immediate postwar years was dramatic. For instance, in 1945 there were twenty-six million cars in service in the domestic United States; by 1950 there were fifty million. Gasoline sales were 42 percent higher in 1950 than just five years prior. Throughout much of the twentieth century the United States had been a net exporter of petroleum, but postwar demands meant that beginning in 1948 for the first time since the end of World War I the United States became a net importer of the valuable resource.[6]

Because the United States, Western Europe, and Japan all required extensive and consistent flows of oil and coal to sustain economic growth, a new geography of power emerged based on access to energy. In the immediate postwar years, the United States expanded its control over Middle Eastern oil, oversaw the slow rewriting of earlier concessions to increase its access points, and worked to stymie further

Soviet control over energy-rich lands. The Soviet Union, after all, controlled many important sites of energy extraction, including the vast coal deposits in Poland and oil reserves scattered throughout Eastern Europe.[7] In addition, the US government forged closer ties with major private oil interests, linking state policy and corporate strategy. The big "Seven Sister" oil companies—five American companies and two European-owned ones—accounted for 90 percent of oil reserves outside of the United States, Mexico, and the communist countries in the late 1940s and nearly 75 percent of refining capacity.[8] US leaders recognized that access to cheap energy was a vital component of postwar recovery and the precondition for growth; more than 10 percent of total Marshall Plan aid, for instance, was spent on oil.[9] The US government facilitated private purchases, as federal agencies supported financing for nearly 60 percent of all oil supplied to the Marshall Plan countries by US companies. This backing gave the companies, and, by extension, the US government, great leverage over countries desperate for energy to fuel power plants and factories, heat homes and offices, power televisions and ovens, and support growing numbers of cars, trucks, and airplanes. As a result, the major national suppliers of oil—Saudi Arabia, Kuwait, Iraq, Iran, and Venezuela—became strategically significant for the long-term economic viability of fossil-fuel-driven expansion in the United States, Europe, and Japan.[10]

All the while, technologies to transport petroleum reshaped landscapes. By the mid-1970s, gigantic oil supertankers that held half a million tons of oil crisscrossed the world's oceans to supply distant locales with fossil fuel energy. Vast pipeline networks created webs of oil that stretched across continents.[11] These technological innovations, combined with the strategic pressure from oil-producing governments to increase output, kept prices of oil low. Even as demand rose, oil prices fell from the late 1940s through the early 1970s, a trend that encouraged ever more oil-intensive technologies (from "lawn mowers to power plants" in John McNeill's words).[12] The supply of energy seemed endless. In the words of political theorist Timothy Mitchell, "If the economy appeared capable of unlimited growth," it was because of "the mid-twentieth-century energy regime."[13]

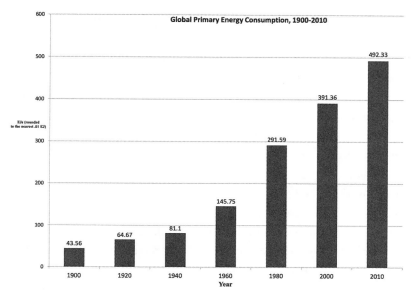

(5) Global primary energy consumption measured in exajoules. As a percent of total energy consumption, coal, crude oil, and natural gas skyrocketed from a combined 48 percent in 1900 to 67 percent in 1940 to 76 percent in 1960 to 83 percent in 1980. They remained 83 percent of the sources of total energy consumption in 2010. All figures from Smil, *Energy Transitions*, 242–43.

The scale of the transformation in energy consumption was enormous. Energy historian Vaclav Smil estimates that global primary energy consumption skyrocketed from 81 exajoules (EJ) in 1940 to 223 EJ in 1970. Global coal output soared from 762 million metric tons in 1925 to 1.36 billion in 1950 to 3.26 billion in 1975.[14] From 1940 to 1970, the share of oil and gas in total primary energy consumption worldwide jumped from 25 percent to 64 percent.[15] The growing demand for oil wove producing countries, corporate interests, and consumers into a web of interdependence that made the pursuit of national economic growth of any one country necessarily a matter of geopolitics. Cheap and plentiful fossil fuels were inextricably bound to the growth paradigm. The pursuit of growth required the expansion of energy, and the expansion of energy production sustained the growth process.

In addition to increased dependence on fossil fuels, the growth paradigm also led to a frantic search for other strategically significant minerals and spurred the construction of a vast expanse of infrastructure around the globe, as well. Postwar industrial production required huge inputs of copper, zinc, lead, and iron for manufacturing and nitrogen for fertilizers used in large-scale agriculture the world over.[16] For instance, world use of refined copper, which had been consistently under two million metric tons each year from 1900 up until World War II, reached over eight million metric tons by 1975.[17] World production of crude steel expanded from 189 million tons in 1950 to 644 million tons in 1975.[18] In the Western industrial countries, imports of raw materials alone soared from 299 billion tons in 1950 to 1.282 trillion tons in 1970.[19] Moreover, the pursuit of GNP growth around the world meant that countries needed to trade with each other and identify new markets for goods and services. National economic growth and increasing world trade were mutually reinforcing goals. Total merchandise exports worldwide, for instance, ballooned from $59 billion in 1948 to $157 billion in 1963 to $579 billion in 1973.[20] Moving goods within and across borders demanded a vast global infrastructure of shipping vessels, cargo planes, roads, and railways that further deepened the dependence on fossil fuels and raw materials.[21] Economic growth required an expansive investment in physical infrastructure that reshaped the natural world in innumerable ways.

While environmental critics of growth long recognized these dramatic material changes, by the early 1970s the connection between economic growth, energy use, and environmental damage became increasingly visible to the public. Major smog problems in cities such as London and Los Angeles during the 1950s; mercury poisoning from chemical wastewater in Minamata Bay, Japan, during the late 1950s; the growing recognition of toxic threats to everyday life after the publication of *Silent Spring* in 1962; the shipwreck and oil spill in 1967 of the *Torrey Canyon* supertanker off the coast of Cornwall; and a major oil spill off the coast of Santa Barbara, California, in 1969 all gave credence to environmentalists' claims that fossil fuels, industrial chemicals, and extensive resource consumption had imperiled the natural world and human health.[22] The same technologies that had made possible cheap energy and rapid economic growth now became sites of contestation as they laid bare the brute material realities of the growth paradigm. These ecological catastrophes were all easily understood and legible downsides to economic growth premised on cheap, dirty energy use.

In addition to these visible signs of growth's downsides, the arguments made by growth critics gained further traction amid the growing public prominence of population control advocates. The UN continually raised its projections of global population growth in the postwar years. In 1953, the UN's median projection for the world population in 1980 was 3.28 billion; just five years later, it increased that projection to 4.22 billion. It had taken almost all human history up to 1800 to reach a population of one billion people, and 130 more years for population to grow to over two billion, but from 1930 to 1960 alone the world population increased by a another billion.[23] For many observers, these trends portended a dark future. Population became a "problem" and an object of policy intervention just as the national economy had decades earlier.[24]

Population control advocates seized on this data to link the growth in human population with environmental concerns about resource overexploitation. Early postwar conservationists such as Fairfield Osborn, William Vogt, and Julian Huxley all warned that rapidly growing human populations would generate crises (especially in the Third World) as growth-oriented economies demanded ever more raw materials and foodstuffs for consumption and production. Over the 1950s and 1960s, growth critics continued to identify population growth as a concern insofar as it highlighted potential future limits to growth. What changed during the late 1960s and early 1970s was a broader public perception, and one shared by many elites, that population growth was an urgent and essential challenge to social and political stability. By the late 1960s, such fears reached a fever pitch among Malthusian true believers who pushed population control arguments to wider popular audiences. Stanford University biologist Paul Ehrlich was an important figure in these efforts. His 1968 book *The Population Bomb* foretold of grave ecological, economic, political, and social consequences if societies did not rapidly transition "from a growth-oriented exploitative system to one focused on stability and conservation."[25] Ehrlich argued that aggressive population control measures—ranging from "compulsion if voluntary methods fail" in the United States to tying food aid to contraception use for the Third World—were necessary to achieve the transition.[26] *The Population Bomb* sold over two million copies and went through twenty reprints by just 1971. Ehrlich became a popular celebrity, making more than twenty appearances on the popular American TV show *The Tonight Show Starring Johnny Carson* and frequently participating in global speaking tours and UN conferences.[27] He gained a wide following, building on the foundation that early population control advocates had laid to suggest not only that excessive energy use was a problem for the environment, but that the very presence of a large number of human beings was a problem. He spread his simple message—that "quantity of life could undermine quality of life"—to the entire world.[28]

Population control advocates engaged in wide-ranging activism, from advising policy makers to grassroots mobilization. Their work took many forms. US economist Stephen Enke calculated the values of "averted births," or how much a country's GNP could grow if families chose *not* to have babies (he calculated that the "worth" of preventing a birth in the typical "less developed country" was about two to six times the output per head). Enke developed computer models and simulations to show off his models, which received grants from USAID and garnered official interest in countries such as South Korea and Taiwan as part of national family-planning strategies.[29] For others, reducing population growth through more direct means offered the surest way to limit resource use and live within ecological limitations. Zero Population Growth, an activist organization that grew to have nearly thirty-two thousand active members by the early 1970s, focused on a wide range of issues from forced sterilization to aggressive promotion of contraception in the Third World. Advised by Ehrlich and Garrett Hardin among others, the group argued that all the downsides of growth—pollution, resource exhaustion, overcrowding, and noise—would be resolved by a future populated with fewer people.[30]

These concerns often resonated with deeply racist fears among North Americans and Europeans who worried that population growth in the Third World threatened traditional hierarchies defined by the long historical legacies of white supremacy. British MP Enoch Powell's hate-filled April 1968 "Rivers of Blood" speech expressed fears about the growing population of immigrants in Britain. French writer Jean Raspail's 1973 bilious novel *Le Camp de Saints* levied similar histrionic warnings, reflecting the racist and eugenicist elements of population control efforts by elite Westerners who saw fertility constraints and fierce limits on immigration as coequal tools for achieving socioeconomic and ecological stability.[31]

During the early 1970s, growth critics also received a boost in prominence as public attention focused on many signs of environmental crisis and resource scarcity. The release of the *Limits to Growth* report in 1972, the first major UN conference on environmental protection in June 1972, and the start of the oil embargo of the Organization of Arab Petroleum Exporting Countries (OAPEC) in October 1973 sparked public fears across much of the wealthy world over the prospects of ecological constraints on future growth. Was the United States "running out of everything?" asked the editors of the popular American magazine *Newsweek* in November 1973.[32] A range of scholarly initiatives analyzed the merits and limitations of the Club of Rome study through the mid-1970s. Debating whether there were clear limits to economic growth became a major preoccupation of many experts.[33] The American Academy of Arts and Sciences sponsored an international symposium in 1973 on whether "no growth" was an advisable economic strategy. The inconclusive results were later published as a book.[34]

The rise in oil prices after the 1973 oil embargo brought abstract notions about limits into the everyday lives of citizens in the Western countries. Waiting in gas lines and struggling to pay for oil-fueled amenities made the notion of resource scarcity resonate for many citizen-consumers accustomed to the promises of future abundance. In late 1973, for instance, reporters for the popular US periodical *Time* magazine noted the myriad effects of the crisis. The Italian government had put curfews on many stores and restaurants while limiting drivers on the *autostrade* to a "rather un-Italian 75 m.p.h."; the Japanese government had mandated "neon lights . . . being turned off earlier along

Tokyo's gaudy Ginza" district and shortened store hours across the country; West Germany reported a 30 percent decline in automobile sales amid fears of limited gasoline; and Americans, for whom energy-intensive consumerism had become synonymous with growth, faced a "baffling" situation as millions reconciled themselves to a "time of learning to live with less."[35] For many experts, the effects were no less profound. "The environmental crisis, the Arab oil embargo, and the subsequent reanalyses of our resources, technologies, and institutions have swept us over an awareness threshold toward the 'economics of the coming spaceship earth,'" economist Richard Norgaard wrote in 1975 in a reference to Kenneth Boulding's pioneering work.[36] OECD official Alexander King, once a growth enthusiast who became one of the key founders of the Club of Rome, recalled in his memoirs that he questioned the virtues of growth as he witnessed environmental decline, student revolts, the hippie movement, and "technology out of control" all punctuated by the visible signs of how energy scarcity could limit future prosperity.[37]

As these concerns intensified, the arguments of growth critics reso-nated with leaders and everyday citizens alike. The *Limits to Growth* report garnered front-page headlines in the United States, Europe, and Japan.[38] The book sold over twelve million copies and was translated into over thirty languages.[39] It also prompted wide-ranging debates over the future of growth among a variety of political parties across the world, even piquing the interest of conservative intellectuals and poli-ticians in countries such as the United Kingdom and West Germany who embraced the book's thesis as part of a broader critique of indus-trial modernity, consumerism, and materialism.[40] Beyond the *Limits to Growth* report, the UN sponsored a 1974 conference on population growth, which in turn prompted US secretary of state Henry Kis-singer to commission a major confidential study on how future growth might threaten US interests and stability.[41] Research into possible futures other than that of one of declining fortunes and biophysical limitations—often grouped under the rubric of "futurology" or "futures research"—flourished across the world during the 1970s as experts and citizens alike clamored for models and approaches to futures that might resolve or transcend the flaws of the growth paradigm.[42]

Another measure of the growth critics' increasing public profile was the strength of the progrowth backlash. After the *Limits to Growth* report began to attract major media attention, for example, the Mobil Oil corporation, whose future profits depended on energy-intensive growth, took out a large ad in the February 17, 1972, *New York Times* to declare that growth was "not a four-letter word" and that "only growth" offered "hope for solving many of the problems mankind faces."[43] American economist Julian Simon likewise made a famous bet with Paul Ehrlich that technological advances would overcome limits, and Simon spent much of the 1970s traveling the world and speaking to audiences arguing that they should not lose faith in growth. "If enabling as many people as possible to have life is taken as the purpose of the economy," Simon suggested, then population growth, so fearful to many, was a "triumph rather than a disaster." Economic growth, by extension, enabled the most possibilities for the most people.[44] Herman Kahn, the most enthusiastic progrowth voice at the 1975 "Alternatives to Growth" symposium in Houston, was a recurring figure on speaking circuits and media outlets. He argued that capitalism and technological innovation could overcome any ecological or energy limits to growth, an argument he made in full through his popular 1976 book *The Next 200 Years*.[45] Multiple scholars even wrote metacommentaries about the public "growth debate"—the pros and cons of growth—that sought to clarify the stakes and arguments of the many participants from economists to radical activists to oil company marketing teams.[46] Growth critics gained prominence as such public-facing debates brought to the fore questions over the future of economic policy and national strategy in ways that had seemed unlikely just a decade earlier.

Growth Critics and the Uncertain Futures of Capitalism and Communism

In debating limits to growth, the stakes were high. Within the wealthy countries, concerns not only about the future of growth, but also about the future of capitalism itself, hinged on energy use and environmental cataclysm. Global capitalism was in turmoil. In addition to the oil shock, the Bretton Woods system of fixed exchange rates came to an end in the early 1970s. US spending on the Vietnam War generated inflation. Increasing activity in offshore markets for US dollars—dubbed "Eurodollars"—added pressure. By March 1970, the Euro-dollar liabilities of US banks approached $25 billion. Bankers and financial analysts worried about a dollar crisis. In early 1971, the situation became untenable. West European countries, led by West Germany, abandoned the stable exchange rates and floated their currencies. In August, the United States responded by announcing it would abrogate its obligation to exchange dollars for gold at a fixed rate. By 1973, the Bretton Woods system of tightly managed international monetary policy was over, replaced by a loosely coordinated system of floating currencies. A crucial piece of the international architecture that had structured the growth paradigm fell apart, just as the era of cheap energy seemed to be waning.[47]

Within just a few years, the future of capitalism appeared bleak. In the summer of 1975, for example, US unemployment reached its highest levels since the Great Depression, peaking at over 9 percent. Inflation soared, hovering around 10 percent. The same was true for much of the Western world. Inflation hit 28 percent in Great Britain, and the pound fell to an all-time low at $2.19. Italy, France, Canada, Australia, and even West Germany and Japan searched for palliative measures to rein in inflation and curb unemployment. Looking at these trends, a special issue of *Time* magazine that July asked a simple question: "Can capitalism survive?"[48] Growth had been the answer to questions about capitalism's viability amid domestic strife and international discord during the 1940s. A generation of leaders who came of age during the growth paradigm viewed growth as the only bedrock of political stability and geopolitical order. Speaking to the OECD in 1975, US national security adviser Henry Kissinger put the matter frankly. "Stagnation magnifies all our difficulties," he proclaimed. "Stable growth enhances our possibilities."[49] But if stagnation and low growth were going to continue, what were the implications for capitalism more broadly?

For environmental growth critics, the flaws of capitalism had

(6) The cover of *Time* magazine from July 14, 1975, when the future of capitalism in the United States and Western world seemed uncertain.

become clear. Herman Daly argued that growth had allowed capitalists to engage in an "evasion" that "the sins of present injustice were to be washed away in a future of absolute abundance by the amazing grace of compound interest." The ecological crises of the 1960s and early 1970s rendered such claims "absurd."[50] Moreover, just as Marx saw "capitalists exploiting the soil as well as the laborer," Daly wrote, environmental critics saw "capital and labor maintaining an uneasy alliance by shifting the exploitation to the soil and other natural resources. It follows that if some institution were to play the role of the landlord class and raise resource prices, the labor-capital conflict would again become severe." For Daly, there were "radical implications of the ecological crisis," such as the "need for some distributist institution" to redress the inequalities capitalism created and the "essential cessation" of "gross physical accumulation."[51] Nicholas Georgescu-Roegen likewise stated that "the market mechanism cannot possibly be relied on for avoiding ecological catastrophe" because the market's time horizon was defined by a single generation, "just a brief spell in comparison with the life-span of the whole species," and thus "future generations" could not "bid on the scarce resources side by side with the current generation."[52] Kenneth Boulding argued that the *Limits to Growth* conclusions were right to suggest that "we cannot go on increasing capital and income the way we have been doing without reaching the limits of the niche of the earth's resources and capabilities," though he cautioned against neglecting the "real advantages of market-type societies" such as "individual freedom and social adaptability" in efforts to imagine economic systems beyond capitalism.[53]

For many social critics of growth, capitalism seemed, at least, to be transitioning to a new form. The sheer range of names given to describe the new form of political economy attested to the widespread sense that capitalism had undergone a major transformation. John Galbraith and David Riesman adopted the term "post-industrial society" to describe the world wrought by rapid growth, a phrase that earned a fuller theoretical exploration by American sociologist Daniel Bell.[54] Socialist thinkers deployed the phrase "scientific technological revolution" to describe how the application of advanced science and major technologies (such as computers) had reshaped society after decades of rapid economic growth. Others, such as C. Wright Mills and Amitai Etzioni, opted for "post-modern society" as the preferred term of art, while German social theorist George Lichtheim preferred the phrase "post-bourgeois society."[55] Likewise, the very term "technocracy"—initially conceived in the early twentieth century by progressive reformers hoping to inject scientific knowledge and management techniques into government—became a term of opprobrium. French political scientist Jean Meynaud's 1964 book on the topic studied the growing debate over the place of expert guidance of social planning.[56] Daniel Bell's 1973 book *The Coming of Post-industrial Society* expressed skepticism over the prominence of technocrats in managing postindustrial society, and fierce technology critics such as American political theorist Langdon Winner railed about "technocrats" just as earlier theorists such as Ellul had done about similar terms such as "technique."[57] Some social theorists even argued for "convergence" theories that suggested both capitalist and communist countries were moving toward similar forms of social organization as vast administrative institutions ruled society through technical control.[58] In all these instances, intellectuals had recognized that capitalism had evolved in ways that seemed to pose great peril for social life.

For a growing number of Marxist thinkers in the West, the years of high growth rates had been exposed as a new and especially dangerous phase of global capitalism. "Capitalist economic growth" threatened "human survival," explained Belgian economist Ernest Mandel, because it depended on "maximizing profit" using the "measuring rod of money." The reliance on money meant the exclusion of otherwise valuable aspects of life that had no price—"human values, air, water, beauty, landscapes, solidarity," and much else—and were thus devalued on a global scale.[59] South African intellectual Michael Kidron likewise saw capitalist growth as an urgent global threat. In his writings, he recast the postwar growth paradigm as a deceitful repackaging of older capitalist imperatives with new components that carried myriad social ills. "Capitalism depends for survival on the growth of its productive apparatus," he wrote in 1974, and the nature of that apparatus had changed dramatically. For Kidron, the "permanent arms economy" driven by World War II and the Cold War had been important in forestalling declining rates of profit but created new perils. Spending on armaments stabilized national economies by justifying continued public investment but threatened to destabilize international relations by the prospect of cataclysmic nuclear war. The pursuit of growth also masked persistent class tensions. "As a system of competition capitalism depends on the growth of capital," he wrote, and "as a class system it depends on obscuring the sources of that growth."[60] Kidron argued further that the Soviet Union had become a form of "state capitalism," sharing similar characteristics to the West. The laborers tasked with "pumping out surpluses from the mass of producers" faced "as oppressive a compulsion to fast economic growth" as workers anywhere else. Definitions of success were similar, too. Even if the main Soviet criterion for economic accomplishment for enterprises had been "the volume of gross physical output rather than money profits," that distinction was "one of detail not essence" because high output "served the bureaucracy perfectly well."[61]

One especially significant component of modern capitalism that alarmed many growth critics was the large-scale, hierarchical corporation. Popular criticisms of corporate power stemmed, in part, from Marxist economists who decried the monopolistic tendencies of contemporary capitalism. At the forefront of this were American economists Paul Baran and Paul Sweezy, who developed a systematic critique of the "monopoly capitalism" through which post growth had taken place. In his 1957 opus *The Political Economy of Growth*, Baran wrote that the social costs of "monopolistic business" were clear. Workers toiled in the "degrading, corrupting, and stultifying mill of vast corporate empires" while the "ordinary man and woman" had been "warped and crippled by the continuous exposures to the output, the propaganda, and the sales efforts of big business."[62] Baran and Sweezy's 1966 book *Monopoly Capital* extended these arguments and criticized the excessive economic waste that countries produced in their quest for growth.[63] Such concerns were widespread, even among popular commentators. John Kenneth Galbraith, for instance, decried the power of corporations to shape consumer taste through large-scale centralized planning in his 1958 book *The Affluent Society* and his 1967 book *The New Industrial State*.[64] So too had social critics of growth such as C. Wright Mills, David Riesman, and Jacques Ellul. In many cases, these critics were blunt. "The human and social effects" of the concentration of capital into large corporations, Ellul wrote, "are, on the whole, evil."[65]

These critics held a wide variety of opinion about how best to respond to the problems spawned by capitalist growth. David Riesman and Herbert Marcuse, for example, shared a critique of corporate mass culture brought on by the embrace of rapid economic growth and its dehumanizing consequences. Yet they differed in their relationship to the capitalist system more broadly. Riesman often levied his criticisms in a plaintive tone as he pondered how Americans might redress the "satisfactions missing in our economic and general social life" and confront the fear of "total meaninglessness" amid rampant consumerism, suburbanization, and ongoing economic expansion.[66] There was scarcely a call for revolution in his thinking. Riesman believed that change should come at the level of individuals seeking more authentic and fulfilling selves in a postscarcity world; he sought to reform the existing order.[67] Marcuse focused his critique more pointedly on how modern white-collar work engendered a social crisis. In *One-Dimensional Man*, he argued that "domination" had "transfigured into administration," in which "capitalist bosses and owners" assumed "the function of bureaucrats in a corporate machine" that obscured ongoing exploitation behind a "technological veil" that concealed "the reproduction of inequality and enslavement."[68] The only way out was through a "totalizing analysis of the structural apparatus" that had caused alienation, the "ideological apparatus that hid this structure, and the overall historical consequences" of this particular formation.[69] And more broadly, Marcuse believed that only through "fundamentally redirecting economic growth and economic activity" toward "the abolition of poverty and inequality the world over" through a "revolutionary situation" could the necessary changes actually take place.[70]

The student protest movements exposed some of the core differences between Riesman's and Marcuse's differing outlooks over how to challenge society. Whereas Riesman had been an initial sympathizer to the New Left in the United States, by the late 1960s he believed student radicals had fallen victim to peer pressure and diverted from a path toward individual authenticity and autonomy. He viewed their disrespect of existing norms and authority as an affront to the university. He even wrote to political scientist Seymour Martin Lipset to wonder whether tear gas was a "humane" method to disperse student protests.[71] When Theodor Adorno told Marcuse of his decision to call the police on student protestors in Frankfurt in 1969, Marcuse, in contrast, sided with the students. "If the alternative is the police or left-wing students, then I am with the students," he wrote Adorno. For Marcuse, the state of affairs was "so terrible, so suffocating and demeaning" that "rebellion against it" was acceptable.[72] In his view, to change the world wrought by growth—the world Riesman also critiqued—required a response beyond the bounds of acceptable norms to fashion an entirely different set of structures for governing social relations. It was a far more revolutionary call to action than what Riesman had in mind. It attested to the range of critiques of not only the world the growth paradigm had wrought but more pointedly the scale of change necessary within capitalist societies.

The crises of the growth paradigm invited reflections about the future of capitalism and the capacity of nation-states to manage it on a global scale. American linguist and activist Noam Chomsky suggested that when "limits to growth" were "seriously faced" a "violent class war might erupt" from "a Third World country trying to separate itself from the Western-controlled global economy" or from "disaffected groups in the industrial societies themselves." He believed there would be a "significant social upheaval" among the "underprivileged dispossessed, and oppressed" citizens of the industrial countries to challenge the "institutional structures" that were "oppressive and unequal."[73] Aurelio Peccei, the founder and chairman of the Club of Rome, claimed that the capitalist countries needed to reorganize all aspects of how they managed global capitalism—monetary policy, trade, investment, fiscal policies, social and environmental policy standardization, rules for corporations, and much else—in order to survive the crises of the growth paradigm. Western leaders had failed "to grasp that the problems cramming their agenda" were "eminently political" and "a touchstone against which the capacity of industrial civilization to put its house in order [would] be measured."[74] Such fears—of budding class war and the monumental scale of political changes required to resolve the perceived crises of the moment—indicated that for some observers the crisis of the growth paradigm was a crisis of capitalism itself.

The debates in the West over the future and nature of capitalism mirrored debates within the Soviet world over the nature of Soviet communism. "The economists are arguing that improved yearly growth rates have not yet translated into general well-being," wrote Soviet KGB chief Yuri Andropov to General Secretary Leonid Brezhnev in 1968. In addition to a series of economic reforms to boost consumer goods production and stimulate technological innovation, Andropov also noted the need for improved youth education and bolstering "democratic institutions" within the Soviet state. These reforms did not amount to a radical set of changes. According to historian Yakov Feygin, Brezhnev-era Soviet leaders distanced themselves from the more radical restructuring of the Kosygin reforms and instead pursued "gradual, legally grounded improvements in administrative practices." This conservative approach to reform took note of entrenched interest groups in the Soviet Union but also reflected a faith that socialism was well suited to adjust to the problems of abundance and slackening growth.[75]

Soviet bloc social scientists wrestled with the social consequences of rapid growth but did so largely without abandoning faith in core socialist principles. Socialism, in their line of thinking, was effectively positioned to adopt such techniques and apply them through centralized planning agencies. Czech philosopher Radovan Richta explained, there was "unceasing conflict between capital and science, since the latter, being essentially a social productive force, calls for more far-reaching forms of social integration than those offered by the capitalist private-property relations." Whereas socialist countries could inject new scientific techniques into central planning agencies to account better for social downsides of growth, the capitalist countries faced more intractable troubles. He claimed it was only a matter of time before "the industrial system of capitalism begins to misfire," while socialists would adopt a more "flexible system of management extending to all areas of social labor" and respond to the downsides of growth more effectively.[76]

Similar thinking shaped the reactions to the threat of possible limitations to future growth. While the *Limits to Growth* report was translated into Russian, it was distributed only within limited circles within the Soviet Academy of Sciences, and the public received only ideological commentaries on it.[77] Soviet scientist Mikhail Millionshchikov brushed aside the report's finding for the Soviet Union because the Soviets had a political economic system that enabled them to "see everything from the point of view of all society" and manage "problems of economic development." Any short-term problems of economic growth would be solved over the long term, claimed the deputy director of Moscow's Institute of Marxism-Leninism in 1972, because "technological revolution" would be "combined with the advantages of the socialist economic system."[78] Soviet scientists did debate whether their ultimate goal would be more growth or something closer to "ecological and resource balance," but for many experts a continued faith in planning obviated fears of long-term trade-offs.[79]

Soviet dissidents, who had become increasingly popular in the West, unsurprisingly differed in their assessment about socialism's adaptability. By the mid-1970s, Aleksandr Solzhenitsyn had come to believe that the Soviet belief in economic growth was "not only unnecessary but ruinous" and that the country needed to renounce Marxism-Leninism altogether in order to redress its myriad social and political problems.[80] Andrei Sakharov was less intent on such revolutionary changes but recognized that the Soviet system's "excessive centralization, party domination, bureaucratic privilege and inertia" all required major reforms to democratize the Soviet system in radical ways.[81] Soviet leaders' crackdown on the dissident figures indicated that no such change was in the offing, content as they were to make piecemeal and conservative reforms bolstered by an ongoing faith in socialist planning.[82]

Although Soviet leaders appeared to maintain faith in their planning techniques and caution in their reforms, behind the scenes they faced difficult choices over challenging material realities. The 1973 oil embargo forced Soviet leaders to rethink spending priorities. Initially, the embargo and the quadrupling of oil prices meant that the Soviets could sell their own oil abroad for far greater profit than they had previously. Soviet oil and gas production expanded throughout the 1970s. The Soviet leadership used the revenue to purchase much-needed grain from the West and buy the advanced technology needed for oil exploration in western Siberia. By selling more energy abroad, however, the Soviets held a reduced supply available for its allies in Eastern Europe, who relied on cheap Soviet oil and gas to fuel their own growth. Eastern European demand outpaced Soviet supply in the 1970s. Soviet leaders ultimately chose to raise the price of oil and gas within the Council of Mutual Economic Assistance (CMEA) countries. Eastern European governments, in turn, turned to Arab exporters to buy their oil in greater numbers, and they increasingly relied on commercial loans to pay the high costs. As a result, the Soviet leadership faced a narrowing window of policy options that limited their ability to maintain domestic growth and continue to support their broader empire. By borrowing money from foreign commercial banks, the Eastern European states faced a burgeoning sovereign debt problem. In other words, like their Western counterparts, Soviet and Eastern European leaders over time experienced the oil crisis as evidence of limits to growth with serious political ramifications.[83]

The North-South Conflicts and New Visions of International Order

As experts and policy makers pondered the future of national economic growth, the crisis of the growth paradigm also prompted wide-ranging debates over relations between the wealthy countries and those of the Global South, as well as the nature of international order more broadly. International organizations and national governments responded to the crisis of the growth paradigm by constructing new venues for studying and debating alternative approaches to development. The World Bank was a first mover. It initiated a "grand assize" of its activities in 1968, led by a commission chaired by former Canadian prime minister Lester Pearson. The Pearson Commission found that while most Third World countries witnessed high growth rates during the 1960s, they also experienced many problems such as rapid population growth that was "nullifying much of the development effort," unemployment levels that had "reached critical proportions," and rising foreign indebtedness that had absorbed a large portion of many countries' export earnings. Despite these important issues, the commission proposed only mild reforms and remained focused on high growth rates (6 percent for developing countries during the 1970s) as its main strategy.[84] Frustration with the Pearson Commission report inspired many experts to debate its findings and explore why so many countries' actual experience had deviated from theoretical expectations. In 1970, Barbara Ward hosted an important conference at Columbia University. Ward and her colleagues took a dim view of the prospects for North-South collaboration and the continued pursuit of high growth rates, stressing that the Pearson Commission's recommendations would only lead to "growing confrontation between the developing and developed countries of the world."[85]

The Columbia Conference presaged a range of debate over the future of economic growth in the Global South. One axis of conflict pitted environmental growth critics against Third World intellectuals and government officials who sought to give priority to poverty reduction and industrialization. By the late 1960s, many Third World intellectuals acknowledged the ecological downsides that stemmed from the prioritization of GNP growth as a developmental goal, although many remained wary of northern environmental protection efforts. These tensions became apparent as countries prepared during the late 1960s and early 1970s for the UN's first major conference on environmental protection, the 1972 Conference on the Human Environment. In the lead-up to the conference, representatives from Third World countries, such as Brazil and India, argued that aggressive global environmental protection schemes would unfairly impair their development. They demanded additional foreign aid and compensation for lost revenue from any protection policies put in place.[86]

To reconcile these tensions, a handful of intellectuals attempted to link environmental protection with the need for alternative development approaches focused on poverty instead of aggregate growth. In June 1971 in Founex, Switzerland, the secretary-general of the UN conference, Maurice Strong, organized a workshop featuring Third World intellectuals such as Mahbub ul Haq, Spanish Uruguayan economist Enrique Iglesias, and Sri Lankan policy maker Gamani

Corea to meet with environmental and development experts from the First World, such as Barbara Ward. The gathering produced a report, authored principally by Haq, that asserted that the major problems facing developing countries were of a different kind than the ecological issues plaguing the industrialized North, but that the growth paradigm was not the answer for the problems afflicting the Global South. The report claimed that "the integration of environmental concern with development planning . . . require[d] a broader definition of development goals than a mere increase in gross national product." Though high growth rates seemed "necessary and essential," the choice to strive for GNP growth rather than poverty alleviation both exacerbated environmental destruction and reinforced income disparities between and within countries. Only by launching a "selective attack" on mass poverty, rather than continuing to embrace the growth paradigm, could Third World countries eliminate "the worst forms of malnutrition, squalor, disease and ignorance."[87] The Founex report attempted to reconcile the tensions between the developing countries continued pursuit of growth and environmental concerns by refocusing foreign aid policies and development strategies toward antipoverty and redistributive programs.

Within just a few years of the Founex meeting, international politics underwent a series of seismic shifts with wide-ranging implications for the growth paradigm. In May 1972, the United States and the Soviet Union formalized a major détente agreement to curtail the arms race and improve relations. The next month, the UN Conference on the Human Environment, however, revealed that international tensions between the North and South remained as fierce as ever. The Founex report had done little to assuage Third World government concerns that environmental accords would impair their ability to pursue development as they saw fit.[88] The collapse of Bretton Woods ended a remarkable period of international monetary cooperation and regulation. The outbreak of war between Israel and its neighbors in 1973 and the subsequent OAPEC oil embargo in 1973 marked a final decisive event that revealed that the postwar order was under great strain. "We are now living in a never-never land," US secretary of state Henry Kissinger remarked, "in which tiny, poor, and weak nations can hold up for ransom some of the industrialized world."[89] In this moment, a range of experts and leaders believed entirely new forms of world order were necessary to govern economic relations between countries.

During the early 1970s, many Third World leaders argued the international economic order inhibited the ability of their countries to pursue growth and development on their own terms. Whereas some development experts and intellectuals such as Dudley Seers and Mahbub ul Haq critiqued the growth paradigm within Third World countries because of persistent poverty and deepening inequality, for others the core problem was that the wealthy countries had constructed a set of international rules designed to enrich the West at the expense of the rest. Raúl Prebisch's work with UNCTAD in the 1960s grew in popularity among many Third World counterparts amid international commodity price instability, the collapse of the Bretton Woods system of fixed exchange rates, and the 1973 oil embargo. In April 1974 at the Sixth Special Session of the UN General Assembly, the Group of 77 (G-77) countries announced a call for a "New International Economic Order," or NIEO. The NIEO was a plan to restructure the rules of the international economy. The NIEO's prescriptions included greater regulation of multinational corporations, price stabilization mechanisms for primary products, increased aid from the First World, and the promotion of producer cartels, among many other recommendations. The NIEO did not include a call for countries to limit the pursuit of growth. Rather, the NIEO's supporters endeavored to change the international legal, political, and economic framework in which it existed to enable the "promotion of sustained growth of the world economy and [accelerate] the development of developing countries."[90] A companion document, the Charter on the Economic Rights and Duties of States (CERDS), contained a similar claim that adopting the NIEO was necessary to promote the "acceleration of the economic growth of developing countries with a view to bridging the economic gap between developing and developed countries."[91] Both documents passed the UN General Assembly with overwhelming support.

The arrival of the NIEO piqued concerns in the global North over the future of global economic governance and its relationship with national economic growth.[92] The United States, in particular, feared the implications of the NIEO and devised a strategy of "direct opposition" to the G-77 bloc. Nor would the United States and many of its closest European allies countenance the more radical redistributive claims put forth in the NIEO and the CERDS. Instead, the US worked to develop a less regulated form of global economic and energy policy coordination through organizations such as the International Energy Agency (IEA) and the G-7 summits in which heads of states and central bankers of the wealthy industrialized countries, not the UN General Assembly, would maintain the authority to manage the global economy and adjust to a new world defined by perceived limits.[93] In 1975 the OECD also launched its "Interfutures" project, a scenario-based modeling of the world economy that the organization hoped would revive faith in the "Western world." OECD officials sought to reaffirm the "Western world" as a stable category amid international strife and internal division and coordinate member states' responses to the Third World by nurturing a vision "that emphasized a positive image of a future world market and that saw the future world as divided between those world actors who were willing to embrace this market and those who were not."[94] These initiatives sought to revive the growth paradigm and blunt the effectiveness of the Third World's collective actions.

Alongside the G-77's world-making efforts, there were other important attempts to rethink the nature of international order. Three years after the Founex workshop, in 1974 the United Nations Environment Programme funded a similar gathering of experts in Cocoyoc, Mexico, including Barbara Ward, Maurice Strong, Gamani Corea, and Mahbub ul Haq. The Cocoyoc meeting was a "systematic attempt" to state the "connections between the issues of environmental protection and the distribution of global economic and social resources." Unlike the NIEO, which reflected an effort of nation-states, the Cocoyoc meeting brought together nonstate experts to define guiding principles for the future of international relations. The group produced a lengthy declaration, largely authored by Barbara Ward, that endorsed the NIEO and the CERDS.[95]

The Cocoyoc declaration, however, took a less sanguine view of economic growth. "We believe that thirty years of experience with the hope that rapid economic growth benefiting the few will 'trickle down' to the mass of the people has proved to be illusory," the declaration stated. Rather, it claimed that while the NIEO struck an effective balance for reorganizing economic policy between countries, within countries it was necessary to "redefine the whole purpose of development." Development should no longer be equated with economic growth, but instead focus on the "satisfaction of basic needs," "freedom of expression and impression," and a "right to work" that included "self-realization" and the right "not to be alienated through production processes that use human beings simply as tools." It melded the international politics of the NIEO, the reformist thinking of social critics of growth, and an ecological sensibility that sought to limit First World consumption so as not to violate the "outer limits of nature."[96] The Cocoyoc group called for changes in international economic policy, the lifestyles of individuals in the wealthy countries, and the development priorities of most Third World governments. As they had with the NIEO, US officials worked with their Western European allies to levy critical diplomatic demarches toward any government that endorsed the Cocoyoc declaration as they hoped to blunt its appeal in halls of power around the world.[97]

The Club of Rome even explored possibilities for structuring a new international governing order. After the Mexican government first proposed the CERDS in early 1974, Aurelio Peccei, the Club of Rome's president, tasked Jan Tinbergen, a Dutch economist and early pioneer of econometric models of national economies, to study ways to reform global governance. Tinbergen organized multiple working groups over the next couple of years to help prepare a final report, published in 1976 as *Reshaping the International Order*. Bringing together reformist development experts such as Mahbub ul Haq, critics of the Bretton Woods system such as Belgian American economist Lionel Tiffin, and Club of Rome regulars such as OECD science director Alexander King, Tinbergen's group largely avoided the language of growth and instead advocated for "the establishment of an equitable international social and economic order" to ensure "that a life of dignity and well-being be attained by all by the end of the century."[98] Tinbergen's report contained a diverse range of proposals and policies, ranging from the adoption of the CERDS, to reforming voting rules in the IMF, to increasing foreign aid, to price guarantees for foodstuffs, to the creation of new institutions to manage global resources to nuclear disarmament.[99] It was an ambitious agenda that proposed a set of institutions and organizations designed not just to generate economic growth but to reshape how individuals lived across the world.

The debates over international order and the varied proposals for alternative frameworks struck to the core of the paradigm. The pursuit of national economic growth depended on the particular form of macroeconomic management that emerged during and after World War II. As that order crumbled during the late 1960s and 1970s, the G-77, the Cocoyoc group, and the Club of Rome put forth alternative orders with distinct attitudes toward growth. As political theorist Adom Getachew has argued, while the NIEO was "Marxist in its diagnosis of economic dependence, drawing on traditions of dependency and world systems theory," its prescriptions were "articulated within the terms of a liberal political economy."[100] Furthermore, the NIEO was ultimately premised on the centrality of growth for developing countries. Its advocates aspired to change the rules governing the global economy to allow for growth unfettered by aid tied to geopolitical imperatives of northern governments, freed from the gains won by multinational corporations, and with terms of trade more suitable to the long-term interest of primary producers than to those of their industrialized counterparts. The Cocoyoc team held a more critical view of growth. They argued that reforming international economic relations would allow countries to make new priorities for development besides those associated with the growth paradigm. Similarly, the Club of Rome report proposed a world oriented toward improving social well-being rather than economic goals alone. The three visions shared a core belief that the world needed a new form of international order to reshape international economic relations.

These efforts to reimagine and reconstruct international order sat uneasily with many leaders, especially in the wealthy countries, who believed major transformations were unnecessary. In a high-level cabinet meeting in May 1975 to discuss the NIEO, US president Gerald Ford made clear that his primary objective in debates over the future of growth and the international configuration of economic power was to "defend our system without establishing a new world economic order." Ford recognized that the "free enterprise system" of global capitalism the United States had constructed was under threat, but he saw "no reason for changing" its basic structure.[101] At the inaugural Group of Six (G6) Summit in November 1975 in Rambouillet, France, Ford reiterated this point. After meeting with leaders from France, West Germany, Italy, the United Kingdom, and Japan, Ford announced that through cooperation on trade, energy, North-South politics, and monetary policy the six countries would pursue a common objective of stimulating "sustained, stable economic growth."[102] Not all prominent leaders would share this line of thinking—Ford's successor, Jimmy Carter, would stand out a few years later in his exceptional calls for economic sacrifice and restraint—but the dominant theme among the G6 was to find ways to restore growth without radical change and with few compromises.[103]

Crisis and Conflict: Growth Critics between North and South

For many growth critics, however, radical changes were indeed required. But there were strong tensions between the differing approaches to reorganizing world order and the more vocal growth critics who aspired to a world defined by limited growth in the future. Conflicts between the most committed environmental growth critics and Third World intellectuals and leaders were especially acute. At the 1972 Stockholm conference, peace activist Tom Artin, a friend and colleague of Georgescu-Roegen, Daly, and Boulding, wrote of a palpable disagreement between the strongest ecological arguments about limiting growth and Third World governments who "feared the zero-growth ideology as another guise of imperialist oppression."[104] The *Limits to Growth* report exacerbated these fears. Mahbub ul Haq argued that the report's "basic weakness" is not that "it is alarmist, but that it is complacent. . . . The industrialized countries may be able to accept a target of zero growth as a disagreeable, yet perhaps morally bracing, regime for their own citizens. For the developing world, however, zero growth offers only a prospect of despair and world income redistribution [as] merely a wistful dream."[105] Haq, of course, had long argued that development policy in the 1970s needed to dethrone "the goddess of GNP" and focus instead on the "satisfaction of basic needs," but he believed that doing so first required a major shift in First World aid and trade policy to provide the Third World with more resources before seeking to place firm limits on their economic policy.[106] Léopold Sédar Senghor, the president of Senegal, echoed these concerns, arguing that while the report was valuable for drawing "attention to the fact that quantitative growth is by no means sufficient," it was ultimately a "problem of the West" because countries such as Senegal needed a "minimum of growth" to meet basic needs before adopting any of the report's more stringent zero-growth recommendations.[107]

The *Limits to Growth* report prompted a strong backlash from experts in the Global South who crafted their own models from futures research premised on redistribution and basic needs rather than Malthusian limits. The most notable of these alternative models, presented in a report produced by the Fundación Bariloche in Argentina, echoed many of the themes of the NIEO and called for a tightly managed global economy. The Bariloche Report's authors believed that the zero-growth mentality underlying the *Limits to Growth* report would lead to "perpetuating the misery of the Third World," thus their model sought to craft newly "egalitarian" societies designed to achieve justice and environmental protection.[108]

How to balance and even reconcile these competing visions for the global economy, national consumption patterns, and international order was a vexing problem. One major issue pertained to democracy. It seemed to many that the quickest way to the steady side was through antidemocratic means. Kenneth Boulding, for instance, wrote that it "could well be, for instance, that the easiest way to achieve a steady-state economy would be to set up an unshakable tyranny with a very small world-ruling class, which would be able to keep the vast mass of mankind in steady-state poverty."[109] No less an establish-ment figure than George Kennan, the architect of the US Cold War containment strategy, advocated that to limit environmental degra-dation worldwide the ten wealthiest industrialized countries should construct an "International Environmental Agency" defined "not on the basis of compromise among governmental representatives but on the basis of collaboration among scholars, scientists, experts," who would be "bound by no national or political mandate" and serve as a global watchdog to track resource use, set priorities and standards, and pressure governments to adopt its recommendations.[110] Governing the global environment, in this view, required a supranational techno-cratic elite with broad powers.

Yet such antidemocratic means sat uneasily against Third Worldist arguments for not only economic justice, but also political empower-ment. Key advocates for the NIEO such as Jamaica's Michael Manley and Tanzania's Julius Nyerere linked the redistribution of economic resources and a new economic order with political enfranchisement. They viewed this "anticolonial worldmaking" as necessary to "real-ize political and economic equality."[111] For environmental growth crit-ics, the conflict between supranational ecological imperatives and national empowerment was clear. In discussions with activists at the Stockholm Conference, Herman Daly acknowledged that a core prob-lem of building a steady-state economy was that it required planning and control, although he and many others preferred more democratic decision making. Tom Artin put it succinctly: "How can decentral-ized decision-making effectively control the planned economy these independents were advocating?"[112] The coercive and often violent cam-paigns of forced sterilization in the Third World on behalf of popula-tion control efforts provided a vivid example of how efforts to manage growth could be antidemocratic and racist.[113]

Growth critics also worried that low economic growth rates would aggravate the tensions surrounding redistribution. The NIEO and CERDS made redistribution between countries a central topic of inter-national concern. Reform-minded development experts such as Dud-ley Seers and Mahbub ul Haq had emphasized inequality as a core concern in domestic politics, as well. Environmental growth critics often sympathized with these arguments but acknowledged how fiery political debate over redistribution would become in a world of limits. Kenneth Boulding claimed, "The problem of distribution becomes much more acute as the rate of economic growth slows down and poverty can only be diminished by relative distribution. Our society seems to be extremely unprepared to deal with this and if any relative redistribution is to take place this almost requires some kind of political consensus which we do not have now."[114] The NIEO's commitment to the ongoing growth of the global economy did not align with environmental critics who argued that a reduction in production and consumption patterns, at least in wealthy countries, was necessary for environmental harmony. Herman Daly conceded that experience of GNP growth was a probably a "good thing" for poor countries, although it was "a bad thing" for rich countries. He suggested that poor countries should be allowed to pursue growth as wealthy countries moved toward a steady-state economy, though he cautioned that ongoing population growth would stultify poor countries' economic development.[115]

There was also a related debate as advocates for the NIEO challenged the growth critics who had argued that addressing inequality within countries and satisfying basic human needs deserved priority. As Hans Singer explained after the declaration of the NIEO, many Third World governments resisted claims on their leadership to organize domestic policy in any particular vein determined by Western experts or foreign aid agencies. "On their part, the developing countries tend to be deeply suspicious of the tendency of western governments to talk about poverty and human needs instead of, say, a Common Fund or voting rights in the I.M.F.," Singer wrote. "They consider this preference of the West partly as an intervention in their own internal affairs, and partly as a device to avoid the discussion of really important questions which are much more awkward for the industrial countries" such as those raised by the NIEO.[116] Thandika Mkandawire noted that for many African leaders, moving away from the growth-oriented strategies warranted skepticism "founded not only on the dismal performance by the advanced countries as supporters of the poor but also on the justifiable fear that the sudden interest of the rich countries in 'poverty' was a ploy, a means of diverting attention from the real issues, namely the need for the restructuring of the world economic order" through the NIEO.[117] This conflict derived partly from different priorities, but also from NIEO advocates' desire to remake the configuration of international power and emphasize "collective self-reliance" over reformist efforts by development experts that did not directly redress an unequal international system.[118] Mahbub ul Haq believed the conflicts between basic needs advocates and NIEO advocates would fade only if basic needs was "accepted as a primary objective which should be met both by reforming the national and international orders and by the more automatic provision of additional financial support for the developing countries."[119]

With little clarity on the political steps to reconcile a commitment for growth alternatives, and with much of the world impoverished and yearning for growth on their own terms, many growth critics recognized the importance of promoting, nurturing, and sustaining new values. In 1973, Kenneth Boulding's concerns about the potentially antidemocratic dimensions of the steady-state led him to call for economists to pay closer attention to the ethical implications of their work, what he called "justice research."[120] In the same year, British economist and growth critic Ezra Mishan added that only once "the ethics of a no-growth economy are accepted and the competitive striving for more, ever more, is a thing of the past" would it be easier to "redirect expenditure away from current extravagance and waste, and to bring about a more equal distribution of income."[121] Throughout the 1970s, Daly wrote often of new "moral resources" needed in wealthy countries that attuned citizens to current-day inequalities instead of focusing on future gains from growth.[122] Nicholas Georgescu-Roegen argued, "A new ethics is what the world needs most," because "economists have preached for two long that one should maximize his present gains. It is high time that people realize that the most rational conduct is to minimize regrets."[123] Perhaps, these critics wondered, it was in the realm of morality, less so politics, that a transition away from the growth paradigm would have to be built.

Conclusion

The rise of the growth critics and the power of their arguments reflected a larger epistemic crisis. The growth paradigm was in large part a story of the growing prominence of economic expertise in public life. Though there had long been dissenters to the growth paradigm, the unrest and uncertainty of the 1960s cut to the core of experts' capacity to manage modern life. Experts and policy makers had promised that growth would alleviate social and political conflicts, but by the 1960s the pursuit of growth had generated its own set of problems. The energy crisis and perception of hard material limits to growth, the debates over the future of capitalism, the endeavors to envision new forms of world order in the wake of the collapse of the Bretton Woods system, and Cold War détente all reflected a broader flux in who could make claims about power and who could define the forms of knowledge necessary to make sense of this new world. There was a range of different international development strategies, visions for a future international order, and rich debates over the meaning of justice for contemporary inequalities and protecting future generations (and the nonhuman world). Yet throughout the 1970s, there was little international or domestic consensus over how to move past the growth paradigm.

What, then, were experts to do? As Ezra Mishan put it in 1977, "the study of economic growth" had become "too serious to be left to the economists" alone.[124] Over the 1970s and 1980s, many growth critics embraced this way of thinking as they imagined and worked to implement alternatives to the growth paradigm focused on issues of measurement and assessment. All growth critics shared one common critique: that GNP, the primary indicator of economic success, was flawed, incomplete, and unsuitable as a measure of progress. Although there was little agreement over how to reform or reject capitalism or reorganize the international configuration of power, there was a shared sense that new metrics were necessary to move beyond the growth paradigm.

FIVE

The Search for Alternatives

For many reformers, the crisis of the growth paradigm opened up intellectual and political space to explore new ways to quantify progress and well-being. "That economic growth will not in itself end poverty now seems so obvious that the extent of the revolution in approach to development is being missed," Dudley Seers wrote in 1973. "The much-publicised 'dethronement of GNP' goes only a small way in explaining the demoralisation; the whole edifice of ideas has been undermined."[1] Despite the crisis, Seers claimed, "we must not fall into the familiar trap of criticizing statistics to the point where we deny them any meaning."[2] So which statistics might replace GNP? The opportunity that lay before experts such as Seers was to construct and promote new indicators that could be used to tell a different story about who had benefited from growth, who had not, and what new frameworks—from alleviating poverty and reducing inequality to protecting the environment— might supplant the growth paradigm. In other words, growth critics had the opportunity to imagine alternative ways of measuring society and defining what constituted well-being.

During the 1960s and 1970s, growth critics sought to counter the use of GNP in many different ways. To capture the social aspects of life left invisible by economic accounts and the persistent poverty and inequality within countries, a transnational movement of experts sought to introduce "social indicators" in public policy. There was also renewed interest in quantifying aspects of labor and economic activity that was unwaged and not expressed in market relations, such as "informal" labor and women's household work. Environmentalists sought to redress the ecological crises by pricing environmental externalities and constructing alternative models and metaphors for economic activity that linked economic and biophysical systems into a cohesive whole. While these alternatives are not a comprehensive list of the range of alternative goals and indicators put forth in the 1970s, they all drew widespread international attention, reflected the most prominent arguments among growth critics, and revealed the range of debate over the meaning and measurement of economic growth during the decade.

All these reform efforts shared common aspirations. The reform movements that crafted alternative indicators captured genuine frustration with the growth paradigm and promoted alternative metrics to use for new goals in public policy. Their work often reflected earlier criticisms of economic growth and alternative ways of measuring progress. The social indicators movement and the attempt to shift public attention to the "basic human needs" of the poor advocated for more bespoke and subnational social indicators, such as those that were central to early twentieth-century standard-of-living metrics. The feminist activists who advocated for the measurement of women's work and the anthropologists and economists who sought to quantify the "informal" sector mirrored Phyllis Deane's arguments about the need for inclusive metrics that quite literally accounted for all people's contributions to the production process. In these cases, reformers hoped to use new and alternatives sources of data to draw attention to aspects of the social world that GNP excluded or occluded.

While these social movements challenged the growth paradigm, they did not amount to the "revolution" that Seers identified. The alternatives put forth by growth critics represented a large spectrum between those who sought only to tweak existing metrics to become more inclusive of various "variables" or "factors" understood to be part of a discreet growth "process" and those who sought to eliminate and move past the growth paradigm altogether, embracing and celebrating the prospect of "zero growth" and a vast change of lifestyles. Ultimately, though, most of the notable new metrics, such as the Physical Quality of Life Index (PQLI), had little long-term effect on national policy or international strategy as national leaders revived the growth paradigm during the 1980s. Moreover, these reform efforts were largely expert driven. In one sense, this enabled growth critics to gain cultural and political attention, much as the expert-led efforts to quantify national income and product had helped endear it to policy makers and the public. Yet it also limited the effectiveness and reach of the reforms. At root, the growth critics often sought to replace one set of numbers in governance with another. They mounted a technocratic critique of technocracy that claimed the basic problems of contemporary life could be resolved through the use of socially relevant and more specialized data. Absent broader political mobilization to sustain and promote the values that the new numbers represented, the growth critics struggled to maintain a lasting effect on those in power.

Accounting for Social Change and Inequality

One major theme of the growth critics was that policy makers had for too long assumed that economic policy could produce positive social outcomes. Dudley Seers, for instance, argued that "social targets" in planning, such as helping people live longer or encouraging more leisure time, "were usually subsidiary to growth" in the 1950s and 1960s. Planners mistakenly believed that high GNP growth rates alone would achieve these other goals and that economic growth "was almost a synonym for development."[3] In addition, by relying on national aggregates to reveal well-being, inequalities within countries were too often hidden from public view. Seers claimed that the system of national accounts was flawed because it was "monistic, treating the whole nation as an appropriate object of analysis and of policy prescription."[4] Instead, Seers argued that governments needed to rely on social indicators that would paint a richer depiction of development and overall well-being.

Seers was one of many intellectuals and activists who sought to develop and promote social indicators as an alternative to GNP during the 1960s and 1970s. "Social indicators" was a broad category that encompassed a range of statistics on various aspects of life that related to how people lived in society: literacy rate, education level, access to housing, life expectancy, and so forth. Social indicators advocates were often sociologists, heterodox economists, or other social scientists who charged that policy makers needed new methods and data to make sense of the problems that afflicted modern society.[5] In contrast to GNP and national economic aggregates, social indicators mirrored the standard of living research from the early twentieth century by allowing for clear comparisons of various social groups within and across countries.

Early research into social indicators came from a technical critique of development economics. A handful of economists and sociologists wanted to improve growth theory by quantifying "social" factors that contributed to how national economies expanded. A milestone in this line of inquiry came in 1964, when a grant from the Dutch government funded the United Nations Research Institute for Social Development (UNRISD) to study "social factors" in economic growth.[6] A Polish economist named Jan Drewnowski spearheaded the UNRISD effort. His research explored "the measurement of social elements of development with their relations to economic variables and the problem of giving social orientation to development planning." He wanted to identify the various social factors in growth (such as education, for instance), quantify them, and inject them into the modeling and planning process.[7]

Shortly after the UNRISD began its research into social indicators for "social" development, the civil unrest, student protests, and sense of anomie that had animated so many growth critics led experts to embrace social indicators less as corrective growth theories than as tools to understand the sources and nature of this discontent. In 1966, American sociologist Raymond Bauer, in an influential study on the domestic social impact of the space race and the militarization of the Cold War, called for social indicators to supplement economic ones.[8] The Department of Housing, Education, and Welfare began systematic collection and analysis of social data.[9] In 1967, US senator Walter Mondale sponsored a bill to adopt national social indicators alongside economic ones and to create a "Council on Social Advisers" to provide advice similar to the Council of Economic Advisers (CEA) in the United States amid urban rioting and growing student protest.[10] In the early years of Richard Nixon's presidency, sociologist Daniel Patrick Moynihan oversaw an effort to use newly collected social indicators to define a set of national social policy "goals" for the Nixon administration.[11]

During the early 1970s, collecting social indicators became a common strategy for other governments seeking to limit social unrest and protest, as well. In 1970, the UN Statistical Commission noted that "national statistical offices are under great pressure to develop social statistics which relate directly and immediately to social concerns of the general public and political authorities," and it sought to increase the collection and promote further standardization of social data.[12] Between 1970 and 1975, the governments of Canada, France, West Germany, Italy, Japan, the Netherlands, Norway, Sweden, Spain, the United Kingdom, Malaysia, and the Philippines also carried out studies on social indicators.[13] Soviet sociologists collected social indicators and used them to anticipate "young people's needs" as Soviet forecasting evolved to try and improve economic planning in the Brezhnev era.[14] The Hungarian Economic Planning Institute devised a "level of living" index based on social indicators to promote "industrial development alternatives" amid weak growth.[15] The Council for Mutual Economic Assistance (Comecon) in the Eastern bloc collected reports on social data, which the UN Economic Commission for Europe (ECE) used to chart Western Europe's "social progress" against economic and social data from the Soviet Union and Eastern European countries.[16] So too did international organizations such as the OECD, with a focus on how they could help leaders understand growth's "unfavourable side effects on society and the lives of individuals."[17] Writing in 1975, a member of India's Planning Commission noted the "much greater degree of awareness about problems connected with inequality in income or in the distribution of public expenditure" in the Third World and endorsed the creation of an international standard system of social and demographic indicators.[18]

For the many experts wary of the growth paradigm, social indicators offered a better way to measure and thus tell the story of developmental change. Development economists Norman Hicks and Paul

Streeten celebrated social indicators because they reflected concerns "with ends as well as means, or at least with intermediate ends nearer to the ultimate end of a full and healthy life" and because such numbers were "capable of catching something of the human, social, and cultural costs of opulence . . . as well as poverty."[19] Social indicators would help policy makers identify social priorities and make targeted policy interventions to improve their populations' well-being, just as liberal experts in the League of Nations and ILO had hoped for with standard-of-living statistics. The similarities between the revived focus on distribution and basic needs and the earlier work on standard of living were not lost on contemporary observers. American researchers Robert Parke and David Seidman wrote in 1978 that the "concerns of the social indicators movement" were "not new" and reflected the social research initiatives of the early twentieth century.[20] "It is clear," development economist Douglas Rimmer wrote in 1981 while reflecting on the research of the previous decade, "that much recent thinking on development objectives covers ground traversed by international agencies in the 1930s."[21]

The social indicators movement garnered widespread interest because it resonated with a growing concern about the "quality of life." The phrase "quality of life" was a broad term that captured a popular sentiment that policy needed to shift away from increasing output toward a more thoughtful reflection on how people lived. Scarcely employed in public discourse before the 1960s, by the 1970s talk about the "quality of life" was ubiquitous. Environmentalists adopted the phrase to emphasize the noneconomic sources of enjoyment that warranted greater protection.[22] In late 1974, the United States' Public Broadcasting Service (PBS) debuted a multi-episode documentary on the future of the country entitled *The Quality of Life*.[23] Studies designed to measure quality of life proliferated. "The assumption that the quality of life could be assessed by counting the national income has proven an overly simple and disappointing delusion," wrote Angus Campbell, the director of the University of Michigan's Institute for Social Research.[24] A 1972 *Wall Street Journal* report chronicled efforts to collect survey data on the quality of life by a range of institutions from the *Economist* magazine in the United Kingdom to the National

Wildlife Foundation in the United States.[25] The OECD noted the growing interest in the concept and commissioned a working party to establish a consensus definition for it, the results of which included twenty-
four "social concerns" in eight "goal areas" ranging from good health
to "social opportunity and equality."[26] The phrase resonated because it
captured growth critics' desire to shift public focus from the *quantity*
of output to the *quality* of life.

Another new focus for policy makers that sustained interest in
social indicators was poverty alleviation. By the middle 1960s, the
growing interest in poverty found statistical expression in a range of
attempts to measure poverty levels. In 1965, economist Mollie Orshan-
sky of the US Social Security Administration developed the first "poverty line" metric for the country based on survey data of household consumption patterns and income levels.[27] Third World countries such as
India also began to set a poverty line as a function of income, and South
African reformers revived earlier efforts to quantify a "poverty datum
line" to estimate "the lowest possible cost for maintaining a household in health and decency under Western conditions."[28] Defining a
poverty line as a function of income and purchasing power, however,
revealed a narrow vision. It excluded "broader indicators of inclusion
and opportunity such as access to education, adequate health care,
transportation, and housing, or other amenities considered basic to
social citizenship" and reified "the poor as a separate, easily definable
social group."[29] Poverty lines also illuminated little about distribution
for those who lived beneath them, as Amartya Sen argued in numerous
venues during the 1970s.[30] This frustration led to a widespread search
for other ways to measure poverty and distribution, especially in the
Third World countries. Social indicators held promise by touching on
the nonmonetary dimensions of poverty and the distribution of access
and outcomes across income levels.[31]

Social Indicators for Redressing Inequality and Poverty: The PQLI

Over the 1970s, there were many attempts to construct new metrics
based on social indicators that linked concerns about persistent pov-

erty with the quality of life, to quantify what were the "basic human needs" of the poor. The most successful of these in terms of funding and popularity came in 1977 when the Overseas Development Council (ODC), an US-based think tank set up to revive support for development assistance in the wake of the growth critics, tasked Morris David Morris, an economist from the University of Washington with a background in sociology, to construct a "Physical Quality of Life Index," or PQLI. Morris drew inspiration from the growing emphasis on both the "quality of life" rhetoric and the basic human needs approach in development policy. He linked both with the social indicators movement. "To the extent that development planners within poor countries and aid dispensers in donor countries now focus more directly on projects that emphasize distribution of benefits," Morris wrote, "they need not only new planning strategies but also additional measurement systems."[32] He designed the PQLI to fill that void. Morris's work on the PQLI drew the attention of the US Agency for International Development (USAID). In the mid-1970s, much like the World Bank, USAID had shifted its funding to include more "basic human needs" projects, but the organization lacked an effective metric to measure their efforts.[33] The PQLI fit well with the mandate. Morris won a grant from USAID, which helped him complete his research and publish the first version of the new index in 1979.

The PQLI rested on a very simple set of numbers. It was based on infant mortality, life expectancy at age one, and literacy rate. Morris transformed each indicator into an index by comparing the level of the indicator to a fixed range of possible levels, and then taking the average of the three components. Morris intended for the PQLI to serve national governments for making comparisons, but also for subnational analysis of regional and local results according to gender or income levels. He viewed it as "a practical measure of social distribution that will avoid the limitations of the GNP, that will minimize cultural and developmental ethnocentricity, and that will be internationally comparable."[34] As with GNP, Morris sought clarity, simplicity, and comparability. In contrast to economic aggregates, he hoped that the PQLI would give more insight into the social health and well-being of a country's population. The metric had a very specific purpose. Morris wanted it "to help focus the search for strategies that might yield quicker improvements in the condition of the very poorest than can be expected if we wait for benefits to flow 'naturally' from increases in national income."[35]

Morris's index garnered institutional and professional acclaim from around the world, especially among international development specialist who saw it as particularly valuable for Third World countries. James Grant of the ODC hailed the PQLI, because it depicted "a stereoscopic view—a way of looking behind the façade of the GNP numbers."[36] Dudley Seers eagerly anticipated the PQLI's arrival, as did many other development experts who saw it as "vastly more illuminating in some respects than GNP."[37] The PQLI data suggested, for instance, that countries with high growth rates, such as Brazil, appeared far lower on their index than their GNP would suggest. A few small countries, notably Sri Lanka, with a history of investing in basic needs scored far better than large countries with high GNP growth rates such as Brazil, Mexico, Egypt, and India. The data on Sri Lanka, according to one observer, told "a success story, in terms of human welfare, more truly remarkable than the more widely publicized stories of countries which are far wealthier in terms of per capita GNP."[38] The PQLI offered a different way to compare countries. It provided, according to Indian journalist M. V. Kamath, "a fascinating and largely accurate picture of nations as they are, not what their GNP alone would make us believe."[39] In the tradition of early standard-of-living indicators, it gave analysts confidence that they could measure and thus improve material well-being of different social groups in a country.

After Morris published his initial methods and finding, he hoped to persuade governments to use the new index. Shortly after his initial research was complete, USAID sent Morris to India to explore options for making the PQLI central to Indian development plans. His visit came at a propitious moment. In the years after independence, postcolonial countries had often relied on colonial-era statistical offices and technical assistance from the wealthy countries to build up their statistical capabilities. By the 1960s, India had crafted an extensive statistical service, which featured a formal national Department of Statistics for national income data collection and calculations as well as the National Sample Survey (NSS) to gather information on the country's socioeconomic circumstances.[40] Over the 1970s, Indian economists debated how to use this data. Poverty persisted following the country's first four five-year plans, leaving nearly two hundred million people in precarious condition. India had developed income-based "poverty line" measurements. But economists such as Pranab Bardhan and Amartya Sen questioned the existing metrics and expressed frustration at disappointing results from conventional policies. "The Indian poor may not be accustomed to receiving much help," Sen wrote in 1974, "but he is beginning to get used to being counted."[41] All the new data and metrics garnered intellectuals' interests, but to little overall effect.

In India, Morris and his wife, economist Michelle McAlpin, traveled around the country for two weeks to meet with statisticians, collect data, and visit various government agencies. The trip resulted in a book that offered national- and state-level PQLI metrics for both men and women throughout the country and compared India's results against other countries. The PQLI varied considerably from state to state, with communist Kerala registering a high ranking. Because India as a whole ranked quite low, Morris and McAlpin hoped the data would provide valuable information for a policy revolution. They wanted useful data for targeted, state-level policies designed to raise the PQLI and, in particular, to alert policy makers about the need for policies to improve "the status of women."[42]

In the end, however, the PQLI did not become an important tool in Indian politics. The absence of data for the index's key indicators was one problem. India lacked reliable statistical information for many of its states, and Morris had to use some guesswork to reach his initial index for the country. Morris admitted as such, acknowledging that his initial data was "not good."[43] Scholarly reviewers in India of Morris's work lamented how troublesome this was. One reviewer suggested that it would be "prohibitively expensive" for the Indian national government to set up a statistical apparatus to collect all the necessary information. Yet without greater administrative capacity, to make policy on the "poor data" that actually existed would be "disastrous."[44] Replicating Morris's initial findings proved difficult, too. Indian economists argued over Morris's weighting system for the three key indicators, and by the mid-1980s multiple efforts to try and repeat Morris's initial work yielded different results than he had achieved just a half decade prior.[45]

The PQLI's challenges went beyond data availability. Critics argued that the focus on physical traits alone did not suffice as "satisfactory measures of human welfare."[46] For instance, one Indian observer lamented that the PQLI could not measure other important aspects of life also neglected by GNP such as "justice, political freedom or a sense of participation" in politics.[47] While Morris never designed the index to do so, the social indicators movement had been predicated on redirecting policy makers' focus to "subjective" aspects of life instead of economic notions of value.[48] Moreover, it was unclear how the PQLI's publication would connect to policy changes. "A successful policy," Morris and McAlpin concluded, "requires a high degree of popular participation and self-administration." However, in a country as administratively complex as India, this was no easy task. It was not clear how their new statistical techniques would alone engender greater participation.[49] The fate of the PQLI in India played out in debates in economic journals, but not on government balance sheets.

Morris's struggles with the PQLI in India spoke to broader concerns about social indicators. Were they, and indexes such as the PQLI, meant to replace growth and GNP? Or simply to help policy makers ensure that the benefits of growth were more widely shared? How one answered that question suggested the priority of distributive or basic needs concerns compared to larger national economic production. Morris himself described the PQLI in contradictory ways. In some instances, Morris referred to the index as a "practical measure of social distribution that will avoid the limitations of the GNP."[50] Yet he also often referred to it as a tool to expose previously hidden or underappreciated "factors" in spurring conventionally understood economic growth. For all the rhetoric of the PQLI as an alternative to GNP, its advocates often described it in terms of growth. Morris suggested as much. With regard to India, he and McAlpin claimed, a "proper emphasis on raising the PQLI" was "likely to make possible a higher rate of growth." While also hoping that it would "ease the tensions that such growth must necessarily generate," they framed PQLI in terms of growth just the same.[51] Subsequent observers would reiterate such criticisms, especially noting that the PQLI had little to say about distributional questions.[52] Others expressed a similar frustration that social indicators, as with GNP, defined poverty just as a state of being, rather than an outcome of historical and structural forces. Economists Keith Griffin and Azizur Khan wrote in 1978 that "perhaps it would be better, however, to work with a structural definition of poverty, in which poverty is regarded as a product of a social system and reflects differences in access of various groups to sources of economic and political power" rather than one that led to indicators that provided a snapshot of consumption habits or social traits.[53]

There was also concern that indexes such as the PQLI and the many new social indicators led to a surfeit of tools for policy makers to use. "What has been created so far," Jan Drewnowski wrote in 1972 following the explosion of social indicators, "is an incoherent maze of variables, the definitions of which are muddled, quantification procedures questionable, and practical uses, if any, extremely doubtful. . . . What is badly needed is the establishment of some ordering principles which would make possible of selection of useful indicators, and rejection of the ill-conceived and inapplicable ones."[54] There was a clear normative element to social indicators, but no universally agreed-on definition to what constituted a high "quality of life." The lack of consensus was a core issue that had plagued debates over standard-of-living statistics during the 1920s. Identifying the ordering principles, as Morris discovered, was a contentious process, too. Ongoing debates over which indicators and variables to emphasize hamstrung some of the ambitious social indicators research programs, such as the OECD's.[55]

The PQLI faced an even larger challenge. Many leaders in developing countries viewed it, along with the basic human needs approach to development, with suspicion. Critical reviewers of the PQLI pointed out that it played down "the sensitive issue of income" and thus diverted "attention away from a fundamental problem" of economic inequality.[56] Morris also came under fire for his attempts to explain divergences in PQLI rates with peculiar and often racist generalizations about social organization ("tribal" African configurations generating lower PQLIs than "village systems" in Asia) and for his broader economic history work on India that many critics saw as far too laudatory of British colonialism and neglectful of its invidious legacies.[57] Indian economist Ajit Singh claimed that Third World leaders feared that metrics such as the PQLI and the basic human needs approach would "discourage industrial development" and place too much emphasis on rural and informal employment strategies.[58]

Though the PQLI never achieved the status Morris and its advocates had hoped, the debate it generated over the possibilities and limits of social indicators marked an important moment in the history of the growth paradigm. The PQLI and the social indicators movement more broadly were attempts to contest the hegemony of GNP by collecting different data to reveal persistent inequalities and poverty within countries that economic indicators had obscured. It was not the only such method for doing so, however. During the 1970s, another set of reforms confronted the growth paradigm by revealing the range of putative economic activities that GNP left out altogether.

Measuring Informal Economies and Women's Labor

In 1965, a British anthropologist named Keith Hart traveled to Ghana to conduct dissertation research. He studied how migrants who moved from the rural northern parts of the country adapted to the growing urban areas around the capital city of Accra. After over three years of fieldwork, Hart realized that development experts had misunderstood the nature of work there. Contrary to what modernization theorists expected, the migrants he studied often struggled to find wage-earning jobs in the "modern" sectors of the urban economy. These were the types of enterprise that ran "with some measure of bureaucracy" that were "amenable to enumeration by surveys," or in other words, that would be included in the country's GNP. He argued further the Western category of "unemployment" did not fit with the migrants' experiences either, as many still found income-generating work in the city from off-the-books businesses.[59]

Hart proposed that the migrants' work should be classified as "informal" activity. For Hart, informal labor included subsistence farming; the service work in the slums that included those working as barbers, maintenance workers, and petty traders; and many "illegitimate" and often illegal activities such as prostitution, gambling, and protection rackets. Rather than cast these forms of income generation as "traditional," as modernization theorists would have it, Hart explained that these were productive endeavors that by their nature happened to "escape enumeration" and remained outside the purview of the national accounts.[60] By naming these activities, Hart imbued this labor with greater significance for scholars and policy makers and revived the effort that Phyllis Deane had begun decades prior to give "standing" to those whose labor did not appear in official accounts and to make count—literally and figuratively—the range of actually existing economic activities.[61] Calculating GNP figures required first and foremost the classification of some activities as economically productive, which generally meant those "formal" activities expressed with money and exchanged through markets. Granting visibility to people whose putative economic activity was not legible in conventional accounts illuminated entire communities that had been overlooked by policy makers.

During the early 1970s, informality became an object of study for many development experts. Their interest stemmed from the criticisms of existing development theory and policies by scholars and practitioners such Mahbub ul Haq and Dudley Seers, and in particular, from the problems surrounding employment that the International Labor Organization (ILO) and Seers's Institute of Development Studies (IDS) had begun to study. As workers in the Global South increasingly experienced the precarious and uncertain employment prospects that Hart diagnosed in Ghana, ILO officials and development experts feared that rising unemployment would produce social and economic crises. They recognized, too, that the existing categories used to describe the absence of formal waged labor—such as unemployment and underemployment—did not match the reality of actually existing labor across the world.[62] In response, the ILO crafted standards for conceptualizing and measuring labor and unemployment. It also partnered with the IDS to study employment issues in new ways.

The two organizations homed in on informal activities in their research collaborations, especially in the ILO mission that Hans Singer and Richard Jolly led in Kenya. The mission derived from frustrations by the Kenyan government that there was "a situation of serious and rising unemployment, particularly among younger people and more recent migrants" to urban areas even "in spite of an absence of precise quantitative data."[63] For Singer and Jolly's research team, the goal of the research mission was to offer a new "interpretation of the development picture in Kenya with employment as the yardstick" and shift away from the country's prior focus on growth.[64] Their 1972 report on the mission was significant not only for its emphasis on poverty alleviation but for its focus on informal work.[65] The report noted that while the informality conjured images of "petty traders, street hawkers, shoeshine boys and other groups 'underemployed' on the streets of the big towns," in fact their research suggests that informal labor was "far from being only marginally productive" and "economically efficient and profitmaking, though small in scale and limited by simple technologies, little capital and lack of links with the other ('formal') sector."[66] The research team estimated that between 25 and 30 percent of total Kenyan urban employment was "informal" in 1969.[67]

The Kenya team's definition of informality differed from Hart's in that it was used to describe a "way of doing things" that created a discreet "sector" of the economy, thus bringing the concept into the language of planning and one subject to formalized accounting procedures. That the report even attempted an estimate of its total size attested to their view that it held promise as a category that could—and indeed should—be enumerated for the purposes of reducing inequality and moving past a narrow focus on "formal" sector activities as the core of GNP growth.[68] The ILO report recommended that the Kenyan government adopt a "positive attitude" toward the informal sector. Rather than seeking to move people into formal jobs, it sought instead to encourage government subcontracting to local informal suppliers, curtail occupational licensing for informal businesses, and cease demolition of informal housing to enable the long-term viability of such activities.[69]

The results of the ILO report were mixed. In one sense, it succeeded in establishing the "informal sector" and made its quantification part and parcel of development research across the world. Over the 1970s, the ILO made the study of informal labor central to its research, departing from its long tradition on focusing on codes of conduct for waged labor.[70] Other researchers hailed it as a breakthrough in statistical work, suggesting even that it portended "the abandonment of the all too prevalent mailed questionnaires, and the establishment of groups within the statistical offices who would monitor, on a continuous and permanent basis, the growth and development of particular sectors of the economy."[71] The informal sector became an object of study and research in many First World countries, as the concept became crucial to the study of poverty, inequality, and employment from the 1980s onward.[72] The Kenya report also spawned not only new research by organizations such as the OECD into the "informal" sector broadly, but also research reminiscent of Deane's work on the incorporation of nonmonetary "subsistence" activity into national accounts.[73]

Yet those in power did not embrace the informal sector in policy to the extent scholars did in their research. Most notably, while the Kenyan government did increase its support for small-scale and informal agricultural activities, it did not embrace many recommendations of the report, especially its calls to redistribute resources from wealthy landowners and for an aggressive land tax.[74] Other critics suggested that the embrace of the informal sector provided a thin guise for exploitation. Economist Colin Leys believed that granting legitimacy to informal activities would glorify low-wage work and low-price goods and enable their exploitation by the wealthy. "The 'informal sector' of the mission's report," he wrote, "is only a—somewhat romanticized—part of the whole range of low-return activities which generate surplus for appropriation by the owners of foreign capital and by the compradors."[75] In this view, measuring the informal sector was the first step not to empowerment, but to reinforcing unequal power relationships between social groups that further deepened inequality.

During the 1970s, feminist activists drew attention to a similar category of work that national accounts and national policy makers had neglected: women's unpaid household labor. The quantification and formal valuation of women's labor had long been understood as a controversial topic in national accounting. Even before Phyllis Deane's efforts to incorporate various aspects of nonmonetary production (such as firewood collection) in national accounts for the colonies, economists recognized that women's daily activities for the household were excluded. Arthur Pigou observed back in 1920 that "if a man marries his housekeeper or his cook, the national dividend is diminished."[76] Over the late 1960s and early 1970s, feminist critics of national accounts expanded on these earlier debates to launch powerful criticisms about how the growth paradigm had devalued and exploited female labor.

The feminist critiques of national accounting and growth models stemmed from broader arguments against domesticity and patriarchy. In the words of activists Lisa Leghorn and Katherine Parker, "traditionally social scientists and economists have looked at women's lives through male eyes," which led many to discount and devalue the work women contributed to the functioning of modern society.[77] Part of this derived from a gender imbalance in the economics profession. In the first three UN experts group tasked with standardizing the system of national accounts (in 1947, 1953, and 1968), 91.7 percent of participants were men.[78] Many feminists further explained the exclusion of women's labor from the accounts by pointing to prevailing patriarchal norms and misogynistic patterns of thinking, which the second-wave feminist movement critiqued in postwar breadwinner liberalism and the cult of domesticity that limited women's participation in formal labor markets.[79]

In response, one vein of feminist research over the 1970s sought to put a price on women's unwaged work. Drawing on a 1970 survey of Wall Street workers' domestic habits by Chase Manhattan bank, Lisa Leghorn determined that American women spent an average of 99.6 hours a week at housework (with poor women often working far more). Based on wages that professional contract workers earned for each task (from dry-cleaning to cooking), they estimated that the women's work had an unpaid value of $257.53 each week in 1970 dollars (about $1,668.59 in 2018 dollars).[80] Ann Oakley published a similar study for the UK in 1974 that found British women with at least one child worked an average of seventy-seven hours a week on unwaged housework.[81] In the early 1970s labor economist Reuben Gronau drew on such studies to conceptualize and develop methodologies for calculating the price of the extensive time women spent on household work.[82]

Over the 1970s, a radical transnational movement built on these arguments to argue on behalf of "wages for housework." Beginning with an Italian feminist group called the Power of Women Collective, the movement spread across Western Europe and North America. The International Feminist Collective (IFC) officially launched the Wages for Housework campaign. The movement used the absence of women's work from national accounts as an entry point into a larger set of concerns about gender. Italian Marxist feminist Silvia Federici argued that women's work in social reproduction effectively subsidized officially accounted for (and largely male) production in national accounts.[83] Making visible such labor, Federici argued, was necessary for women to show "our capacity to expose what we are already doing, what capital is doing to us and our power in the struggle against it."[84] Activists not only demanded recognition and compensation for women's labor but also sought to "end the essentialized notions of gender that underlay why women did housework in the first place, and thus amounted to nothing less than a way to subvert capitalism itself."[85] Members of the movement carried out seminars and international conferences, led major strike campaigns for homemakers in countries from Italy to Iceland, published extensively on women's labor issues, and contributed to local, national, and international governmental organizations.

While the IFC focused largely on the First World countries, there was also widespread criticism about the absence of women's work in

(7) Supporters of the Wages for Housework campaign in a march for International Women's Day in New York City, on March 12, 1977. Photograph by Bettye Lane and courtesy of the Schlesinger Library, Radcliffe Institute, Harvard University.

Third World growth policy. A Danish economist named Ester Bos-erup led the way with a pioneering 1970 book entitled *Woman's Role in Economic Development.* Over the late 1960s, Boserup traveled across Asia and Africa to study how women had been characterized by development experts and what role they actually played in development projects. She noted that although women performed a range of productive activities, the "conventional method for estimating incomes in kind in developing countries considerably under-estimated" women's labor. The present system not only made "under-developed countries seem poorer" than they were, she wrote, but it also made their "rate of economic growth appear in a more favourable light than the fact warrant[ed] since economic development entails a gradual replacement of the omitted subsistence activities by the creation of income in the non-subsistence sector."[86] Absence of unwaged labor not only had created adverse conditions for women but led to larger problems for how countries understood the nature of economic and social change within their borders.

Boserup's work and the feminist activism about unwaged labor sparked a series of campaigns surrounding gender and development. New programs on "women and development" and "women in development," designed to empower women and increase their role in development initiatives, proliferated alongside basic needs and employment projects.[87] Spanish economist Lourdes Benería published research for the ILO that highlighted the persistent "ideological bias" against women in national accounts, extending beyond their role in unwaged production to include activities such as care giving and small home repairs, as well.[88] New studies illuminated deep gender inequalities. A 1980 UN report revealed that women amounted to about a third of the world's formal labor force and accounted for four-fifths of all "informal" labor but received only 10 percent of the world's income.[89]

Feminist activists working in informal activities took stock of the new social scientific category granted to their labor and used it as an organizing tool. In India, during the late 1960s a lawyer and activist named Ela Bhatt noticed all the "informal, home-based jobs" many women workers held around the textile hub of Ahmedabad. Bhatt had worked as a research assistant for data collection in the early post-independence censuses. While the workers she encountered were "unprotected" by the law and uncounted in national statistics, she knew they still contributed to the economic health of the area.[90] After studying cooperative movements for a few years, in 1972 she founded the Self-Employed Women's Association of India (SEWA) to act as a labor union for the millions of workers who otherwise had no such organization to build their power. Existing trade union organizations did not recognize the many "embroiderers, cart pullers, rag pickers, midwives, and forest-produce gatherers" as workers. Bhatt believed that without such formal representation, "dividing the economy into formal and informal sectors" served to perpetuate poverty by denying to the informal workers the same protections and opportunities as those afforded other workers by the trade unions. She worked through

SEWA to blur the distinction between formal and informal to ensure that all laborers, regardless of the administrative categories grafted onto their work, could promote their collective interests.[91] Over the following years, SEWA expanded from its initial rural focus to encompass agricultural laborers, casual laborers, and service providers who worked on the margins of the measured and waged economy. These "informal" workers increasingly "mapped their world less by its relation to a formal state-regulated economy than by its workplaces," while challenging the precariousness that such workplaces granted to them.[92] Similar groups emerged during the following years, such as a transnational domestic workers' organization in Latin America called the Latin American and Caribbean Confederation of Household Workers (CONLACTRAHO).[93]

By the end of the 1970s, the UN's SNA and most national accounts had done little to incorporate this new research into their framework. There were renewed calls to incorporate domestic unpaid work in national accounts throughout the early 1980s, but these amounted largely to "many suggestions concerning the method" of calculating such value but importantly "no practical initiatives."[94] The urgency of the Wages for Housework campaign faded from public view in the United States and Western Europe, as well, leaving the politics of household labor with "the status of a curio" by the end of the twentieth century, in journalist Barbara Ehrenreich's words.[95] There was also mounting disapproval of the new "women in development" programs. Lourdes Benería and economist Gita Sen argued that development policies aimed at empowering women were too often "motivated by a perception that women are instrumental to programs of population control, increased food production, and the provision of other basic needs" with scarce attention on "the subordination of women" that took place in these particular social roles.[96] Feminist critics also contested development agencies that continued to assess progress by studying households as a single unit without differentiating women and men's gains and losses and called for more detailed accounting, but these criticisms had little policy impact during the 1970s.[97] Yet feminist activism—especially the growth of groups such as SEWA—

and the growing interest in women and development reflected widespread frustration with conventional economic accounting practices that neglected women's unwaged labor.

Quantifying the Environment

While advocates for measuring informal labor and unwaged work sought to identify how people engaged in such activities contributed to total production, the environmental critics of growth sought to make visible how economic activity influenced ecological processes and vice versa. "The very biological existence of mankind as a species is threatened by mankind's economic activity as practiced today," Nicholas Georgescu-Roegen wrote to friend and colleague Kenneth Boulding in 1974. Economists needed to reject their conventional ways of defining value and measuring change. Instead, he argued they should "study the problems raised by economic activity of mankind within a finite supply of terrestrial free energy and of nicely arranged matter," or, in other words, redirect their attention to biophysical processes rather than what economists had come to identify as purely "economic" behavior.[98] Over the 1970s, environmental growth critics followed this line of thinking to challenge the growth paradigm by attempting to delink energy use from economic production, craft entirely new metaphors and models for economic activity, and find ways to price the unwanted "externalities" such as pollution in economic accounting.

One strand of thinking among environmental critics of growth was to decouple energy use from economic expansion. The oil embargo of 1973 had brought to the fore of international politics the core material element of the growth paradigm: it was possible only with an unusually cheap and vast supply of oil. For many environmental activists, moving past the growth paradigm meant moving beyond fossil fuel energy sources. The most notable success in shifting energy policy came in West Germany, where an active environmental movement pushed the Social Democratic Party (Sozialdemokratische Partei Deutschlands, or SPD) to imagine that decoupling—reducing energy use while expanding economic activity—was feasible. A key figure was

SPD leader Erhard Eppler, who "wanted to orient policy around the more fluid concept of 'quality of life' instead of around GDP" as Germans pondered the limits and downsides of growth.[99] Over the 1970s, the SPD debated the virtues of growth and the plausibility of decoupling, with environmental experts working with party leaders to criticize old assumptions about supposed inelasticity of energy and minimize fears about the effects of conservation on employment. The new thinking won out, and German energy consumption began to decline from its high point of 1979 (which it has since never exceeded).[100]

Few major countries, however, made that shift in practice besides West Germany. The United States, for instance, responded with minor attempts at conservation, but leaders largely emphasized expanding domestic sources of fossil fuels (such as coal) and reorienting foreign policy strategy to ensure even greater access to Middle Eastern oil.[101] Great Britain turned to oil exploration, which led to the discovery of vast reserves in the North Sea during the 1980s.[102] French politicians pushed through a dramatic expansion of nuclear power, over the objections of a robust domestic protest movement.[103] A mixture of a renewed reliance on fossil fuels and embrace of nuclear energy outpaced conservation initiatives and investment in renewables.

A second alternative to traditional growth theory and politics put forth by environmental critics to growth came through the burgeoning study of ecological economics. Herman Daly's advocacy for a steady-state economy set the stage for a wide-ranging set of criticisms about economists' disregard for the natural world. Over the late 1960s and early 1970s Daly built on Georgescu-Roegen's earlier research to incorporate insights from the second law of thermodynamics into economic analysis to highlight the material limits and theoretical flaws inherent in what Daly called "growthmania."[104] Central to this work was Daly's belief that economists needed to incorporate biological metaphors and analogies into their research to capture the ways in which economic activity necessarily shaped and was shaped by biophysical processes of the planet.[105] Doing so, he argued, would help economists better account for the entropic nature of the life process and the vast waste produced by modern economic systems. The steady-state economy, he believed, would achieve such a change by encouraging the mainte-nance of "the stock of wealth" instead of maximizing flows of resources through the production and consumption process.[106]

During the 1970s, the first generation of self-identified ecological economists advanced the stock-flow metaphor as a way of express-ing their critique of growth. Alongside Daly in this effort were econo-mists such as his graduate adviser Nicholas Georgescu-Roegen, the environmental convert Kenneth Boulding, and Robert Costanza, an economist who worked with Daly at Louisiana State University during the 1970s and 1980s. Building on Daly's work, ecological economists argued that nature was a fixed stock of capital that could sustain a flow of "services" from ecosystems and that those services could be calculated in terms of their monetary value.[107] Scholars also began to identify the long-term costs of eroding or using up available flora and fauna, from trees for timber to coal for fuel to fish for food. The hetero-dox economist E. F. Schumacher wrote in his popular 1973 book *Small Is Beautiful*, "the modern industrial system . . . consumes the very basis on which it has been erected." Schumacher identified three catego-ries of "irreplaceable capital"—"fossil fuels, the tolerance margins of nature, and the human substance"—for which economists did not account.[108] Subsequent studies in the late 1970s and 1980s carried out research designed to calculate this "natural" capital.[109] This research represented a major challenge to existing growth theory. Building on Robert Solow's research that depicted technological progress as the key driver of growth, economists identified knowledge as the major limiting factor of growth. As knowledge improved and people created new technologies, the conventional wisdom held, growth would occur. Daly and other ecological economists countered that there were eco-logical limiting factors to this process. Depletion of natural capital limited future growth by undermining the capacity of ecosystems to regenerate and sustain the biophysical basis for life on the planet.[110]

The focus on ecosystems and the "services" they provided set the grounds for a new set of valuations about the nonhuman world. Attempting to estimate prices for ecosystem services became a minor cottage industry. Ecological economists sought to determine how much monetary value, over the long term and in relation to future generations, the natural world offered to humankind. For instance, ecologist Walter Westman carried out a study for California and published an early framework for quantifying ecosystem services that included the absorption of air pollutants, radiation balancing, soil binding, and nutrient cycling in an article for *Science* in 1977.[111]

A related but distinct movement of environmental growth critics sought to incorporate environmental factors back into national accounts by pricing natural resources. One branch of this research dovetailed from Ezra Mishan's work on "disamenities" and what natural resource economists had termed "externalities." Resources for the Future economist Allen Kneese published a series of pioneering works that established a framework analysis for pricing the costs of pollution in national accounts.[112] Economists William D. Nordhaus and James Tobin revised GNP to craft a new metric that included leisure and nonmarket activities but subtracted "disamenities" and capital consumption (but not, significantly, natural capital depletion) called the Measure of Economic Welfare (MEW).[113] Japanese researchers constructed a metric termed Net National Welfare (NNW) that subtracted the costs of pollution and environmental "maintenance," revealing a growth rate lower than the net domestic product for the boom years of the 1950s and 1960s (5 percent compared to over 7 percent).[114] These attempts to account for resource use and environmental "externalities" were fiercely debated among scholars during the 1970s, though they made little headway into official policy.[115]

In addition to the technical aspects of contriving new theories and accounting practices for economists to adopt, environmental growth critics also sought new policy frameworks and promoted new concepts to describe the connections between environment and economy. The most notable of these efforts took place during the 1980s, as environmentalists adopted the phrase "sustainable development" to link the desire for planetary well-being over the long term with the reality of historical and contemporary inequality within and between countries. Environmental thinkers such as Barbara Ward and Kenneth Boulding attuned to the global political debates over environmental protection had used the phrase sparingly across the 1970s. A 1979 expert report published by the UN Environment Programme called the *World Conservation Strategy* explicitly used the phrase to call for principles of conservation and preservation over the long term across the globe while also supporting the New International Economic Order (NIEO) to promote greater international inequality in the short term. Sustainable development became popular over the 1980s, entering into international discourse as an alternative to the growth paradigm that highlighted that faith in exponential economic growth absent sound ecological protection would undermine the possibilities of long-term production and consumption and render much of the world worse off in the future.[116]

Such arguments did little to assuage the frustrations of Third World leaders, however. As environmental thinkers embraced the sustainability concept as a way to reconcile many Third World leaders' desire for growth with ecological principles, many intellectuals, activists, and leaders critiqued it as insufficient. When a few countries, such as Zambia and Tanzania, attempted to implement sustainable national plans in the 1980s, they struggled to fund the expensive process of reorienting national economic activity along ecological lines. Absent a vast increase in foreign aid and reorientation of investment patterns to promote alternative development, transcending growth remained easier to imagine than implement in policy.[117] As with the different attempts to quantify different aspects of the nonhuman world in economic terms, sustainable development was far more popular in scholarly and activist circles than in reshaping how governments pursued development strategies throughout the 1970s and 1980s.

Conclusion

Across the world during the 1970s, activists and intellectuals proposed new goals for development besides growth and constructed new statistical tools to measure those goals. Advocates for social indicators made "quality of life" and poverty central concerns for policy makers and used a range of new tools, such as the PQLI, to measure them.

Third World development experts hoped to replace the growth paradigm with the focus on basic human needs, poverty, and employment.
They recognized that existing conceptual frameworks and income and
wealth metrics were ill suited to this task, so they sought new ways to
quantify economic activity and work in Third World countries and
tie those with new social indicators to depict what GNP had concealed. Similarly, feminists highlighted gender inequalities by revealing in monetary terms just how much women's unwaged work shaped
national well-being. And environmental growth critics believed that
that the growth paradigm had created a global ecological crisis. New
models and metaphors to characterize the relationship between economies and the ecology of the planet were necessary to contend with
the fallout.

Collectively, though, all these reform efforts encountered common
challenges. In many cases, they remained wedded to a national frame
of reference that made it difficult to see what Dudley Seers called the
"total relationship" between everything from tariff and trade policies to shifting commodity prices to monetary policy to foreign aid
policy.[118] Third World critics of social indicators and environmentalist arguments made similar arguments. As Mahbub ul Haq wrote in
1980 over the fledgling North-South conflict, "the world's economic
and political crisis is not a temporary one. It is deeply rooted in present international structures and institutions.... What is really at issue
is a sharing of economic and political power, within nations as well as
internationally."[119] Displacing the growth paradigm required a reformation of the relationships of power—between First and Third World
countries, between capital and labor, between men and women, and
much beyond—that had structured and sustained national and international governance for decades.

Few leaders were willing to countenance such a revolutionary set
of claims. By the early 1980s, many alternative indicators and the
movements that sustained them had been assimilated into scholarly
research and government bureaucracies, but major funding for continued research dried up. As inflation and unemployment ticked up,
many governments in the wealthy countries also began to curtail their

social spending and development aid. The communist bloc faced continued stagnation. Third World countries became increasingly reliant on commercial lending and sovereign debt skyrocketing. Rather than increasing public spending to redress the myriad problems that alternative indicators and approaches revealed, leaders instead called for quantitative growth once again to boost their fortunes.[120] Thus those promoting alternatives to growth found themselves locked between publics anxious about the limits and downsides of economic growth and leaders who worried about the long-term implications of a world without growth. While research into alternative indicators flourished and new metrics became important in many different activist groups and international organizations, national leaders rarely accepted them as equivalent in significance or national purpose to the still popular GNP. And by the 1980s, the growth critics ran up against an even greater challenge to their reform efforts: a widespread revival of the growth paradigm.

SIX

Revival and Debate at the
End of the Twentieth Century

While during the 1970s leaders around the world feared a world of limits and stagnation, by the late 1980s and 1990s optimism about a future of limitless growth returned. In late 1979, US president Jimmy Carter spoke like a growth critic. The United States had developed a "keener appreciation of limits" as it struggled "with a profound transition from a time of abundance to a time of growing scarcity in energy," he claimed. "We can no longer rely on a rising economic tide to lift the boats of the poorest of in our society," he added. "We must focus our attention and our care and our love and concern directly on them."[1] Yet in 1992, former British prime minister Margaret Thatcher gleefully looked back on the 1980s as "one of the longest periods of economic growth with stable prices."[2] This new growth era, however, came with a twist. Whereas the growth paradigm had been forged in a statist era, defined by national technocratic planning and strong government intervention, the embrace of growth in the 1980s and 1990s was, in historian Robert Collins's words, an "anti-statist growthmanship."[3] Leaders hailed growth as a solution for political and social problems as earlier generations had done, but they now described an idealized "free market" as its source. As US president George H. W. Bush said in May 1990, "in the long term, the free market remains the only path to sustained growth."[4] The perception that unleashing market forces had conquered the stagflation of the 1970s renewed faith in the possibility of limitless economic growth as the market became the "dominant social metaphor of the age."[5]

Western elites held up growth as the premier goal for everyone else, too. In the Second World, the 1980s and 1990s were a period of stagnation, revolution, state collapse, and instability. As former communist countries began the tumultuous transition to capitalism, a common refrain held that the promise of future growth justified short-term difficulties. US president Bill Clinton captured such thinking when he told a room of Belarusian policy makers during a visit to Minsk in January 1994 that although they faced a "hard transition," there was "cause for hope because, as you privatize more of your economy, as more of it works in a market system, people will have reason to invest more and generate more economic growth."[6] For the Third World, a wrenching debt crisis rendered the 1980s a "lost decade" for development.[7] By the early 1990s many moved, through a mixture of brute international coercion and national experimentation, toward liberalization. As major countries such as China, India, and Brazil began to restructure their national economies, growth served a similar function as the reward for painful recoveries from fiscal crisis and stagnation. As George H. W. Bush told Jamaica's socialist prime minister Michael Manley in May 1990, if Jamaica embraced "more privatization" and structural reforms to wrest open the economy to investment, the country would receive the gift of "more economic growth."[8]

Yet as so many leaders once again sang the gospel of growth, those who had spent much of the 1970s searching for alternatives continued their quest to craft new goals and metrics to define development anew. For instance, in 1989 Herman Daly teamed up with American theologian John B. Cobb Jr. and his son, Clifford Cobb, to construct an alternative to GNP they called the "Index of Sustainable Economic Welfare." Later revised as the Genuine Progress Indicator (GPI), this new metric incorporated unpaid labor, environmental pollution, natural capital depletion, and a range of other indicators into a holistic measure of social progress.[9] Clifford Cobb wrote with colleagues in 1995 that the GPI reflected a growing sense that "pronouncements from economic experts are fundamentally out of sync" with how people understood their own lives and that the world needed "larger goals and better ways to measure our achievements" than economic indicators.[10]

Similarly, in May 1990, Mahbub ul Haq released another new measure of progress. The Human Development Index (HDI) used life expectancy at birth, literacy rate, and purchasing power–adjusted real GDP per capita to form a composite indicator of well-being to show that "development" was "more than GNP growth, more than income and wealth and more than producing commodities and accumulating capital."[11] Thus even as leaders placed growth atop their policy agendas, the growth critics continued to promote alternative ways of describing and valuing the world.

The faith in growth revived because of policy changes designed to promote private enterprise and investment, the collapse of communism as an alternative model of development, and newfound sources and declining prices of fossil fuel energy. Growth became for many leaders a means and an end, a way to overcome the doldrums of the 1970s and the primary goal to which national resources should be directed. Tensions persisted, however, over the meaning and measurement of growth as technological and political changes bedeviled conventional accounting techniques. As had been evident when the growth paradigm took initial shape in the 1930s and 1940s, experts debated how to quantify economic activity and how best to value economic life amid growing financialization, globalization, and digitization of economic activities. Questions over what to count and how to assign value still left "the economy" far from a stable entity. So too did the ongoing challenges to the growth paradigm, which built on the legacies and insights from earlier growth critics on issues such as environmental degradation, social dislocation, and inequality.

With its revival during the 1980s, the growth paradigm has faced criticisms from contemporary growth critics. As was the case in the 1960s and 1970s, today's growth critics flourish in the context of crisis: growing wealth inequality within countries, the continuing fallout of the great recession of 2007–8, and the gradual recognition that global climate change has already begun to reshape planetary life in profound ways. Amid this economic and ecological uncertainty, two decades into the twenty-first century many experts and activists are again raising questions that were so crucial to the making of the twentieth: how best to measure society, what values to adopt to structure the organization of resources and power, and how to make sense of world in turmoil and define national purpose in the context of global crisis.

The Growth Paradigm and First World Recovery

Beginning in the late 1970s, leaders in the First World embraced a series of rhetorical, intellectual, and policy shifts designed to tamp down inflation and revive faith in economic growth as a universal goal. Often termed the rise of "neoliberalism," these transformations in the United States, Western Europe, and Japan are too complex to explain in full detail here. But there are a number of key shifts worth summarizing.[12] To redress the range of economic problems afflicting countries in the 1970s—high unemployment, flagging exports, inflation—countries responded with experiments in deregulating capital controls and financial markets, which led to looser credit and greater monetary flows across borders in the wake of the Bretton Woods system's collapse.[13] Governments across the capitalist world deregulated many different industries to spur competitiveness and increase economic activity.[14] The US Federal Reserve's strategy to tamp down inflation by raising interest rates from 1979 to 1982 accelerated this redirection, marking a turning point in global capitalism.[15] The consequences for global investment were dramatic. In the 1970s, the G-7 experienced a net outflow of capital of $46.8 billion; in the 1980s, they benefitted from a $347.4 billion inflow.[16]

In addition, national governments adopted a range of other market-oriented policies. In the United States and many other countries, conservative politicians hailed tax cuts, especially on wealthy individuals and corporations, as keys to increase productivity, boost investment, and create jobs.[17] Many countries, especially those in Western Europe, privatized state-owned enterprises in industries such as telecommunications and energy.[18] In the United States, the embrace of privatization took many forms, even including a debate about whether all government economic data collection should be privatized.[19] Governments across the wealthy, capitalist world privatized over a trillion dollars' worth of assets during the 1990s alone.[20] In both the United States and Great Britain, conservative governments curtailed the power of unions as part of broader campaign to empower business over labor.[21] The First World also promoted formal integration, especially with regard to international trade. Over the 1980s and 1990s, regional trade pacts proliferated. The Uruguay Round of GATT during the 1980s and the establishment of the formal World Trade Organization (WTO) in 1995 set new rules to structure freer and nondiscriminatory trade. In Europe, the creation of the European Union in 1992 culminated a decades-long trend toward economic and political integration.[22]

Multinational corporations (MNCs) exploited the changing rules and regulations that enabled greater transnational capital mobility. The number of MNCs worldwide rose from about seven thousand in 1970 to nearly sixty-three thousand parent companies with nearly 690,000 affiliates by 2000.[23] Foreign direct investment by MNCs surged from around $10 billion annually during the early 1970s to around $1 trillion annually by 2000.[24] During the 1980s and 1990s, MNCs developed extensive production and supply networks as they outsourced operations in search of lower labor costs and acquired material inputs from around the world. In many countries, independent suppliers and distributors bid for entry into these networks of integrated production, which reinforced both the MNCs and local companies' desire for continued economic growth to sustain this integrated form of global capitalism.[25] MNCs also increased lobbying efforts, bolstering their newfound structural power in the global economy with the instrumental power gained by influencing the policy process.[26] Because of the growing scale of their investment and scope of their activities, the United Nations described MNCs as "engines of growth" in the global economy.[27]

All these transformations reshaped the role of the state in many countries, although governments still embraced government spending as a political necessity. In the United States, for instance, the Reagan administration's embrace of deregulation was matched by a desire to stimulate the economy through increased military spending so large that one historian termed the president "one of the most profligate peacetime spenders in the history of the republic."²⁸ And in most countries, welfare spending as a percentage of GNP rose during the period as the WWII generation aged into retirement.²⁹ Yet throughout the 1980s and 1990s leaders and policy makers saw the mixture of major policy trends—trade and investment liberalization, deregulation, privatization, integration—as core elements of a new growth paradigm. Altogether, these policy changes empowered investors, speculators, and business owners over workers. Economic growth was "back on track" by the late 1980s and 1990s, but in a different form than before.³⁰

This period also marked a triumph for economists who sought to revise or reject the Keynesian economics and growth theories that had dominated the profession a couple decades earlier. Economists developed new approaches at universities such as the University of Chicago, the University of Virginia, and George Mason University. Adherents of "public choice" theory brought market logic to bear on a range of noneconomic social and political issues. Many economists also touted the importance of assuming the "rational expectations" of economic actors. They promoted the virtues of free market exchanges in an idealized setting of intrinsically rational individuals possessing full and clear information and following agreed-on rules. Markets left unfettered would permit these rational actors to optimize the distribution of goods and produce efficiency; government officials' interventions to remediate market outcomes would only make matters worse.³¹ In the United States and the United Kingdom "rational expectations" economists displaced the older generation of managerial Keynesian thinkers in key advisory government roles.³² These intellectual projects reinforced and granted even greater public legitimacy to many of the new policies being put into place. Likewise, during the 1980s, experts who had stated that there were insurmountable ecological limits to growth lost influence in public discourse to the more hopeful views of technological optimists, such as economist Julian Simon, who argued that a combination of innovations and proper market incentives would create technological "fixes" to overcome environmental constraints.³³

Undergirding these policy and intellectual shifts was a radical transformation of energy markets and a shift in public fears away from looming energy scarcity. The oil shocks prompted many governments to promote efficiency standards and embrace other sources of energy (mainly natural gas, coal, and nuclear power). Diversification altered the global oil market. Oil's share of the total energy market in the industrialized countries shrank from 58 percent in 1978 to 43 percent in 1985. The geography of oil production shifted, too, after the discovery of untapped petroleum reserves in the North Sea provided a valuable new source of raw output. Technological advances in energy exploration also generated optimism. Extraction and transportation advances around Alaskan reserves led to an increase in total US production during the 1980s. Between 1987 and 1990 alone, estimates of proven recoverable reserves of petroleum, for example, rose 11.4 percent and those of natural gas by 17.9 percent. Finally, there were important changes in the international politics of oil pricing. In 1983 the New York Mercantile Exchange introduced a futures market in crude oil, which undermined OPEC's price-setting powers.[34]

These changes reshaped how most people understood the relationship between economic growth and the material world. The technological advances in energy production coupled with the revolution in electronics, computing, and communication technologies gave further evidence to claims of growth enthusiasts that technological advance and infinite substitution had overcome the doldrums of the 1970s and that growth had returned once more.[35] The US-based environmental think tank World Resources Institute claimed in 1994 that, "the world is not yet running out of most nonrenewable resources and is not likely to, at least in the next few decades," because of technological change, increasing stocks of strategic reserves, and growing "competition among suppliers."[36] William Nordhaus and a group of ecological economists wrote in a 1992 report that in contrast to the early 1970s even many environmental thinkers had started to think that while "long-run constraints upon economic growth might well exist" they would be "unlikely to arise because of intrinsic limitations of natural resources."[37] The fears heightened by the *Limits to Growth* report and the oil shocks gave way to optimism that energy scarcity and resource depletion no longer posed such severe threats.

Taken together, these political and intellectual shifts revived popular faith in economic growth. Barely a decade after President Carter called for an era of limits, George H. W. Bush declared in 1990, "The primary economic goal of my Administration is to achieve the highest possible rate of sustainable economic growth."[38] Likewise, the EU's Stability and Growth Pact, signed by the eurozone countries in 1997, required countries to keep budget deficits below 3 percent of GDP and defined EU's goals and rules in terms of economic growth.[39] Altogether, in the OECD countries leaders defined progress in terms of "sustained non-inflationary growth" based on integrated global trade, deregulation, "flexible" labor markets, budgetary discipline, privatization, and higher investments and profitability.[40] Such rhetoric and policy choices revealed that the concerns over limits to growth, zero growth, or alternatives to growth had receded for many leaders in the wealthy countries by the 1980s and 1990s. Policy reforms were both cause and consequence of the revived faith in the growth paradigm. Policy makers turned to market-oriented policies to combat the stagflation of the 1970s, and over time they pointed to low inflation and declining unemployment as further evidence to empower the private sector as the key driver of future growth.

The Debt Crisis, Structural Adjustment, and Growth in the Global South

The revived growth politics in the wealthy, capitalist world had significant ramifications for the Third World. During the 1970s, Third World countries faced declining direct foreign aid amid the "basic human needs" reforms, as well as general resistance, rather than sustained cooperation, toward the NIEO.[41] To finance development initiatives, they increasingly turned to commercial banks, which were flush with recycled OPEC earnings—"petrodollars"—available on relatively favorable terms. Yet the economic crises that struck the developed world in the 1970s exacted a heavy toll on much of the Third World. Rising inflation, the end of the Bretton Woods system of exchange rate convertibility, and the oil shocks all hampered the non-OPEC countries.[42]

While at the international level many self-identified Third World countries supported the NIEO, by the late 1970s many responded to domestic struggles and the vicissitudes of global currency and commodity markets by experimenting with market-oriented reforms to fit their own needs. Financial liberalization, openness, and decentralization were parts of a new development strategy to counter the perceived downsides or unmet expectations generated by state-led attempts at growth. Over the course of the 1970s and early 1980s, countries such as Chile, Brazil, Uruguay, and Turkey experimented with reforms ranging from currency devaluation to limiting capital controls before external aid packages from international organizations required similar shifts.[43] Faith in large-scale, state-led industrialization waned. Leaders in countries such as Mexico and regions such as Soviet Central Asia spoke of individual entrepreneurialism and a reduced role for state agencies in promoting social mobility.[44] These liberalizing strategies appeared attractive to elites as ways to revive growth, build national and transnational alliances, and often "stay in power despite broad public dissent."[45]

The growing sovereign debt held by many Third World countries coupled with tumult in global markets created domestic and international conditions for crisis. While the liquid capital sloshing around petrodollar banks briefly sustained solvency, by the early 1980s the stage was set for a vicious and debilitating collapse.[46] The global oil shock of 1979, the fall of commodity prices in the global recession of 1981–82, and the rise in interest rates after 1979 made debt servicing increasingly difficult. Third World governments faced declining revenues and limited lending options as debt obligations increased.[47] Outstanding debt for non-OPEC developing countries increased from $130 billion in 1973 to $664 billion in 1983. Mexico defaulted on its debt servicing obligations in 1982, and thereafter dozens of other countries reached a crisis point as much of the Third World fell into fiscal turmoil.[48] The scope of the debt crisis was vast, covering much of the Global South. For countries facing insolvency, the International Monetary Fund (IMF) offered Structural Adjustment Loans (SALs). In return for loans to service their debts, developing countries accepted predefined "conditions" such as interest rate and trade liberalization, privatization, deregulation, and cuts to public spending that often spurred short-term hardships for many citizens.[49]

The SALs, coupled with the experiments toward openness and deregulation prior to the debt crisis, led to widespread liberalization.[50] "The 'planning and control' mentality and approach to economic development," two World Bank economists wrote of the Third World in 1986, "is clearly giving ground to the acceptance of market forces."[51] The bank mirrored the larger changes taking place. At the head of the organization, A. W. Clausen, a prominent banker, replaced Robert McNamara, who had spearheaded the basic human needs shift, in 1981. Clausen accelerated bank's embrace of structural adjustment.[52] There were important intellectual changes among development experts, as well. Arguments about limits of statist intervention and planning using aggregate indicators that colonial economists such as S. Herbert Frankel and P. T. Bauer made during the 1940s and 1950s moved from the fringe to the fore of development economics. Experts in the World Bank had by the early 1980s begun to trumpet the need for sub-Saharan African countries to reduce public sector spending and encourage the private sector. Bank economists stated the thinking bluntly in their 1981 "Berg Report" for the region. "A reordering of postindependence priorities" away from statist intervention and direct antipoverty programs, they claimed, "is essential if economic growth is to accelerate."[53] Moreover, arguments by development economists such as Deepak Lal, who called for an end to state-led planning, provided intellectual fodder to justify many of the structural changes taking place.[54] Often called the "Washington Consensus," the cluster of policies put forth for the Third World reflected a new "dogma" that "universal virtue resided in the market" as the source for economic growth.[55]

As fiscal and social policies shifted in the late 1980s, so too did trade policy. The Uruguay Round in GATT, out of which grew the WTO, reinforced financial liberalization with lower tariffs world-

wide. By shifting rules to stimulate investment and by making liberal
trade policies a prerequisite for inclusion in the global economy, the
Uruguay Round "undermined the viability of inward-oriented economic development."[56] Moreover, a series of regional free trade pacts—
NAFTA (1994), the Southern Common Market (MERCOSUR, 1991),
the Common Market for Eastern and South Africa (COMESA, 1994)—
that coincided with the Uruguay Round emphasized the acceptance of
liberalizing trade in the developing world. Multinational corporations
took advantage of this liberalization; foreign direct investment in the
Global South by MNCs skyrocketed from around $2 billion annually
during the early 1970s to over $250 billion annually at the turn of the
twenty-first century.[57] This confluence of fiscal and trade liberalization
brought widespread instability and tumult across the Third World as it
deepened and expanded the liberal capitalist order that the First World
countries had reshaped in the wake of the crises of the 1970s. Often
recast as "emerging" economies, these countries faced a difficult "balancing act" between deepening their integration, stimulating exports,
mitigating their debt, and keeping currencies stable in the name of
generating economic growth.[58] Growth remained the overarching goal
for national economic policy, but the means to achieve it had shifted
dramatically away from earlier statist and import-substitution models
toward liberalization.

The End of the Soviet Union

As the capitalist First World embraced growth and the Third World
wrestled with debilitating debt, the Second World foundered. Leaders in the Soviet Union and Eastern Europe debated how to respond
amid lagging production, limited innovation, and a disastrous war in
Afghanistan that drained Soviet state resources.[59] Economists and
enterprise managers debated government bureaucrats over the direction of reform. As Johanna Bockman has shown, these conflicts often
focused on possible democratic "market socialisms." Reformers hoped
managerial changes and the injection of market mechanisms within a
socialist framework would improve on the centralized bureaucracies

and top-down planning. Polish and Hungarian officials, for instance, carried out reforms designed to hand over sclerotic state-owned enterprises to workers (based on policies of a similar orientation in Yugoslavia) to decentralize production. During the late 1980s, the Polish government also loosened restrictions on private entrepreneurs and lifted price controls on agricultural products to stimulate economic growth, while the Hungarian government abandoned its guarantee of full employment for every adult and opened its borders to foreign direct investment. Mikhail Gorbachev's more widely known reform efforts, glasnost and perestroika, were also attempts to construct a market socialism characterized by greater engagement with the global economy and pluralistic domestic arrangements with greater democracy and worker empowerment. These initiatives in transitioning to different forms of socialism were experiments to reconfigure past developmental strategies designed to stifle domestic dissent and overcome international constraints.[60]

It was, ultimately, the political crisis within the Soviet state and revolutions across Eastern Europe that ended the Soviet Union and its broader empire. Over the 1990s, the former Soviet Union underwent an abrupt and chaotic transition to market capitalism. Newly independent Russia experienced vast capital flight, lagging production, political unrest, and declining living standards measured by economic and social indicators (including a precipitous drop in male life expectancy).[61] The country underwent "the biggest peacetime setback for a major economy in modern history" as plutocratic elite passed state industries into a few private hands. By 2004, thirty-six billionaires had amassed nearly $110 billion, about a quarter of the country's total national product.[62] In the 1990s not only did people lack access to cheap, effective, and desirable consumer goods; they could no longer earn unemployment protection in a consistent way. Poverty rates shot up from 3 percent to 25 percent during the 1990s throughout the Warsaw Pact countries as transitional policies struggled to fund social security programs.[63]

Western leaders often cast these struggles as necessary sacrifices to bring about long-term growth. "I believe," US president Bill Clinton told Russian leaders in Moscow in September 1998, "you will create the conditions of growth if, but only if, you continue to move decisively along the path of democratic, market-oriented, constructive revolution."[64] Economic growth was the goal for the countries of the former Soviet bloc, the promise for which present-day suffering needed to be endured. The Cold War conflict imbued the pursuit of growth in both the capitalist and the communist worlds with clear ideological significance. In its aftermath, Western leaders accepted as an article of faith that "free markets" had "outgrown" the Soviet model. They argued that the former Soviet world had to adopt Western prescriptions to enjoy the fruits of future growth, even if those benefits seemed distant amid the tumult of the 1990s.[65] In time, growth did revive in many transition countries, especially those in central Europe, such as Hungary and the Czech Republic. Overall, though, the transition to market capitalism painted a "highly ambivalent picture," according to historian Philipp Ther. Economic prosperity and democracy remained "precarious" over the two decades after the revolutions of 1989.[66]

As the Soviet Union and its satellites collapsed, communist China reformed. Beginning in 1978, Deng Xiaoping and his allies promoted stability and renewed prosperity through economic reforms. Over the next two decades, the Chinese government passed farmland to private farmers. It established a dual price system to introduce market prices for goods sold beyond government-set quotas. The government also set special economic zones with limited regulation to promote export-oriented production, invited foreign investment, and initiated decentralization of bureaucratic regulation and management. By the late 1990s, China had surpassed Japan as the world's second largest economy in terms of GDP, increased its exports from nearly $20 billion near the start of its reforms to over $200 billion, and brought in over $35 billion a year in foreign corporate investment.[67] The reforms led Chinese leaders to speak the gospel of economic growth as a symbol of national vitality and avoid the social unrest that had pervaded Eastern Europe in the late 1980s. For the Western countries, the collapse of the Soviet Union and its liberalization coupled with Chinese reforms meant that by 2000 most of the world fit within a broad capitalist order committed to pursuing robust economic growth. Growth was a unifying purpose for states across the world once again.[68]

Globalization, Finance, and Measurement Problems

With the communist alternative in collapse and the liberalization of many Third World countries, by the early 1990s the popular embrace of "globalization" recast the growth paradigm.[69] During the Bretton Woods era, international cooperation and rules shielded nation-states from many globalizing pressures. In the globalization era, national leaders and officials in international organizations restructured international rules to promote global integration by stimulating free trade, removing controls on capital flows to promote international investment, and supporting the growth of MNCs. US president Bill Clinton captured the soaring and quixotic rhetoric of globalization's enthusiasts when he told the WTO in 1998 that "globalization and the technology revolution are not policy choices, they are facts." Tearing down barriers to trade would "spur growth in all countries," just as "private capital markets" would "spur rapid growth while minimizing the risk of worldwide economic instability."[70] In the 1990s, leaders across the world embraced globalization as a driving source for national economic growth and as an antidote to the ills that had plagued capitalism and sustained the growth critics during the 1960s and 1970s.

Alongside globalization, financialization marked a second important feature of the revised growth paradigm. In many of the wealthy capitalist countries, a considerable portion of the aggregate economic growth experienced since the 1970s derived from the "financial sector," or the institutions and instruments that permit transactions through credit extension. In the United States, by 2001 the financial sector earned over 40 percent of total profits, up from below 20 percent in the 1980s.[71] Between 1990 and 2007, while world trade grew at an impressive annual rate of 8.7 percent, cross-border financial flows grew nearly 14.5 percent annually. The turnover of derivatives reached a mind-boggling daily level of $5 trillion on the eve of the 2007–8 financial crisis. For the Global South, financialization facilitated the outward flow of capital as countries purchased large shares of US treasuries to guard against runs against local currencies. Many countries, especially those in South and Southeast Asia, drew on international investors and MNCs to become manufacturing hubs as countries such as the United States increasingly generated high aggregate growth rates from the expansion of the financial and service sectors.[72]

Globalization and financialization prompted debates over how best to measure and give meaning to the nature of economic activity in the new era. One question focused on the "N" in GNP. GNP referred to *national* product, which statisticians defined as all goods and services produced by the national residents of a given country, regardless of whether that activity took place within its border. By the 1980s, however, many experts began to emphasize the use of Gross Domestic Product (GDP), which focused on the economic activity within a given nation-state's borders regardless of whom contributed to it. Thus, for instance, while an MNC's profits under the GNP framework would flow back to the country in which its owners were based, under GDP the profits would count toward the country in which they occurred. The United States began to highlight GDP over GNP in December 1991, and the UN's System of National Accounts began to employ GDP after its 1993 revisions.[73]

The result of this shift was complicated. For critics, the change served to reinforce the "dominant perception that globalization was in everybody's interest and that stronger trade ties held the potential to bring development everywhere," in Lorenzo Fioramonti's words.[74] It had an especially distorting effect for poorer countries that experienced a boom in international investment in extractive industries such as mining. While switching to the new GDP framework, these countries watched their national growth rates go up compared to conventional GNP numbers. The shift to GDP, Clifford Cobb, Ted Halsted, and Jonathan Rowe charged in 1995, hid a "basic fact" that "the nations of the Global North are walking off with the South's resources, and calling it a gain for the South."[75] According to Zachary Karabell, the ever-expanding global supply chains for major companies rendered the compilation of basic trade data (an important component of GDP metrics) far more difficult with national and international statistical offices struggling to respond. Globalization meant that national economic indicators had "not kept up with the changing world."[76]

Another major source of tensions surrounding the measurement of the new growth paradigm related to banking. As financialization grew in policy significance, the question of whether banking was "productive" became an important topic of discussion. Statisticians had long debated whether banking should be considered as economically productive and how to classify it in terms of income, product, or transfers.[77] The globalization of finance and services trade coupled with the push of British, French, and American banks' internationalization left national accounts even more unstable. Bankers and statisticians alike struggled to measure the vast quantity of transactions and argued over whether such activity fit within the production boundary in national accounts.[78]

Yet for some experts such an exercise was foolhardy. Drawing on a long history of Marxian analysis about banking, economists Anwar Shaikh and Ahmet Tomak suggested that financial services did not fit within the production boundary. They argued that since banking revenue derived from "recirculation of money flows" within primary sectors, it served to preserve wealth and social power while not contributing to otherwise desirable economic activity. Thus it was not, in their view, "part of the total value or total product."[79] Few official statisticians, however, accepted these arguments. As economic geographer Brett Christophers has detailed, the majority of statisticians and economists managing national accounts and the UN SNA ultimately decided in the 1990s to classify most financial services as formally productive. These changes had clear political implications. Making financial institutions appear "economically vital" in maintaining economic growth often left them "politically untouchable."[80]

While finance became "productive" in national accounts, the place of government remained largely fixed to the position granted to it during the 1940s. John Maynard Keynes had argued that public spending was necessary to safeguard economies. In accounting terms, government added to GNP on the expenditure side by purchasing goods to make up for weak private investment. In the national accounts, the method was "simply to add up the costs of government production, subtract intermediate material inputs and equate the difference— basically, government employees' salaries—with the output of government." Political economist Mariana Mazzucato has argued, however, that this approach does not "capture the full amount" of value created by government activity. Contemporary national accounts too narrowly define government's role, excluding vital actions—such as public investments that produce positive returns, productivity increases sparked by public spending, or profits earned by government-owned entities—from the national accounts. In an era in which political arguments that depict government spending as wasteful have been used to justify ever deeper austerity, such accounting conventions both reflected and exacerbated "fables about government told over centuries" and impaired the ability of policy makers to adduce the myriad ways in which government had contributed to broader notions of economic and social value.[81]

One final problem for the measurement of the growth paradigm in recent decades stemmed from the rise of digital transactions and new information technology. National income and product accounts did not effectively capture rapid increases in technological quality and decline in prices. For instance, a 1996 commission found that the US Consumer Price Index had overstated the rate of inflation by 1.3 percentage a year because what appeared to be rising prices (or less rapidly declining prices) were in fact improvements in quality and consumer benefit for popular technologies such as cameras, computers, and telephones. In turn, this exaggeration led to an understatement of real GDP growth as official statisticians compensated for these "phantom" price increases. US statisticians responded by calculating "hedonic" price indexes to ascertain the "true" price of such goods by assessing prices for all the components and characteristics of such objects that users find beneficial, from built-in wireless internet capabilities to large memory capacity. A related issue concerned how to classify software. Statisticians debated whether to deem it as an investment (as many do now) or the purchase of an intermediate good (as most originally had done), reflecting a deeper uncertainty about how to render legible components of economic activity that were becoming increasingly salient to everyday life but which were not present when national accounts had been constructed back in the 1940s to measure the production of physical objects. GDP simply did not capture "all the incremental value-added" benefits of an "increasingly weightless economy," in economist Diane Coyle's words.[82]

What these issues reveal was that throughout the revival of the growth paradigm, the object of growth—the national economy—was still subject to contestation and revision. As before, too, the choices over what to measure reflected dominant values, which, in turn, prompted critics to highlight the ways in which metrics concealed the ideological commitments of those who had constructed them. There are persistent problems with data collection in many countries, as well.[83] In China, for example, critics have for decades lamented poor data in constructing GDP estimates and the ongoing efforts of enterprising officials to manipulate data to meet growth targets.[84] Even in spite of the growth in administrative and technological capacity worldwide to collect and analyze economic data, choosing what to count and what to exclude from official accounts remains a subject of ongoing debate.

Growth Critics at the End of the Growth Century

As the growth paradigm revived across the world in the 1980s and 1990s, criticisms of it persisted. In many ways, the most successful of the alternative metrics from the 1970s were the social indicators advocates. Over the 1970s and 1980s, most governments and international organizations began to actively compile social data, building institutional momentum behind their use in academic research if not in public policy. The World Bank, for instance, adopted a "dashboard approach" to the use of indicators in project assessment that drew on a range of economic and social indicators.[85] In 1995, the bank introduced a "wealth index" based on four categories (natural capital, produced assets, human resources, and social capital). Countries and localities experimented with such dashboards. Jacksonville, Florida, for instance, introduced in 1983 a dashboard approach in its "Quality Indicators for Progress" project, which included up to one hundred indicators recalibrated annually with citizen input.[86]

Though many of the most popular alternative social indexes of the 1970s, such as Morris David Morris's PQLI, did not replace GDP, there were multiple efforts to construct similar metrics during the 1980s. The most famous and influential of these was led by Mahbub ul Haq. Over the course of the 1980s, Haq worried that "human costs" of the debt crisis and subsequent structural adjustment policies "were extremely harsh."[87] In 1985, Haq returned to Pakistan, where he served for four years as the country's finance minister to engineer adjustment policies while maintaining the country's focus on social services and antipoverty policies. Haq and many like-minded growth critics, such as Amartya Sen, also continued to revise and rethink the "basic human needs" approach. By the late 1980s, Sen advocated for a new approach to development, often called the "capabilities approach," based on the belief that the purpose of development should be to enlarge each individual's capabilities to enjoy a full and meaningful life.[88] Haq's thinking moved in a similar direction. He wrote about "human development," which Haq's friend and colleague Paul Streeten described as "providing all human beings . . . with the opportunities for a full life."[89]

After leaving the Pakistani government in 1988, Haq accepted a position as a consultant for the UN's Development Programme. He initiated research to expand the human development approach and construct a metric that would give statistical expression to the underlying ideas. Working with many other reform-minded development experts such as Sen, Streeten, Frances Stewart, and Gustav Ranis, Haq's research led to the inaugural *Human Development Report* of 1990. The report included a new metric designed to measure well-being and assess levels of human development called the Human Development Index (HDI).[90]

The HDI was an aggregate index that linked health, education, and "standard of living." In the index, health was represented by life expectancy, education by literacy rate (and, after a few years of adjustments, school enrollment), and standard of living by GDP per capita at purchasing power parity.[91] Haq believed these three indicators would capture "the many dimensions of human choices" and inspire action to build a "conducive environment for people, individually and collectively, to develop their full potential and to have a reasonable chance of leading productive and creative lives in accord with their needs and interests."[92] The purpose of human development, Haq said at the HDI's official launch, was not "just in the expansion of national income, but in the extension of human wellbeing."[93] Over the 1990s, the HDI became a popular metric in UN policy and achieved widespread recognition by scholars and development experts around the world. Similarly, the focus on small-scale and humanistic development priorities in the UN's Millennium Development Goals and Sustainable Development Goals bore the hallmark of the many reform efforts from 1970s and attested to international organizations' deepening use of social indicators.[94]

As with social indicators, though, the HDI was not without its critics. Economist T. N. Srinivasan charged that claims of the HDI's originality were overblown, since the metric had a clear debt to earlier social indicator movements and because of its resemblance to the standard of living measures of the 1920s and 1930s.[95] Srinivasan and many others also were quick to point out the often-flawed social data on which it rested.[96] World Bank economist Martin Ravallion identified several issues pertaining to the index's "implicit monetary valuation of an extra year of life," which, based on his calculations, was far greater for rich countries than for poor ones.[97] Libertarians critiqued it for implicitly holding as a normative national ideal the Scandinavian social democracies, which explained why those countries so often had the highest HDI scores.[98] Yet the metric remains popular in international development circles today as a useful counterpart to GDP and the main metric for assessing the still popular "human development" paradigm.[99]

Ecological economists also continued their efforts to quantify environmental damage and provide new metrics and models for understanding the connections between the human and nonhuman world. Herman Daly continued to promote the steady-state framework over the course of the 1980s. He also took a job with the World Bank's environmental department, where he worked on the intersection of global poverty, lending policies, and environmental issues.[100] In the late 1980s, Daly teamed up with theologian John Cobb Jr. to craft a wide-ranging critique of growth that fused ecological economics with a communitarian philosophy, a project that included their new "Index of Sustainable Welfare" (ISEW) as a challenge to GNP.[101] The ISEW built on Nordhaus and Tobin's Measure of Economic Welfare and the Japanese Net National Welfare to create an index that included estimates of unwaged labor and leisure alongside deductions for pollution and natural capital depletion. The ISEW showed that while US GNP had grown considerably since the late 1960s, US overall welfare had not.[102] Refashioned as the Genuine Progress Indicator in 1995, the metric drew increasing attention as statisticians in US states such as Maryland and Vermont began to make official GPI estimates.[103]

Ecological economics also gained adherents. Daly and his colleague Robert Costanza, together with scholars in Europe such as the Spanish economist Juan Martinez-Alier, built up ecological economics as a small but dedicated subdiscipline with its own journals and professional organization. During the 1990s, the Ford Foundation funded a research institute at the University of Maryland, where both Daly and Costanza worked. Their institute nurtured transdisciplinary dialogue about "new economic concepts that take into account environmental and natural resources, features, and processes" and played a "central role" in coordinating research efforts with similar institutes in Sweden, Italy, and Canada.[104] Even the *Economist* conceded in 2015 that the growing number of ecological economists are "asking some important questions" about the relationship between economic life and "planetary boundaries."[105]

As ecological economics drew greater public and scholarly attention, critics pondered its potential downsides. Many economists pointed out that the many predictions of the *Limits to Growth* report had been proven wrong by time. As a result, they suggested that technological innovation and effective pricing techniques would clear any scarcity hurdles.[106] Ecological economists countered that while there may no longer be clear hard-and-fast limits to growth, the combined effect of paying for responses to climatic changes, pollution abatement and minimization, and other important environmental protection policies would limit future growth. William Nordhaus, for instance, estimated in 1992 that per capita output growth would slow by one-fifth in major OECD countries by the middle twenty-first century.[107] Such figures prompted economists to make counterprojections about economic damage from any interventions in markets and to highlight the importance of relying on market-based solutions to environmental problems. In 1995, for instance, Nobel Prize-winning economist Kenneth Arrow and a team of researchers published a popular article in the journal *Science* on optimizing the "incentives" and "signals" for economic actors to value environmental protection.[108]

Other critics suggested that the problems with ecological economics were primarily philosophical. Many environmentalists asked whether it was wise or just to use the language and techniques of economics to convey the value of nature. In 1995, philosopher Mark Sagoff published a searing essay in which he castigated ecological economics for treating environmental protection with a utilitarian conception of value, departing from earlier luminaries such as Henry David Thoreau and John Muir who celebrated its intrinsic value. Daly, Nordhaus, Arrow, and their like-minded colleagues had adopted "the very economic or utilitarian approach their predecessors deplored."[109] A similar debate emerged in 1997, when Robert Costanza published a study using neoclassical utility theory to assign an economic worth of $33 trillion to the world's natural capital and ecosystems. For Costanza, it was a valuable way to draw attention to natural capital and ecosystem services because they were too often ignored or undervalued, which led policy makers "to the error of constructing projects whose social costs far outweigh their benefit."[110] For critics such as Sagoff, however, the estimates defanged the moral bite of the ecological economists' message. "Ecological economists ended up fully embracing the slogan of mainstream welfare economics that protecting the environment is a matter of getting the prices right," Sagoff wrote of the Costanza study. "A discipline that just a decade or two earlier had insisted the market was embedded in nature had learned how to embed nature into the market."[111] Even Herman Daly, Costanza's longtime colleague, was skeptical of the effort after his long career of challenging mainstream economics' claims to "numerical precision."[112] Other critics charged that the dominant metaphors of ecological economics—that nature was a stock that provides a flow of services—were too reductive and schematic to address the depth and range of ecological and economic predicaments facing the twenty-first-century world.[113]

As these debates raged, ecological economists struggled to make significant headway in reshaping national accounting practices. Robert Repetto, a resource economist, pioneered research into natural capital depletion that exposed how long-term natural degradation actually undermined growth potential, using 1980s Indonesia as a case study.[114] Yet the study and many others like it established wild swings in country's net value, depending on new discoveries of key materials. For instance, one study of Indonesia showed that the discovery of new oil reserves in the early 1970s coupled with oil price hikes led the country's green GDP to increase more than 50 percent over one year. When oil prices fell and the suspected new reserves were downgraded in quantity and quality, the country's green GDP fell back to its preboom levels, leaving scholars and policy makers with "erratic and economically meaningless" figures.[115]

A few countries experimented with "satellite" national accounts that supplemented income and product figures with environmental depletion metrics, first through the UN and then in a few major countries. In the first years of the Clinton administration in the United States, the Commerce Department's Bureau of Economic Analysis (BEA) produced its own satellite accounts. A team of economists, headed by William Nordhaus, however, argued that doing so would complicate the parsimonious economic metrics. They suggested that satellite accounts should instead remain supplemental. That argument won the day. Green GDP estimates remain a popular subject of study, with international organizations such as the UN producing official but supplemental environmental accounts. They still face the range of technical, methodological, and ethical critiques that have existed for decades.[116]

There were other substantive criticisms of the growth paradigm that pervaded the 1980s and 1990s. One especially popular one centered on the notion of "happiness." A major theme of the social critics of growth had been that the pursuit of material abundance had led to spiritual disengagement, social alienation, and limited satisfaction. In other words, high GNP growth rates did not seem to make a country's population especially happy. In 1965, the Gallup polling company, working with psychologist Hadley Cantril, asked citizens around the world about how they felt about the state of their lives. Cantril then ranked the responses on a "self-anchoring striving scale" to compare the happiness of countries.[117] In a 1974 study, economist Richard Easterlin published a study based on social surveys from nineteen countries that found that after a certain level of per capita income, people no longer reported increasing in satisfaction. He concluded that the pursuit of economic growth generated for many people new desires "that lead it ever onward" in search of a sense of satisfaction few reached.[118] For Easterlin, the study was significant because it imported insights from sociology and psychology that allowed for subjective measures of well-being. "Mainstream economics," he wrote, "spared itself confrontation with the evidence" that many people reported less satisfaction after reaching a certain income limit "by its dogmatic rejection of subjective testimony on well-being."[119] Other experts, such as Hungarian American economist Tibor Scitovsky, engaged in similar research into the 1980s.[120]

The happiness critique of growth entered into national politics. King Wangchuck of Bhutan famously declared in 1972 that the country would measure its development according to "gross national happiness," which the country assessed through social surveys through the 1980s and 1990s.[121] In recent years, other countries have followed. For instance, beginning in 2011 the United Kingdom's Office of National Statistics used social surveys to assess the state of life satisfaction and a sense of well-being in the country.[122] Many university research teams, think tanks, and international organizations carried out similar "life satisfaction" surveys that stem from Easterlin's original argument that subjective measures of well-being need to be incorporated in studies of how people understand their status.[123]

The study and promotion of happiness has also become a booming and controversial industry. Consultants, researchers, and salespeople blend research on consumer satisfaction, psychological data from social surveys, and corporate self-help pabulum in the name of promoting "mindfulness." Many critics have astutely noted that what began as something of a potentially radical critique of the growth paradigm has ultimately been co-opted by those most invested in sustaining it. American historian Jackson Lears argued that the happiness industry today began with the "laudable desire to define happiness as something more than per capita GDP," but it "wants to do so without ever challenging the economic system that produces the GDP."[124] British sociologist William Davies likewise claimed that happiness studies and the rhetoric of well-being cloak an invidious arrangement of psychological surveillance, a misguided conflation of "the pursuit of health" with "the pursuit of money," and a foolish "fantasy of a single measure of human optimality."[125] In this way, the happiness critique of growth has come to serve as a tool for corporate managers hoping to extract greater productivity from their frustrated and anxious workers.

Ongoing Efforts to Measure the Unmeasured

In addition to the work of these growth critics, researchers continued their efforts to quantify informal activity and unwaged household labor, though in both instances the research moved far beyond its radical origins of the 1970s. Experts came to view the informal sector through the lens of property rights and entrepreneurship, as an incubator of a capitalist mindset among the poor. For instance, Peruvian economist Hernando de Soto's 1987 *The Other Path* presented the informal sector as a "rebellion against the status quo" and evidence of need for "economic freedom."[126] In stark contrast to how Keith Hart and the ILO/IDS had depicted informal activity, Soto reframed it as a paragon of market virtue and called on governments to experiment with property titling to spark growth. His work won favor across the world. Speaking to the Council of the Americas in May 1990, US president George H. W. Bush hailed the informal sector not as evidence in support of stronger antipoverty and employment programs, but instead as a holding tank of would-be capitalists waiting to be unleashed. "De Soto's prescription, and mine," the president said, "is to free this economic force, unleash the million sparks of energy and enterprise, let the incentive of reward inspire men and women to work to better themselves and their families."[127] US president Bill Clinton called de Soto "probably the world's most important living economist" at the 2004 World Economic Forum in Davos.[128]

Subsequent analysts of de Soto's work suggested a different story than what the globe-trotting economist had presented. Timothy Mitchell argued, for instance, that his pilot titling programs oversold their ability to make increases in working hours and erased the much more complicated history of structural adjustment reforms that had reshaped Peruvian housing markets in which de Soto claimed to produce undeniable and universal facts about capitalist development.[129] By the 1990s, de Soto's stories continued to resonate because they presented the citizen of the Global South as "a natural entrepreneur, held in poverty by an overbureaucratized developmental state that fails to establish the simple rules that make possible the generation of wealth."[130] For Keith Hart the informal sector simply spoke to the limitations of conventional economic indicators, whereas de Soto and his supporters used it as part of an ideological project designed to delegitimize statist interventions to alleviate poverty altogether.

Measuring women's work followed a similar trajectory. The work of New Zealand economist Marilyn Waring is instructive. Waring had served in the New Zealand Parliament from 1976 to 1984. After her service, she pursued a doctorate in political economy. In her research, she studied how the official UN SNA and national accounting techniques had devalued women's labor. Building on the earlier work of Ester Boserup, Lourdes Benería, and others, Waring published a book in 1988 based on her research entitled *If Women Counted* that argued forcefully for attributing "monetary valuation to unpaid work, productive and reproductive" with the goal of making such work "visible" and "influencing policies and concepts, and questioning val-

ues."[131] Waring's book and similar efforts by labor economists such
as Robert Eisner inspired UN officials to incorporate some of their
research into the 1993 SNA revisions. While UN statisticians did
not agree to incorporate unpaid domestic work, they did encourage
imputing values of household production and "domestic services" into
satellite accounts.[132]

During the 1990s, international development experts similarly
viewed women's domestic labor as an untapped source of monetary
productivity. Many development agencies began to support extending
credit to women to transform them from domestic laborers to full-
blown capitalist entrepreneurs. Popular rhetoric surrounding women
in development often featured financial metaphors, depicting women
as wise "investments" for national governments and international
donors.[133] For example, when US First Lady Hillary Clinton visited
Indian organizer Ela Bhatt's Self-Employed Women's Association of
India (SEWA) as part of a tour of South Asia in the spring of 1995, she
described it as an example of how "women have organized around their
capacity as borrowers, lenders and savers to achieve greater economic
independence." She elided the organization's roots as a trade union
designed to make visible women's labor and build power for women
as workers.[134]

By the end of the 1990s, Waring surveyed all the piecemeal reforms
and concluded that more radical changes were necessary. She had initially sought to make women's work visible in conventional accounting.
In the 1999 revised version of her breakthrough book, however, Waring
worried that by imputing prices on to domestic labor, her work ultimately reinforced the growth paradigm rather than effectively con-
fronting it. "By advocating the inclusion of women's unpaid work in
national income," Waring feared that she and other feminists risked
advancing the idea that GDP maximization should remain the central
focus of economic policy. Waring argued against the national accounting framework altogether in favor of time-use surveys, as many radical
feminists had done in the early 1970s, to show how long people spent
carrying out specific activities and, for instance, how cuts in social
spending increased the time-labor burden on women.[135] In this way,

women's unwaged labor would still be made visible to policy makers, but it would be viewed less as a contributor to overall growth than as a subject of policy intervention that made more clear individual and group injustices.

Both informal activity and unwaged women's labor remain popular topics of study and the basis of grassroots organizing. SEWA grew to include over two million members—the largest "informal" labor organization in the world—by the early 2010s. Ela Bhatt and her allies also helped to create new organizations, such as the Women in Informal Employment: Globalizing and Organizing (WIEGO) network, to highlight the inequalities by making visible such forms of labor and imagining alternative ways of framing the relationship between social and biological reproduction, labor, and well-being. WIEGO included over eight hundred local and national organizations designed to organize on behalf of "informal" workers across the world by 2015.[136] WIEGO has even begun to classify the differing interpretations of the meaning of "the informal sector" to capture the variety of meanings now attached to the concept.[137] Likewise, the ILO's Conference on Labour Statisticians drafted guidelines for measuring informal activity.[138] Grassroots movements to support informal activity broadened into many forms. Historian Michelle Murphy, for instance, celebrates Bangladeshi activist Farida Akhter's eco-feminist movement that supports mixed-crop, seed-sharing organic farming and community building as a model for a "refusal" of GDP-oriented development projects that follow narrow and flawed definitions of progress and success.[139]

Critics of the growth paradigm and those promoting alternatives ways of measuring society continue to this day. They contend with the ongoing power and prominence of growth as a national goal and organizing principle for economic life. The alternatives to GDP have not displaced it in national politics or the public imagination worldwide. These challenges, however, represent a powerful and distinct set of values that threaten, to varying degrees, the core assumption of the capitalist growth paradigm: that maximizing economic output and encouraging productivity reduces political and social conflict.[140] The efflorescence of alternatives and the spread of many complementary research programs and social movements mark a strong countermovement to the growth paradigm. But they will require larger shifts in values and more powerful and sustained political mobilizations to make a lasting impact.

Conclusion

The transformations of the world since the 1970s generated myriad consequences. The antistatist growthmanship embraced by many leaders and policy makers within the wealthy, capitalist world reshaped life at home and reordered global economic relations. The shift from a world defined by fears of energy scarcity to one with a revived faith in energy abundance enabled policy makers to once again promise restive populations that the future was one of limitless economic potential; no more fierce trade-offs or sacrifices would be necessary. The collapse of the Soviet Union and the end of the Cold War reshaped international politics in fundamental ways. The deepening integration of the countries that once composed the Third World into the broader capitalist world order intensified global interconnection. During these changes, leaders revived the growth paradigm. Promoting growth now came through different policies, but as it had in the 1940s and 1950s, the pursuit of national economic growth defined state purpose. In a longer historical view, as the international relations scholar Bentley Allan argues, the variations on the growth paradigm in the capitalist world—"Keynesian" and "neoliberal" are his terms—still required that nation-states "deliver the benefits of scientific modernity." The growth paradigm as it emerged in the 1940s and 1950s and the growth paradigm of the 1990s and 2000s both rested on "modernist epistemic presuppositions" since both "place faith in the idea that expertise and knowledge can advance human progress."[141] In other words, the growth paradigm demonstrated remarkable flexibility and durability. Thus many leaders and citizens alike still place faith in economic growth to resolve social, political, and environmental problems at the turn of the twenty-first century, just as they did many decades earlier.

Yet a distinguishing feature of the revived growth paradigm was the depth and breadth of its critics. While GNP and GDP still dominate how policy makers across the world assess progress, the sheer volume of alternatives used by international organizations, experts, and the wide range of grassroots movements suggest that the many dissidents who criticized the growth paradigm have gained considerable ground since the 1950s and 1960s. Contemporary growth critics often echo the arguments of their earlier counterparts. Phyllis Deane's efforts to measure the unquantified resonate with the ongoing efforts of feminist economists to do the same today; Dudley Seers's critique of GNP growth as a solution for social problems and an avoidance mechanism for redistribution has found many afterlives among development critics such as Sen and Haq; Georgescu-Roegen's and Kenneth Boulding's environmental criticisms of the growth paradigm have been expanded by Herman Daly and an entire generation of ecological economists. The recent spate of books written about the present-day downsides of growth and the flaws of GDP attest to the ongoing influence of growth critics and dissenters in contemporary politics.[142] It remains to be seen, of course, whether today's critics are able to forge the political coalitions with the will to mount a far more enduring challenge to the growth paradigm.

History, Narrative, and Contemporary Growth Critics

The growth paradigm defined the purpose of national governance during the twentieth century. In the capitalist world, policy makers pursued growth because they hoped to redress older distributional conflicts, avoid depressions, and reduce poverty without engaging in the explicitly redistributive nature of intervention that standard-of-living advocates demanded. The faith that a rising tide would lift all boats resonated in a world wracked by depression, social unrest, and war, especially for policy makers hoping to abjure class conflict through the promise of future collective gains. For the Soviet Union and its allies, the pursuit of growth provided a way to compete with capitalism, a tool for rallying citizens to sacrifice, and a justification for collective mobilization in the quest for future glory. For the rest of the world, growth offered the surest path to power and prestige, the way to overcome long histories of exploitation and poverty, and the economic means to gain leverage to push for greater international political power.

All the while, there were many critics of the growth paradigm and many who sought alternative ways of measuring the world. They inspired debates over what the purpose of national governance should be, how government policy should be measured and assessed, and which statistics would best serve the public interest. These thinkers included the advocates for standard-of-living statistics; those who highlighted the people and activities excluded from economic accounting conventions such as Phyllis Deane and Marilyn Waring; the growth critics who lamented the social consequences of growth and the persistence of inequalities that growth did not wash away such as Dudley Seers and Mahbub ul Haq; the ecological economists such as Nicholas Georgescu-Roegen and Herman Daly who presented alternative ways of conceptualizing the relationship between human prosperity and the resources it required. Because these critics did not successfully displace growth as a preeminent goal, it is easy to dismiss them as a failure. But to do so would be a mistake because it would elide the richness, depth, and breadth of the debates over the meaning and measurement of economic growth across the twentieth century world.

The growth critics resonate again today in the face of global conditions that cast doubt on the growth paradigm. Growth critics thrived when the material consequences of growth—from its failure to deliver widely shared prosperity to its visible ecological effects—sparked outrage, especially during the 1960s. The energy shocks, fears of biophysical limits to growth, and collapse of international economic governance during the 1970s gave wide credence to the growth critics and generated a search for alternative paradigms. Over the past two decades, the financial crisis of 2007–8 and the slow public awakening to the realities of global climate change inspire renewed criticisms of the growth paradigm. The high growth rates of the 1990s and early 2000s masked a volatile financial system, deepening inequalities within major countries, and a burgeoning ecological crisis. Consequently, contemporary growth critics seek new goals for national and international life and new ways of measuring progress. Like their predecessors, today's critics use history to critique popular narratives about the benefits of the growth paradigm and to draw public attention to unresolved tensions and flaws. The history told in this book, in other words, is very much a part of our present time.

Over the first couple of decades of the twenty-first century, scholars and activists have continued to challenge the growth paradigm. They do so as a forward-looking endeavor, to create alternative metrics to help contend with the myriad problems of the present and future. But in their critique of growth and the ongoing use of GNP, they also engage in historical revisionism. In order to produce a more compelling basis for potential reforms, today's growth critics craft alternative stories that dispute growth as a narrative of historical change. Throughout the twentieth century, economists, policy makers, and citizens across the world used "economic growth" not only as a policy prescription or a term of economic analysis, but also as a description of the past. Growth critics object to using growth as the dominant narrative of the past by recasting recent history as a far less rosy and simple story of progress.

Much as Simon Kuznets's and Colin Clark's estimates of national income and product figures in the 1940s served as the basis for historical narratives that presented growth as a metanarrative for describing human civilization, in the twenty-first century growth remains a powerful story for charting modern history. For instance, Swedish public intellectual Hans Rosling produced a series of popular videos that portray the last two hundred years as a simple, triumphant story of collective growth. His famous "200 countries, 200 years, 4 minutes" clip, which has over 9 million views on YouTube, depicts countries as small dots on a virtual graph with life expectancy on the y-axis and per capita income on the x-axis. Countries begin "sick and poor" but after "two hundred years of remarkable progress," he says, "everyone can make it" to wealth and good health.[1] Likewise, corporate elites and techno-optimists such as psychologist Steven Pinker agree. They hail economic growth as a dominant story of the last two hundred years and a metonym for human progress.[2] They describe growth as the cure-all for the future. As billionaire investor Peter Thiel told a Harvard University class in March 2019, "if we have enough growth in our society, we can solve all problems."[3]

Over the last two decades, however, critical anthropologists, sociologists, and historians have adopted a historicist perspective that treats economic growth *as* history, not as an ahistorical term to describe a metanarrative of material progress. Timothy Mitchell, Alain Desrosières, Adam Tooze, Manu Goswami, Silvana Patriarca, Scott O'Bryan, Robert Collins, Daniel Speich Chassé, Matthias Schmelzer, and many others have explained that "national economy" and "national economic growth" are contingent historical concepts arising from distinct sociotechnical circumstances.[4] They have challenged simplistic narratives of growth and exposed what economic aggregates occluded. In their work, they have portrayed in subtle and powerful ways many of the arguments that the growth critics in this book articulated long ago. They have illuminated the role of economic reasoning in popular discourse and highlighted the cultural conditions that explain why growth remains so popular.[5] They have even questioned the adequacy of the basic data necessary to make arguments about aggregate economic progress. Morten Jerven's work, for example, cast doubt on conventional narratives that show sub-Saharan Africa as one of consistently low growth rates.[6]

Like their predecessors covered in this book, contemporary economists who study income inequality have revised the popular narrative that sees growth as the dominant story of the twentieth century. French economists Thomas Piketty and Emmanuel Saez, for example, drew worldwide attention for the depth and breadth of their research when they published a paper in 2003 with the shocking conclusion that the top 1 percent of US income earners now received nearly 15 percent of total national income, almost twice as much as they had at the start of the 1970s.[7] Piketty, Saez, and British economist Anthony Atkinson expanded the study of inequality to many other countries.[8] Piketty's 2014 book *Capital in the Twenty-First Century* built on this research to set a new narrative of twentieth-century history.[9] Wealth and income moved briefly toward equality during the Great Depression and World War II but after the 1960s gravitated again toward extreme inequality with the top 1 percent garnering a staggering share of total income. What separated Piketty and Saez's work from previous studies was their ability to make top incomes more visible than had the studies of most of their fellow economists.[10] Branko Milanovic, former lead economist of the World Bank's research department, added to this story by showing that lower-income earners in wealthy countries did not benefit from the growth of the 1990s and early 2000s, deepening inequality within wealthy countries.[11] As a result of this research, the twentieth century appears less as a universal and linear story of aggregate prosperity for all and instead as one of oscillating and uneven patterns of accumulation and increasing inequality within key wealthy countries (especially the United States).

New studies of tax avoidance by large companies also suggest a compelling counternarrative to one of increasing collective prosperity. Economist Gabriel Zucman, a student of Piketty's, broke new ground on this front with a systematic collection of data on corporate tax havens. In a 2015 book, Zucman revealed that nearly 8 percent of all household financial wealth had been hidden away in tax havens and 55 percent of all the foreign profits of US firms had been similarly sheltered offshore.[12] Historian Vanessa Ogle has uncovered the imperial origins of these tax havens, detailing decades-long quests by wealthy elites to squirrel away money from national authorities.[13] These stories suggest that rather than GNP growth perhaps the most salient economic narrative of the past hundred years has been the consolidation of wealth in the hands of very few global elites, their systematic efforts to shield their wealth from national tax coffers, and the inability of conventional economic and statistical methods to illuminate such trends without more attention to issues of distribution and tax avoidance.

Recent research on the size of the financial sector also illuminates the vast inequality worldwide between the major owners of capital and the rest of humanity. As technological innovations increased the speed and frequency of global financial trading, a "shadow banking system" of financial institutions, not subject to conventional regulatory oversight, has become staggeringly large. Including hedge funds, securitization vehicles, money market funds, and other intermediaries outside the traditional system of regulated depository institutions, the shadow banking system contained hundreds of trillions of dollars by 2017.[14] To grasp the scale and meaning of this extensive financial world, scholars have developed a new approach to study it called "macrofinance." As the historian Adam Tooze has noted, macroeconomics stemmed from the premise that "the national economy, national society and national politics formed a coherent whole." Macrofinance, by contrast, acknowledges that "globalization has ruptured those links." It focuses on gross flows on the capital account and corporate balance sheets to monitor the contemporary drivers of international economic activity such as the thirty or so megabanks.[15] From this perspective, the basic units (the national economy) of economic life and tools used to monitor it (national accounts) no longer serve as fully accurate guides for capturing and managing the scale of economic activity today. Macrofinancial analysis speaks to the need for new concepts and accounting frameworks that could serve both scholars and policy makers as they try to render this world more legible and accountable. As with the research on tax havens, this approach suggests that the movement of capital largely freed of domestic fetters constitutes one of the dominant historical stories over recent decades yet too often remains obscured in national economic indicators.

The global financial crisis also generated conditions of uncertainty and instability that revived criticisms of the growth paradigm. As had happened in the 1970s, many experts and activists pondered a future of weak growth and searched for alternative ways to depict economic life. Historian and financial analyst Zachary Karabell, for instance, has studied what a "low-growth" future would look like based on an analysis of Japan during its many years of low GDP growth rates.[16] In 2016, economist Robert Gordon published a massive study of the evolution of US economic productivity and growth that portended a low-growth future, suggesting that the technological advances of the twenty-first century were unlikely to replicate the scale of economic expansion that those of the early twentieth had done.[17] Likewise, while GDP growth rates picked up in the year after the 2008 crisis, inequality increased. "The average American shared only to a small degree in national economic growth measured by GDP statistics" after the crisis. With flatlined wages and with capital receiving far more of the share of total income than labor, Adam Tooze asked, "Could the national economy any longer be plausibly presented as a project common to all Americans?"[18] For the millions for whom postcrisis recovery meant stagnant wages and diminished opportunities, higher growth rates offered little solace. Rather than a consistent narrative of economic growth, the financial crisis and its aftermath have led such thinkers to consider whether more apt narratives would focus on the "rise and fall" of national economic growth as a barometer of collective well-being.[19]

The growing recognition of global climate change inspired another reassessment of the growth paradigm. Global climate change moved into the fore of national and international politics during the 1980s and early 1990s, though scientists had detected links between carbon emissions and rising global temperatures much earlier.[20] By the 2000s, many scholars had linked the pursuit of rapid economic growth with the transformation of the earth's climate and the catastrophe it portended. While environmentalists in many ways echoed the theme of the environmental growth critics of the 1940s, 1950s, and 1960s, the scale of climate change forced a reckoning with human beings not only as ecologically destructive, but also as "geological agents," in the words of historians Naomi Oreskes and Dipesh Chakrabarty.[21] Climate change and the concomitant discussion of dating the "anthropocene" as a new geological age mark another challenge to the growth metanarrative.[22] The pursuit of economic growth premised on cheap fossil fuels has reshaped the earth to the point where disruptions and dislocation from climate change may very well imperil future prosperity. The embrace of economic growth worldwide during the twentieth century, in this story, may simply be the prelude to a gradual cataclysm experienced by many across the world during the twenty-first.

It is important to note, too, that the causes and consequences of climate change are unevenly distributed. For instance, a handful of countries are largely responsible for the increase in greenhouse gases. Since 1850, according to 2011 data compiled by the World Resources Institute, the United States, Russia, China, Germany, the United Kingdom, France, and Japan together accounted for over 65 percent of total carbon dioxide emissions (the United States alone accounted for 28.8 percent of the total).[23] And yet the countries least responsible for generating carbon emissions, from Vanuatu to Bangladesh to Chad, are least able to contend with its myriad consequences and most vulnerable to its immediate impacts.[24] Transitioning to greener forms of energy alone would not redress the already-existing consequences of past fossil fuel use, a realization that led many representatives from

Global South countries to advocate for greater attention to climate adaptation and loss and damage issues in international climate negotiations.[25] The unequal effects and the multidimensional nature of climate change rendered obsolete key aspects of the growth paradigm, such as the notion that growth was a first-order priority to solve all problems. "We can no longer think of things like social and ecological wellbeing as 'post-material' concerns or something to address as a 'justice' bonus after we've gotten the economy growing again," claimed political scientist Alyssa Battistoni in early 2019.[26] Meaningful action on climate change must face up to these realities of inequality in emissions and ecological effects without reproducing the same patterns of behavior that generated the dilemmas in the first place. Climate change provokes a reckoning with the categories so often used to make sense of the world and the foundational assumptions that have long shaped the growth paradigm.

In this context, it is unsurprising that critics of the growth paradigm and advocates for alternative measures of well-being have flourished once again. In 2008, French president Nicolas Sarkozy created a national commission to study the measurement of economic and social progress, chaired by economists Amartya Sen, Joseph Stiglitz, and Jean-Paul Fitoussi. The commission recommended that countries should supplant GDP with new measures of well-being that take greater stock of inequality, consumption, and nonmarket economic activities.[27] In 2009, economist Tim Jackson authored a book that stemmed from the United Kingdom's Sustainable Development Commission that envisioned a world of "prosperity without growth."[28] In 2012, the United Nations launched an "Inclusive Wealth Index" that incorporated countries' "manufactured, human, and natural capital stocks" into a single index number.[29] In 2018, the International Institute for Sustainable Development conducted a similar study to produce a "Comprehensive Wealth Report" for Canada to "balance the short-term view of progress offered by GDP."[30] In May 2019, New Zealand prime minister Jacinda Ardern announced a new national budget dictated by "well-being" of citizens—focused on goals such as "community and cultural connection and equity in well-being across generations"—

rather than "traditional bottom-line measures like productivity and economic growth."[31] All these cases share common criticisms of GDP that have been rehearsed for decades but were revived in the wake of the global financial crisis and the experience of global climate change.

There have also been even more radical movements that confront the growth paradigm directly. Over the last two decades, a loose but growing network of activists and intellectuals have promoted "degrowth."[32] Building on the work of French economist Serge Latouche, who popularized the term *décroissance*, a series of scholars and activists in France, Italy, and Spain embraced degrowth during the early 2000s.[33] Degrowth advocates envision societies in which "the economic is no longer at the center of everything; democracy is direct; surplus is expended for reproduction or fun; income and wealth are distributed according to egalitarian principles; vital resources, infrastructures, and spaces are shared and held in common; technology is convivial and serves social purposes; resource throughput is minimized; and working hours are reduced by cutting consumption, production, and wasteful expenditures."[34] Degrowth is a holistic approach to social organization that draws on ecology, Georgescu-Roegen's bioeconomics, Herman Daly's steady state, the older critiques of modernization theory, the social critics of growth, participatory democracy, and social justice to forge not only another critique of mainstream economics but a broader philosophy for how to organize the social world in direct opposition to the growth paradigm.[35]

Degrowth thinkers and activists have also argued against the more recent efforts by economists and policy makers to promote "green growth." A vague and often slippery term, green growth is generally meant to signify a set of values and policies that render capitalist growth compatible with a transition to more environmentally friendly patterns of energy use, production, and consumption. The phrase became especially popular in the early 2010s, touted by leaders in countries such as South Korea and Brazil and adopted in centrist and center-left think tanks in the United States and Western Europe.[36] Degrowth advocates have criticized the green growth approach for simply repackaging older growth paradigm assumptions and capitalist imperatives (ongoing accumulation, the continuous extraction of surplus labor) and suggest that any energy transition would not occur on the global scale nor the immediate time frame necessary to avoid the consequences of catastrophic climate change. In their view, entirely new patterns of living and, crucially, structures of power and decision making must be conceived and implemented.[37] They have also added a further explanation for why, despite the range of available policy to limit carbon emissions, there has been so little meaningful action. In the words of environmentalist scientist and degrowth advocate Giorgos Kallis, "good climate policies are not adapted because of their [potential] impact on growth, and growth is outstripping the gains made from renewable energy."[38] As a result, as long as growth remains a priority (even if in a "greener" form), it will set the terms of debate and narrow the boundaries of possible policy choice long into the future. Though a diffuse and small movement, degrowth activists and thinkers mark yet another ongoing critique of the growth paradigm and represent an important continuation of older critiques of the growth paradigm that demand serious engagement.

The growth historicists; the new scholars of inequality, tax avoidance, and finance; those mobilizing to redress the terrifying realities of global climate change; and the activists in degrowth movements call into question the centrality of economic growth as a metanarrative for the last century. They constitute another set of powerful challenges to the growth paradigm. But they should not be interpreted as aberrations from past thinking. Debating how to measure and define national progress and well-being has been a central theme of the last century. The social statistics of the progressive era and the transnational movement to quantify workers' standard of living represented alternative ways to measure society that reflected different objects for policy makers to consider. The robust debates about what to include in GNP and the difficulties of extending it to the colonial and postcolonial world during the 1930s and 1940s exposed the value judgments and biases inherent in constructing economic statistics. The diverse growth critics of the 1950s, 1960s, and 1970s decried the flaws and perils of the growth paradigm. The ongoing efforts of growth critics, even amid the revived faith in growth late in the twentieth century, to question its core assumptions expanded on earlier reforms by offering alternative metrics to define and assess progress. The story of the growth paradigm is less one of consensus than of ongoing debate, dissonance, and revision.

As activists and experts continue to ponder the meaning and measurement of economic growth, they would do well to build on an implicit insight from the recent studies that have challenged the centrality of growth as the dominant narrative of the twentieth-century world. Statistics need to serve popular concerns. They are political instruments. They tell stories. To make the case that one's numbers provide valuable insights into the world, advocates for displacing metrics such as GNP and GDP need to couch their figures in similarly powerful counternarratives. Challenging the growth paradigm is not just a matter of finding more effective alternative measurements for the present and future. It also requires retelling the past to offer a convincing set of narratives about how and why to change the contemporary world. The stories we tell about the world and how it has changed over time, just like the concepts and statistics we use to imbue those stories with meaning and evidence, have long been subject to debate. To build a more inclusive, equitable, and ecologically sensitive world as we brace for the environmental realities that await us, we must draw on this long history of dissent as a starting point to move our politics and society beyond the quest for economic growth.

The growth critics provide some insight into possible futures. Growth critics suggest a world in which the state of the nation is not reduced to quarterly GDP reports, where politicians and leaders make policies based on their contributions to social equality and the public good rather than aggregate economic performance. It is a world in which development interventions seek to promote social and ecological compassion rather than boost economic production. It is a world premised on international cooperation designed to minimize international inequalities, curtail fossil fuel use, and democratize global governance organizations to respond boldly to the perils of global climate change.

A greater awareness of the growth critics also lays bare the misguided faith that high growth rates can necessarily redress social, environmental, or political problems. Rather than hoping that a rising tide would lift all boats, taking criticisms of growth seriously should encourage policy makers to make more targeted interventions to diminish wealth and income inequality, reduce poverty, and promote social well-being. Rather than using economic metrics to guide national decision making and shape popular expectations, growth skepticism encourages the use of noneconomic indicators in public policy more widely. Rather than place faith primarily in experts and their social scientific knowledge to generate desirable social outcomes, the history of the growth critics reveals the significance of political engagement and enfranchisement to allow all people to participate meaningfully in shaping the future of the planet. And rather than focusing on short-term material gains, growth critics enable a way of conceiving of politics that defies conventional categories and time frames, to allow citizens to envision their obligations across space and time by caring for distant peoples and future generations in just and sustainable ways. Above all, the history of the growth critics allows us to see that the growth paradigm is neither universal nor natural. With this insight, we can imagine and build better futures.

Acknowledgments

I began working on this project as I finished up a book on the history of sustainable development. I was struck by how many environmental activists had criticized economic growth and its measurement during and after the 1970s. I became fascinated by the ways in which quantification figured in their understanding of environmental politics and wanted to learn more about how and why economic growth came to hold such a powerful place in the twentieth- and twenty-first-century worlds. As I uncovered many more growth critics in my research, the scope of this project expanded in ways I never anticipated at the outset. As I turned that research into this book, I benefited from the gracious support of colleagues and friends.

To begin, I thank the many archivists who helped guide me through the many different collections that shaped my research. I thank Jacques Rodriguez at the International Labour Organisation; Patricia McGuire at King's College, Cambridge University; Jacques Oberson at the United Nations Archives in Geneva; Belinda Spinaze and the staff of the Fryer Library at the University of Queensland; Sandra Willmott at the Organization for Economic Cooperation and Development Archives; Sarah Stevens at the National Institute for Economic and Social Research; Stephanie Watson, Gary Edwards, and Richard Jolly at the Institute of Development Studies; Renee Pappous and the entire archivist staff at the Rockefeller Archives Center; Cheikh Ndiaye at the UN Archives in New York; and Sherrine Thompson and Tonya Ceesay at the World Bank Group Archives.

I am very grateful for the generous scholars who listened to my ideas and offered advice, gave feedback in workshops and conferences, and commented on various draft chapters over the years. My thanks go to Paul Adler, Majed Akhter, Betsy Beasley, Daniel Bessner, Megan Black, Iris Borowy, Jennifer Burns, David Engerman, Nils Gilman, Udi Greenberg, Gretchen Heefner, Daniel Immerwahr, Morten Jerven, Erez Manela, Joanne Meyerowitz, Jennie Miller, Amy Offner, Vanessa Ogle, Tom Robertson, Matthias Schmelzer, Tim Shenk, Brad Simpson, Glenda Sluga, Christy Thornton, and Alden Young. I've especially benefited from working alongside and learning from fellow "growth" historians over the years: Venus Bivar, Stephen Gross, Chris Jones, and Fredrik Albritton Jonsson. Brent Cebul, Nick Cullather, and Mel Leffler deserve special praise. They read many parts of this manuscript (often multiple times) and shared many useful suggestions throughout this project.

Many kind, brilliant, and thoughtful colleagues at Indiana University also aided this project. I thank Huss Banai, David Bosco, Purnima Bose, Sarah Bauerle Danzman, Kon Dierks, Elizabeth Dunn, Stephanie Kane, Padraic Kenney, Rebecca Lave, Adam Liff, Scott O'Bryan, Jessica O'Reilly, Rob Schneider, Jessica Steinberg, Amanda Waterhouse, Ruth Winecoff, Will Winecoff, and John Yasuda for their help, guidance, and insights over the years. Amanda Waterhouse and Geoffrey Heck provided excellent research assistance in the latter stages of drafting this book. Barbara Breitung and Delia Igo helped me organize and manage the logistics of many research trips and travel to conferences and workshops.

I was very fortunate to have the opportunity to present this work to many colleagues over the years. I thank Sarah Milov and the Movements and Directions in Capitalism group at the University of Virginia; Ed Miller, Jennie Miller, Udi Greenberg, Stefan Link, Bill Wohlforth, Stephen Brooks, and the rest of the crew with the Dickey Center US foreign policy and international security fellowship at Dartmouth College; Micol Seigel, Bethany Moreton, and the participants in the Cultural Studies Conference at Indiana University; Iris Borowy and the participants of the conference that launched the Center for the

History of Global Development at Shanghai University; Glenda Sluga, Dirk Moses, Sarah Claire Dunstan, and the attendees of University of Sydney's International History Workshop; Felix Römer, Mary Morgan, and participants at the Global Knowledge of Inequality Workshop at the German Historical Institute London; Joe Parrott and the Mershon Center for International Security Studies at Ohio State; Stephen Gross, Frederick Cooper, Mary Nolan, and the attendees of the New York University Economic History Seminar; and Mark Roseman and the participants in Indiana University's European History Workshop. I've also presented parts of this project to the annual conferences of the Society for Historians of American Foreign Relations (SHAFR) and the American Society for Environmental History (ASEH). My thanks to both organizations, as well as to the audience members who considered my arguments and posed valuable questions in response.

Portions of chapters 1, 3, and 5 appeared in "Whither Growth? International Development, Social Indicators, and the Politics of Measurement, 1920s–1970s," *Journal of Global History* 14, no. 2 (2019). Portions of chapter 3 appear in another article, "Dudley Seers, the Institute for Development Studies, and the Fracturing of International Development Thought in the 1960s and 1970s," *History of Political Economy* 52, no. 1 (2020). I thank Cambridge University Press and Duke University Press for permission to reprint that material in this book.

At the University of Chicago Press, Timothy Mennel has long been an enthusiastic supporter of this book. It has been a pleasure to work with Tim. Susannah Engstrom managed this project through the production process with great skill and care. Kathleen Kageff provided expert copyediting. The anonymous reviewers of this manuscript offered helpful suggestions and criticisms, and I am very grateful for their extended engagement with this project.

Finally, I wish to thank family and friends for their love and support over the years: Mark, Dede, Virginia, Mickey, John, Marty, Richard, Betty, Rick, Louie, Trevor, Anna, Brent, Katherine, Cyd, Jason, Mike, Will, Ruth, John, and Huss. Most of all, I thank Allison and Evelyn, for our past and our future.

Notes

Introduction

1   Dudley Seers, "What Are We Trying to Measure?," in Baster, *Measuring Development*, 21. The first version of this essay appeared in 1969, but the definitive version appeared in print in this 1972 volume.

2   Seers, "What Are We Trying to Measure?," 21–22.

3   Though GDP is far more commonly discussed today, for much of the twentieth century nation-states and international institutions focused on GNP. In this book I use each as they were used in their particular historical context. In brief, the main difference is that GDP is the value of production within a country, while GNP is that value plus net property income from abroad.

4   See, for instance, Stiglitz, Sen, and Fitoussi, *Mismeasuring Our Lives*; Latouche, *Farewell to Growth*; Fioramonti, *Gross Domestic Problem*; Karabell, *Leading Indicators*; Coyle, *GDP*; Higgs, *Collision Course*; Philipsen, *Little Big Number*; Masood, *Great Invention*; Lepenies, *Power of a Single Number*; Pilling, *Growth Delusion*; Hoekstra, *Replacing GDP by 2030*.

5   Schmelzer, *Hegemony of Growth*; Schmelzer, "Growth Paradigm." On the study of economic growth as an object of policy making and political discourse rather than as an ahistorical name used by economists to describe material change, see Arndt, *Rise and Fall of Economic Growth*; Jonsson, "Origins of Cornucopianism"; Schmelzer, *Hegemony of Growth*.

6   Mitchell, "Economentality"; Timothy Mitchell, "Economists and the Economy in the Twentieth Century," in Steinmetz, *Politics of Method in the Human Sciences*, 126–41; Mitchell, *Rule of Experts*; Tooze, *Statistics and the German State*; J. Adam Tooze, "Imagining National Economies: National and International Economic Statistics, 1900–1950," in Cubitt, *Imagining Nations*, 212–28; Speich, "Travelling with the GDP through Early Development Economics' History"; Goswami, *Producing India*; Young, *Transforming Sudan*.

214 NOTES TO PAGE 4

7 Timothy Shenk summarizes this grand transformation in knowledge production and policy as the "three M's": measurement, modeling, and management. Shenk, "Inventing the American Economy," 17–18.

8 On the United States, see Collins, *More*; Yarrow, *Measuring America*;
Shenk, "Inventing the American Economy"; on the United Kingdom, see
Mitra-Kahn, "Redefining the Economy"; on Japan, see O'Bryan, *Growth
Idea*; on Sudan, see Young, *Transforming Sudan*. For recent studies that
highlight the role of economists in forging the national economy as an opera-
tive concept and precondition for the rise of the growth concept, see Shenk,
"Inventing the American Economy"; Mitra-Kahn, "Redefining the Econ-
omy," 210–73; D. Hirschman, "Inventing the Economy."

9 On "keywords" as historical subjects, see R. Williams, *Keywords*. On modernization and development, see, e.g., Gilman, *Mandarins of the Future*;
Stephen Macekura, "Development and Economic Growth: An Intellectual History," in Borowy and Schmelzer, *History of the Future of Economic
Growth*, 110–28.

10 Cullather, "Third Race"; Alessandro Iandolo, "De-Stalinizing Growth:
Decolonization and the Development of Development Economics in the
Soviet Union," in Macekura and Manela, *Development Century*, 197–219;
Engerman, *Know Your Enemy*, 97–128; Fioramonti, *Gross Domestic Prob-
lem*, 33–36. The literature on foreign aid and international development is
growing rapidly. For recent reviews of this literature, see Stephen Macekura
and Erez Manela, "Introduction," in Macekura and Manela, *Development
Century*, 1–20; Hodge, "Writing the History of Development (Part 1: The
First Wave)"; Hodge, "Writing the History of Development (Part 2: Longer,
Deeper, Wider)."

11 McNeill, *Something New under the Sun*, 336. In a similar vein, Nick Cullather studied the concept of development "as history" and an "artifact of
the political and economic context of the Cold War." Cullather, "Development?," 642.

12 Charles S. Maier, "The World Economy and the Cold War in the Middle of the
Twentieth Century," in Leffler and Westad, *Cambridge History of the Cold
War*, 3:48; Maier, "Politics of Productivity"; Milward, *European Rescue of
the Nation-State*, 51–52.

13 Allan, *Scientific Cosmology and International Orders*, 221; Allan, "Paradigm and Nexus."

14 Dale, "Growth Paradigm." See also Purdey, *Economic Growth, the Environment, and International Relations*.

15 Schmelzer, *Hegemony of Growth*, 12.

16 For a recent argument that the desire for growth—if not the calculative practices—has a very long history, see D. Cohen, *Infinite Desire for Growth*.

17 See Daly, "In Defense of a Steady-State Economy," 947. And before that, the term economic "growthmanship" was often used to describe policy makers' and economists' preoccupation with growth. Colin Clark coined the term in Clark, *Growthmanship*.

18 On statistics, aggregation, and accounting in public life, see, for instance, Crosby, *Measure of Reality*; Igo, *Averaged American*; Porter, *Rise of Statistical Thinking*; Stapleford, *Cost of Living in America*; Bernstein, "Numerable Knowledge and Its Discontents"; Rosenthal, "From Memory to Mastery"; Soll, *Reckoning*; J. Kelley and Simmons, "Politics by Number; Fourcade, "Cents and Sensibility."

19 On the importance of economic statistics to modern policy making, see Daniel Speich Chassé, "Use of Global Abstractions"; on economists in governance, see Bernstein, *Perilous Progress*; Markoff and Montecinos, "Ubiquitous Rise of Economists"; Fourcade, *Economists and Societies*; Mudge, *Leftism Reinvented*.

20 This argument follows from Adam Tooze's call to "de-reify the data" by studying "the processes through which quantitative truth claims are made and put to use." Tooze, "Trouble with Numbers," 683.

21 See Macekura, "Dudley Seers."

22 Piketty, Saez, and Zucman, "Distributional National Accounts"; Case and Deaton, "Rising Morbidity and Mortality"; Weller and Hanks, "Widening Racial Wealth Gap"; Lisa J. Dettling et al., "Recent Trends in Wealth-Holding by Race and Ethnicity: Evidence from the Survey of Consumer Finances," *FEDS Notes*, September 27, 2017, https://www.federalreserve.gov/econres/notes/feds-notes/recent-trends-in-wealth-holding-by-race-and-ethnicity-evidence-from-the-survey-of-consumer-finances-20170927.htm.

23 Deringer, *Calculated Values*, 318.

24 Gordon, *Rise and Fall of American Growth*; Piketty, *Capital in the Twenty-First Century*.

Chapter 1

1   On the rise of the concept of "standard of living," see De Grazia, *Irresistible Empire*, 75–129; Coffin, "'Standard' of Living?"; Clavin, *Securing the*

World Economy, 164–79; Glickman, "Inventing the 'American Standard of Living'"; Moskowitz, *Standard of Living*; Berolzheimer, "Nation of Consumers."

2   Soll, *Reckoning*, 3.

3   Scott, *Against the Grain*, 145–46.

4   Soll, *Reckoning*, 15–28.

5   Mitra-Khan, "Redefining the Economy," 70–96.

6   Deringer, *Calculated Values*, 115–52.

7   Karabell, *Leading Indicators*, 16.

8   Patriarca, *Numbers and Nationhood*; Schor, *Counting Americans*.

9   Tooze, *Statistics and the German State*, 5.

10   Studenski, *Income of Nations*, 26–141.

11   Cook, *Pricing of Progress*, 5–7.

12   Cullather, "Foreign Policy of the Calorie."

13   Karabell, *Leading Indicators*, 14.

14   Menand, *Metaphysical Club*, 182.

15   Porter, *Rise of Statistical Thinking*, 6. See also Menand, *Metaphysical Club*, 181–95.

16   Scott, *Seeing Like a State*.

17   Keasbey, "Economic State"; Tooze, "Imagining National Economies," 216–18.

18   Mitra-Kahn, "Redefining the Economy," 154.

19   Jonsson, "Origins of Cornucopianism," 153–64.

20   Tooze, *Statistics and the German State*, 42.

21   Giffen, "Importance of General Statistical Ideas," 445.

22   Shenk, "Inventing the American Economy," 77–78.

23   See, for instance, Moses, "Economic Situation in Japan."

24   Tooze, *Statistics and the German State*, 40–75.

25   Statistics from Chandler, *Scale and Scope*, 4–7. On the global dimensions of the industrial revolution, see Bayly, *Birth of the Modern World*, 170–98.

26   Quoted in Martin Bulmer, Kevin Bales, and Kathryn Kish Sklar, "The Social Survey in Historical Perspective," in Bulmer, Bales, and Sklar, *Social Survey in Historical Perspective*, 15.

27   Cook, *Pricing of Progress*, 100–127.

28   Karabell, *Leading Indicators*, 25–32.

29   O'Connor, *Poverty Knowledge*, 27–28.

30   Kemp, *Housing Conditions in Baltimore*, 11.

31   John Modell, "Patterns of Consumption, Acculturation, and Family Income

Strategies in Late Nineteenth Century America," in Hareven and Vinovskis, *Family and Population in Nineteenth Century America*, 207. There were many subsequent studies of family consumption habits and standard of living. See F. Williams and Zimmerman, *Studies of Family Living in the United States and Other Countries*.

32 O'Connor, *Poverty Knowledge*, 27, 32–33.

33 Karabell, *Leading Indicators*, 30; Stapleford, "Defining a 'Living Wage' in America."

34 Stapleford, *Cost of Living in America*, 59–140.

35 Rauchway, "High Cost of Living in the Progressives' Economy," 900.

36 Cook, *Pricing of Progress*, 275.

37 The notion of an "average" worker was a statistical abstraction, too. See Igo, *Averaged American*.

38 Levy, *Freaks of Fortune*; Bouk, *How Our Days Became Numbered*.

39 Dodge, "Standard of Living in the United States," 131.

40 T. J. Riley, review of *The Standard of Living in New York City*, by Robert Coit Chapin.

41 Leo Wolman, "Consumption and the Standard of Living," in *Recent Economic Changes in the United States*, 13.

42 On labor in the United States during this period, see McCartin, *Labor's Great War*. On class conflict and social strife in this period in Europe, see Maier, *Recasting Bourgeois Europe*, 19–87; Wrigley, *Challenges of Labour*.

43 Quoted in International Labour Office, *Workers Standard of Life in Countries with Depreciated Currency*, ix.

44 "Note on an Interview between Sir Percival Perry and Mr. L. Urwick," September 26, 1929, Series T, file number 101/0/1, International Labour Organization (ILO) Archives, Geneva, Switzerland; see also "Enquiry for the Ford Motor Co. into Relative Cost of Living in Certain European Cities. Preliminary Plan," Series T, file number 101/0/1, ILO Archives. De Grazia, *Irresistible Empire*, 79–81.

45 Clavin, *Securing the World Economy*, 173–74.

46 See, for instance, "Cost of Living Index Numbers" Series T, file number 102/0, ILO Archives; "Summary of an Official Enquiry on Working and Living Conditions and on the Situation of Industry in China," Series T, file number 101/1/13/1, ILO Archives; "Labour Statistics," Series T, file number 102/0, ILO Archives.

47 Coffin, "'Standard' of Living?," 6–7.

48 De Grazia, *Irresistible Empire*, 76–77, 92–93.

49 "Discussion with Mr. Filene at Amsterdam," 4, Series T, file number 101/0/1, ILO Archives.

50 A. W. Flux to R. Meeker, February 15, 1921, Series T, file number 101/25, ILO Archives.

51 Dodge, "Standard of Living in the United States," 133.

52 Hexter, "Implications of a Standard of Living," 222.

53 Coffin, "'Standard' of Living?," 9–16.

54 Tobin, "Studying Society."

55 Mitra-Khan, "Redefining the Economy," 203–5.

56 Fisher quoted in D. Hirschman, "Inventing the Economy," 49.

57 Boumans, *How Economists Model the World into Numbers*, 21–50.

58 Tooze, *Statistics and the German State*, 5–6, 65–66; Bernstein, *Perilous Progress*, 48–52.

59 Mitchell quoted in D. Hirschman, "Inventing the Economy," 44.

60 Tooze, *Statistics and the German State*, 9.

61 On the NBER and its role in the history of national income accounting and economic measurement, see Shenk, "Inventing the American Economy," 35–82.

62 Quoted in Cook, *Pricing of Progress*, 259.

63 D. Hirschman, "Inventing the Economy," 74.

64 Cook, *Pricing of Progress*, 261.

65 Andrew Abbott and James T. Sparrow, "Hot War, Cold War: The Structures of Sociological Action, 1940–1955," in Calhoun, *Sociology in America*," 537–65.

66 Karabell, *Leading Indicators*, 56–57.

67 Coyle, *GDP*, 12–14.

68 League of Nations, "Provisional Minutes of the Fourteenth Plenary Meeting," December 14, 1928, 6, Cotes des Series 180, International Statistical Conference, Geneva, 1928, Cotes des Cartons 2703, folder "Conference de Statistique, 1928," League of Nations Archives, Geneva, Switzerland; League of Nations Economic Committee, "International Conference of Economic Statistics: Introductory Observations," June 23, 1928, Cotes des Series 3911, International Statistical Conference, Geneva, 1928, Cotes des Cartons 2703, folder "Project de Convention Statistique," League of Nations Archives.

69 Clavin, *Securing the World Economy*, 34–39.

70 Clavin, *Securing the World Economy*, 174.

71 On this global context for the New Deal, see Patel, *New Deal*.

72 Statement by Henry Morgenthau Jr., September 25, 1936, https://www.loc
   .gov/law/help/us-treaties/bevans/m-ust000003-0277.pdf.

73 Clavin, *Securing the World Economy*, 174.

74 Patricia Clavin, "What's in a Living Standard? Bringing Society and Economy Together in the ILO and the League of Nations Depression Delegation,
   1938–1945," in Kott and Droux, *Globalizing Social Rights*, 240.

75 "Notes concerning Report on Measures to Improve Standard of Living,"
   1937, Series EP, file number 200/01, ILO Archives.

76 "Note by the Secretariat," August 30, 1939, Series EP, file number 200/01/1,
   ILO Archives.

77 Albert Thomas, "Preface," in International Labour Office, *International
   Labour Organisation*, 12.

78 Noel Hall, "Preliminary Investigation into Measures of a National or International Character for Raising the Standard of Living," May 21, 1938, Cotes
   des Series 1227, "Unification of Methods in Economic Statistics: General,"
   Cotes des Cartons 2694, folder "Enquete sur le niveau de vie," League of
   Nations Archives.

79 "Report of the Meeting of the League Economic Committee," Series EP, file
   number 200/01/1, ILO Archives.

80 "Third Meeting, Sub-committee on the Standard of Living," December 2,
   1938, Cotes des Cartons 2694, folder "Sous-Comite pour l'etude des niveaux
   de vie," League of Nations Archives, Geneva, Switzerland. See also Clavin,
   Securing the World Economy, 177–78.

81 Hall, *Preliminary Investigation into Measures of a National or International Character*, 10.

82 "Economic Committee: Study of the Best Means of Increasing the Standard
   of Living," May 31, 1939, Cotes des Series 1227, "Unification of Methods in
   Economic Statistics: General," Cotes des Cartons 2694, folder "Enquete sur
   le niveau de vie," League of Nations Archives.

83 Hall, *Preliminary Investigation into Measures of a National or International Character*, 16, 26.

84 "Note by the Secretariat: National and International Measures to be
   Employed for Raising the Standard of Living," November 30, 1937, Cotes
   des Series 1227, "Unification of Methods in Economic Statistics: General,"
   Cotes des Cartons 2694, folder "Enquete sur le niveau de vie," League of
   Nations Archives.

85 International Labour Office, *Worker's Standard of Living*, 98.

86 "Note by the Secretariat," August 30, 1939, Series EP, file number 200/01/1, ILO Archives.

87 International Labour Office, *Economic Stability in the Post-war World, Part II*, 20, 22.

88 By the release of Hall's 1938 report, some in the ILO wondered whether "income per head" was preferable to standard-of-living statistics because of its simplicity. "Notes concerning Report on Measures to Improve Standards of Living," Series T, file number 200/01, ILO Archives. In 1946, Simon Kuznets produced time-series estimates for US income per capita back to the Civil War. Over the next two decades, historical reconstructions of income per capita became the basis for a debate among economists about whether industrialization improved "living standards" using GNP per capita as the benchmark. See Pope, "Changing View of the Standard-of-Living Question in the United States." A debate emerged over how to reconstruct historical metrics of standard of living and which metrics should be the basis for time-series comparisons. See Hobsbawm, "Standard of Living during the Industrial Revolution."

89 Milward, *War, Economy, and Society, 1939–1945*, 60–98.

90 Bernstein, *Perilous Progress*, 78. On the debates between Keynes, Richard Stone, Colin Clark, and others that gave rise to this particular formula by 1940s, see Mitra-Kahn, "Redefining the Economy," 213–16.

91 D. Hirschman, "Inventing the Economy," 82–84.

92 Tooze, "Imagining National Economies," 222.

93 Coyle, *GDP*, 17–18.

94 Richard Stone to Colin Clark, January 23, 1942, envelope 3/1/25, John Richard Nicholas Stone Papers, King's College Archive, Cambridge University.

95 E. Barnett, *Keynesian Arithmetic in War-Time Canada*.

96 Simon Kuznets to Joseph H. Willetts, October 7, 1940, Rockefeller Foundation records, administration, program and policy, RG 3, Subgroup 1: Administration, Program and Policy; Series 910: Social Sciences, FA112, box 10, folder 86, Program and Policy—National Income and Wealth, Rockefeller Archive Center (RAC), Tarrytown, NY.

97 Simon Kuznets to Joseph H. Willetts, October 7, 1940, Rockefeller Foundation records, administration, program and policy, RG 3, Subgroup 1: Administration, Program and Policy; Series 910: Social Sciences, FA112, box 10, folder 86, Program and Policy—National Income and Wealth, RAC.

98 Interview with Dr. Simon Kuznets, January 15, 1943, Rockefeller Foundation records, projects, RG 1.1, Series 200: United States; Subseries 200.S: United States—Social Sciences, FA386, box 385, folder 4548 New York University—National Income Comparisons, RAC.

99 On postwar conditions, see Leffler, *For the Soul of Mankind*, 57–62; Judt, *Postwar*, 13–40.

100 Mitchell, "Economentality," 491–92.

101 Duncan and Shelton, *Revolution in United States Government Statistics*, 84. GNP was the total market value of goods and services produced in a territory within a year. It did not include estimates of capital consumption (depreciation), which a rival metric, net national product, did. National income measured total income received. Both rely on the similar definition of the economy as a flow of money; they measure the monetary value at different points in the system. For a full recounting of different debates over calculating GNP, see Carson, "History of the United States Income and Product Accounts," 142–88.

102 Duncan and Shelton, *Revolution in United States Government Statistics*, 86–92.

103 On full employment in the United States, Western Europe, and Japan, respectively, see Collins, *More*, 18–24; Arndt, *Rise and Fall of Economic Growth*, 28–31; and O'Bryan, *Growth Idea*, 109.

104 Collins, *More*, 14–39.

105 Maier, "Politics of Productivity," 618.

106 Milward, *European Rescue of the Nation State*, 41.

107 O'Bryan, *Growth Idea*, 145.

108 For a thorough overview of this process, see Schmelzer, *Hegemony of Growth*, 75–162.

109 Collins, *More*, 14–39.

110 Caldwell, *NSC 68*, 34.

111 Sargent, *Superpower Transformed*, 18.

112 Sargent, "Cold War and the International Political Economy in the 1970s," 397.

113 International Labour Office, *Economic Stability in the Post-war World*, Part II, 20.

114 On economic internationalism in this period, see Thomas W. Zeiler, "Opening Doors in the World Economy," in Iriye, *Global Interdependence*, 210–22.

115 Spulber, *Foundations of Soviet Strategy for Economic Growth*; Michalis Hatziprokopiou and Kostas Valentzas, "Preobrazhensky and the Theory of

Economic Development," in Psalidopoulos, *Canon in the History of Economics*, 180–95; V. Barnett, *History of Russian Economic Thought*; S. Johnson and Temin, "Macroeconomics of NEP."

116   Herrera, *Mirrors of the Economy*, 26.

117   Spulber, *Foundations of Soviet Strategy for Economic Growth*; Engerman, "Price of Success."

118   Engerman, "Bernath Lecture," 620–21.

119   Joseph Stalin, speech before voters of the Stalin Electoral District, Moscow, February 9, 1946, from the Pamphlet Collection, J. Stalin, *Speeches Delivered at Meetings of Voters of the Stalin Electoral District, Moscow* (Moscow: Foreign Languages Publishing House, 1950).

120   Leffler, *For the Soul of Mankind*, 50–52.

121   Quoted in Leffler, *For the Soul of Mankind*, 83. See also Latham, *Right Kind of Revolution*, 36–64; Unger, *International Development*, 79–102; Cullather, "Third Race," 510–12; Schmelzer, *Hegemony of Growth*, 153–66.

122   By the release of Noel Hall's 1938 report, some in the ILO wondered whether "income per head" was preferable to standard-of-living statistics because of its simplicity. "Notes concerning Report on Measures to Improve Standards of Living," Series T, file number 200/01, ILO Archives.

123   "Memorandum on Setting up of a Social Science Research Committee on a Study of Economic Growth," December 8, 1948, p. 1, folder 798, box 144, FA021, Series 1, Subseries 19, Social Science Research Council Records, RAC.

124   Colin Clark, "Economic Life in the Twentieth Century," *Measure* 1, no. 4 (1950): 330–32, box 21B, Colin Clark Collection, Fryer Memorial Library, University of Queensland, St. Lucia, Australia.

Chapter 2

1   Austin Robinson, "Foreword," in Deane, *Measurement of Colonial National Incomes*, x.

2   For recent scholarship on the history of international development within imperial governance, see, for instance, Unger, *International Development*, 23–78; Cyrus Schayegh, "Imperial and Transnational Developmentalisms: Middle Eastern Interplays, 1880s–1960s," in Macekura and Manela, *Development Century*, 61–82; Tilley, *Africa as a Living Laboratory*; C. Riley, "Monstrous Predatory Vampires"; Moon, *Technology and Ethical Idealism*; Hodge, *Triumph of the Expert*; van Beusekom, *Negotiating Development*;

Zachariah, *Developing India*. On debates in African colonial demography and quantification more broadly, see Ittmann, Cordell, and Maddox, *Demographics of Empire*.

3   Historians have challenged the widely held notion that postcolonial independence necessarily meant a world of nation-states. See Cooper, *Citizenship between Empire and Nation*. Yet the desire for territorial state building was strong especially among US officials, who believed the postwar order was ideally one of sovereign nation-states constrained by mutually accepted rules and institutions. See Irwin, "Some Parts Sooner, Some Later, and Finally All"; Mazower, *Governing the World*, 273–304; Charles S. Maier, "Leviathan 2.0: Inventing Modern Statehood," in Rosenberg, *World Connecting*, 272–82.

4   Many studies of the history of national accounting and economic growth note that GNP achieved "world domination" as the dominant way to define national economies, as Dirk Philipsen notes. See Philipsen, *Little Big Number*, 117–42. Yet few studies examine in depth how countries around the world came to adopt such metrics and the struggles involved. On this process, see Speich, "Travelling with the GDP through Early Development Economics' History"; Speich Chassé, "Use of Global Abstractions"; Young, *Transforming Sudan*.

5   Hodge, *Triumph of the Expert*, 26–29.

6   Ekbladh, *Great American Mission*, 14–29; Rist, *History of Development*, 47–58; McVety, *Enlightened Aid*, 36–37.

7   Westad, *Global Cold War*, 8–38; Kramer, *Blood of Government*.

8   Hodge, *Triumph of the Expert*, 42–43.

9   Rist, *History of Development*, 51–55.

10 On development projects, see Macekura, "Point Four Program and International Development Policy"; Rivas, *Missionary Capitalist*. On banking, see Hudson, *Bankers and Empire*.

11 Hodge, *Triumph of the Expert*, 8.

12 S. L. Rao, *Partial Memoirs of V. K. R. V. Rao*, 10.

13 *Economic Survey of the Colonial Empire*. On the role of international organizations in collecting and disseminating quantitative data during this period, especially on issues pertaining to rural spaces, see Forclaz, "Agriculture, American Expertise, and the Quest for Global Data."

14 Davie, *Poverty Knowledge in South Africa*, 103–41.

15 Tilley, *Africa as a Living Laboratory*, 328–29.

16 Hodge, *Triumph of the Expert*, 180. Guidance implied planning. The notion

of national planning was common throughout the midcentury world. Planning required a clear and coherent metric on which to base future growth targets, and thus national income and product statistics emerged as a core way for policy makers to envision the aggregate economy and chart its future evolution. For an overview of planning, see David Engerman, "The Rise and Fall of Central Planning" in Geyer and Tooze, *Cambridge History of World War II*, 3:575–98.

17   National Institute of Economic and Social Research, Annual Report, 1942, 6, National Institute of Economic and Social Research (NIESR) Library and Archives, London, United Kingdom.

18   Deane, *Measurement of Colonial National Incomes*, 2.

19   "The Problem of Raising the Standard of Living in the British Colonial Empire," 1942, 7, CO 852/503/17, National Archives of the United Kingdom (NA-UK), Kew, Richmond, United Kingdom.

20   Austin Robinson to Feodora Leontinoff, September 13, 1941, Minutes of the Meetings of the Executive Committee of the National Institute of Economic and Social Research, 1941–46, NIESR Library and Archives.

21   The National Institute of Economic and Social Research, Annual Report, 1942, 6, NIESR Library and Archives.

22   Messac, "Outside the Economy," 558–60.

23   Gann, *History of Northern Rhodesia*, 209–12.

24   Phyllis Deane, "The Construction of National Income Tables for Colonial Territories," paper draft, August 1944, 6, CO 852/554/2, NA-UK.

25   Deane, "Measuring National Income in Colonial Territories."

26   Deane, "Construction of National Income Tables for Colonial Territories," 2.

27   Deane, "Construction of National Income Tables for Colonial Territories," 9.

28   Colonial Economic Advisory Committee, Research Sub-committee, Meeting Minutes, January 22, 1945, CO 852/554/2, NA-UK.

29   Deane, "Construction of National Income Tables for Colonial Territories," 2.

30   Phyllis Deane, "National Income: Problems of Social Accounting in Central Africa," manuscript draft, November 1945, 26–27, CO 853/554/4, NA-UK.

31   National Institute of Economic and Social Research, Annual Report, 1943, 13, NIESR Library and Archives.

32   Deane, *Measurement of Colonial National Incomes*, 5.

33   Deane, *Measurement of Colonial National Incomes*, 149.

34   Deane, "Measuring National Income in Colonial Territories," 168.

35   Deane, "Measuring National Income in Colonial Territories," 154.

36   Deane, *Colonial Social Accounting*, 120.

37 Deane, "National Income," 28–29.

38 W. Jones, "Colonial Social Accounting," 673.

39 Clark, "Review," 80.

40 Austin Robinson to Feodora Leontinoff, September 13, 1941, Minutes of the Meetings of the Executive Committee of the National Institute of Economic and Social Research, 1941–46, NIESR Library and Archives.

41 Studenski, *Income of Nations*, 443–45.

42 Richard Stone to Joseph Willits, June 19, 1946, envelope 5/1, John Richard Nicholas Stone Papers, King's College Archive, Cambridge University, Cambridge, United Kingdom; Richard Stone, "Some Notes on the Work and Organization of a Department of Applied Economics," envelope 4/10, Stone Papers; Prest and Stewart, *National Income of Nigeria*.

43 Benham, "Estimation of National Product, 7–8.

44 Prest and Stewart, *National Income of Nigeria*, 5.

45 Okigbo, *Nigerian National Accounts, 1950–57*, 41.

46 Seers and Ross, *Report on the Financial and Physical Problems of Development in the Gold Coast*, 175. On Seers's life, see Lehmann, "Dudley Seers (1920–1983)"; Paul Streeten, "Dudley Seers (1920–1983): A Personal Appreciation," *IDS Bulletin* 20, no. 3 (1989): 26–30.

47 Seers, "Role of National Income Estimates," 161–62, 168.

48 Frankel, *Capital Investment in Africa*.

49 S. H. Frankel to Secretary, Social and Economic Planning Council, May 16, 1944, box 10, S. Herbert Frankel Papers, Hoover Institution Library and Archives, Stanford, CA; S. H. Frankel, "National Income—Calculation of the Union of South Africa," box 11, Frankel Papers.

50 Frankel, review of *The Measurement of Colonial National Incomes*, by Phyllis Deane, 594.

51 S. H. Frankel, "National Income Calculation of the Union of South Africa," 3, box 9, Frankel Papers.

52 S. H. Frankel, "National Income and Net Investment in Calendar Years," 3, box 8, Frankel Papers.

53 Frankel, *Economic Impact of Under-developed Societies*, 34–35.

54 Frankel, "United Nations Primer for Development," 314.

55 Slobodian, *Globalists*, 86. For a fuller elaboration on Hayek and the Geneva school of neoliberals' distrust of numbers, see Slobodian, *Globalists*, 55–90.

56 Booker, review of *The Measurement of Colonial National Incomes*, by Phyllis Deane, 320.

57 Rosenstein-Rodan, "Problems of Industrialization of Eastern and South-

eastern Europe"; Paul Rosenstein-Rodan interview transcript, August 14, 1961, World Bank Oral History Program, 2–4, http://documents.worldbank .org/curated/en/540171468320949901/pdf/931650TSCP0Box0transcript t00PUBLIC0.pdf.

58 Dosman, *Life and Times of Raúl Prebisch*, 242–45.

59 Lewis, *Theory of Economic Growth*. Lewis emphasized persistent under-employment in agriculture and argued that rural productivity was low, capital rare, and labor supplies vast in "underdeveloped areas"—a "dual economy" wracked by a traditional, poverty-stricken agrarian "sector" and a nascent, capitalistic, urbanizing productive one. Lewis argued that 10–15 percent of national income should be directed to "productive" investments. This dualistic modeling—which divided the economy into sectors by space, time, and/or type—became the foundational assumption behind growth theories that promised to take lagging sectors and transform them into production-oriented powerhouses through targeted interventions of external capital, knowledge, and careful planning by technocratic elites.

60 Sackley, "Passage to Modernity," 233. See also *Measures for the Economic Development of Under-developed Countries*; Lewis, *Theory of Economic Growth*; Toye and Toye, "Origins and Interpretation of the Prebisch-Singer Thesis."

61 H. W. Singer, "Poverty, Income Distribution, and Levels of Living: Thirty Years of Changing Thoughts on Development Problems," in C. H. H. Rao and Joshi, *Reflection on Economic Development and Social Change*, 31.

62 W. W. Rostow, *Stages of Economic Growth*. See also Gilman, *Mandarins of the Future*, 155–202; Latham, *Right Kind of Revolution*, 51–64; Pearce, *Rostow, Kennedy, and the Rhetoric of Foreign Aid*.

63 Malcolm Hailey to Sydney Caine, February 15, 1946, CO 853/554/4, NA-UK.

64 Engerman, "Bernath Lecture," 619.

65 Tom Mboya, "African Socialism and Its Application to Planning in Kenya," in Mboya, *Challenge of Nationhood*, 103.

66 Young, *Transforming Sudan*, 16.

67 Simpson, "Indonesia's 'Accelerated Modernization,'" 477.

68 Speich, "Travelling with the GDP through Early Development Economics' History," 32.

69 On the ideology animating Point Four, see Macekura, "Point Four Program and International Development Policy"; McVety, *Enlightened Aid*, 83–120; Ekbladh, *Great American Mission*, 77–113.

70 Staples, *Birth of Development*; Helleiner, "Development Mandate of International Institutions."

71 "Estimates of Per Capita Income for Near Eastern Nations," box S-0938-0001, folder 3, "Committee on Contributions," United Nations Archives, New York City, NY; "Suggestions for Method by J. B. Brigden, September 1946," box S-0938-0001, folder 4, "Committee on Contributions," UN Archives.

72 Kapur, Lewis, and Webb, *World Bank*, 1:97; Alacevich, "World Bank and the Politics of Productivity."

73 Duncan and Shelton, *Revolution in United States Government Statistics*, 222–23; Studenski, *Income of Nations*, 497; *Fields of Economic Development Handicapped by Lack of Trained Personnel in Certain Countries of Asia and the Far East* (Bangkok: United Nations, 1951), 97.

74 Herrera, *Mirrors of the Economy*, 71.

75 *Measurement of National Income and the Construction of National Accounts*; *System of National Accounts and Supporting Tables*.

76 *System of National Accounts and Supporting Tables*, 5; Deaton, "John Richard Nicholas Stone."

77 Messac, "Outside the Economy," 572n58.

78 UN General Assembly Resolution 527 (VI), January 26, 1952.

79 The UN's Economic and Social Council convened a working group of experts from the ILO, World Health Organization, UNESCO, and Food and Agricultural Organization in the summer of 1953 with a wide range of experts from around the world: anthropologists, agronomist, sociologists. Chaired by V. K. R. V. Rao, the group issued a report challenging the growing emphasis on national product accounts. *Report on International Definition and Measurement of Standards and Levels of Living*, 5.

80 International Bank for Reconstruction and Development, *Basis of a Development Program for Colombia*, 2.

81 Seers, "Role of National Income Estimates," 168.

82 Speich Chassé, "Use of Global Abstractions," 19.

83 "Notes from April 1962 Data Collection," Ghana Central Bureau of Statistics Files, box 6, Hoover Institution Library and Archives.

84 Mitchell, *Rule of Experts*, 113.

85 Peacock and Dosser, *National Income of Tanganyika*, 12.

86 Jerven, "Users and Producers of African Income," 178–79.

87 V. K. R. V. Rao, "Some Reflections," 178.

88   Oshima, "National Income Statistics," 171.

89   L. Cohen, *Consumer's Republic.*

90   Collins, *More*, 40–97; Cebul, *Illusions of Progress*; Lichtenstein, *State of the Union*, 98–177.

91   Petersen, Glennon, Mabon, Goodwin, and Slany, *Foreign Relations of the United States*, vol. 1, document 85.

92   Rose and Petersen, *Foreign Relations of the United States*, vol. 2, document 101.

93   Milward, *European Rescue of the Nation-State*, 30.

94   Judt, *Postwar*, 325.

95   Oshima, "Reinterpreting Japan's Postwar Growth"; Westad, *Cold War*, 395.

96   Hook, *Rebuilding Germany*; Flora, *Growth to Limits*; Anderson, *Welfare Policy and Politics in Japan*; Nolan, *Transatlantic Century*, 198–201; Mazower, *Dark Continent*, 298–302; Judt, *Postwar*, 72–76.

97   Furukawa, *Social Welfare in Japan*; Gould, *Capitalist Welfare Systems.*

98   C. Howard, *Hidden Welfare State*; Mettler, *Submerged State*; Kessler-Harris, *In Pursuit of Equity*, 150–61; Katznelson, *When Affirmative Action Was White.*

99   Esping-Andersen, *Three Worlds of Welfare Capitalism.*

100 Frieden, *Global Capitalism*, 297.

101 Melvyn P. Leffler, "Victory: The "State," the "West," and the Cold War," in Lundestad, *International Relations since the End of the Cold War*, 80–90; Berkowitz and McQuaid, "Welfare Reform in the 1950s," 47–49; Patterson, *America's Struggle against Poverty in the Twentieth Century*, 77–91.

102 Schmelzer, *Hegemony of Growth*, 137–38.

103 Milward, *European Rescue of the Nation-State*, 31, 41–43.

104 For an overview of US foreign economic policy and the evolution of the global economy during this period, see Zeiler, "Opening Doors in the World Economy," 203–84.

105 Schmelzer, *Hegemony of Growth*, 121.

106 "Memorandum of conversation of Mao Zedong with Six Delegates of the Socialist Countries," October 2, 1958, Woodrow Wilson International Center for Scholars Digital Archive, https://digitalarchive.wilsoncenter.org/document/116826. For a general overview of Mao's development strategy during the 1950s and early 1960s in the context of the Cold War, see Westad, *Cold War*, 233–50.

107 On Chinese state building and statistics, see A. Ghosh, "Making It Count."

108 Feygin, "Reforming the Cold War State," 3.

109 Khrushchev Memorandum to the CC CPSU Presidium, December 8, 1959, Woodrow Wilson International Center for Scholars Digital Archive, http://digitalarchive.wilsoncenter.org/document/117083.

110 Fioramonti, *Gross Domestic Problem*, 35.

111 Discussing the factors and sources of growth even provided a shared language with which Soviet diplomats could engage with foreign leaders in capitalist countries such as Japan. Sanchez-Sibony, "Economic Growth in the Governance of the Cold War Divide," 143.

112 Philip E. Mosely, "Conversation with Arthur F. Burns regarding proposed study of Soviet National Income," Rockefeller Foundation Records, projects, RG 1.2 Series 200, United States—Social Sciences, FA387, box 538, folder 4600, NBER—Soviet Economic Growth, RAC.

113 The socialist calculation debate concerned how to measure and define value in socialist economies that related to how well statistics could express socialist economic performance. Friedrich Hayek and some of his acolytes argued that prices, following laws of supply and demand, allowed for efficient decision making as producers and consumers could read the prices as information then act in their rational interest. By contrast, the absence of markets as information-processing venues in command economies meant that socialist economies could not achieve efficiency. Socialist economists such as Oskar Lange retorted that socialist economies could achieve such efficiencies by mimicking the price system in various ways. The debate raged for decades. It stemmed from the root quandary of expressing communist national economic accounts in familiar Western terms. See, for instance, Cottrell and Cockshott, "Calculation, Complexity and Planning."

114 G. Warren Nutter, Israel Borenstein, Adam Kaufman, "Introduction," in Nutter, *Growth of Industrial Production in the Soviet Union*, 11–12. The most advanced and sophisticated analysis of Soviet statistics at the time was Grossman, *Soviet Statistics of Physical Output of Industrial Commodities*.

115 "US versus Soviet Spending for Major GNP Categories," *Intelligence Information Brief No. 87*, February 24, 1959, RG 56, entry UD-UP 734-H, box 85, National Archives and Records Administration II (NARA II), College Park, MD.

116 Macekura, "Point Four Program and International Development Policy," 153–60.

117 John F. Kennedy: "Letter to the President of the Senate and to the Speaker of the House Transmitting Bill Implementing the Message on Foreign Aid," May 26, 1961, online by Gerhard Peters and John T. Woolley, *The*

American Presidency Project, http://www.presidency.ucsb.edu/ws/?pid=8153.

118 Walter Heller, "Economic Growth: Challenge and Opportunity," May 18, 1961, "OECD/5/30 EPC Working Party #2, Economic Growth, Vol. 1," box 3, entry UD-UP 734-H, RG 56, NARA II.

119 Iandolo, "Rise and Fall of the 'Soviet Model of Development' in West Africa," 692.

120 Westad, *Cold War*, 248–49.

121 "The Economic Relations between the O.E.C.D. and the Developing Countries," June 20, 1963, "OECD/4/10 Council Documents, Vol. 2," box 2, entry UD-UP 734-H, RG 56, NARA II.

122 Domar, *Essays in the Theory of Economic Growth*, 18.

123 Wiles, "Growth versus Choice," 244.

124 Boianovsky and Hoover, "In the Kingdom of Solovia," 201–2; Colin Clark, "Growthmanship: A Study in the Mythology of Investment," Hobart paper no. 10 (Institute for Economic Affairs, 1961), 15–16.

125 Phelps, "Golden Rule of Accumulation, 638; Solow quoted in Robert M. Solow, "United States Economic Growth," in Gutmann, *Economic Growth*, 102.

126 Brick, *Transcending Capitalism*, 168.

127 Sackley, "Passage to Modernity," 256; Engerman, *Price of Aid*, 2, 89–116.

128 Tignor, *W. Arthur Lewis and the Birth of Development Economics*, 109–211.

129 Masood, *Great Invention*, 43.

Chapter 3

1 Packard, *Waste Makers*, 25.

2 Ellul, *Technological Society*, 158. The English translation of his book appeared in 1964. The original version, written in French, first appeared in 1954.

3 Marcuse, *One-Dimensional Man*, ix.

4 Mahbub ul Haq, "System Is to Blame for the 22 Wealthy Families," *Times* (London), March 22, 1973

5 Seers, "What Are We Trying to Measure?," 21.

6 Robertson, *Malthusian Moment*, 36–60.

7 Leopold, *Sand County Almanac: With Essays on Conservation from Round River*, 237–64.

8 Macekura, *Of Limits and Growth*, 17–53.

9   Macekura, *Of Limits and Growth*, 54–90.

10 Jundt, "Dueling Visions for the Postwar World," 46–52.

11 Robertson, *Malthusian Moment*, 36–60.

12 Kenneth E. Boulding, "The Economics of the Coming Spaceship Earth," in Jarrett, *Environmental Quality*, 7–10.

13 Hardin, "Tragedy of the Commons," 1243.

14 Macekura, *Of Limits and Growth*, 137–71.

15 Ehrlich, *Population Bomb*.

16 Schmelzer, *Hegemony of Growth*, 250.

17 Donella Meadows et al., *Limits to Growth*, 23. See also Sabin, *Bet*, 84–87.

18 For a sample of the tenor of the debate around the book, see Peter Passell, Marc Roberts, and Leonard Ross in the April 1972 "Limits to Growth," *New York Times*, April 2, 1972, 1. On the international reception and debate over the report, see Schoijet, "Limits to Growth and the Rise of Catastrophism," 520–21.

19 Grove, *Green Imperialism*.

20 R. Carson, *Silent Spring*.

21 Packard, *Waste Makers*, 316.

22 Marcuse quoted in Gottlieb, *Forcing the Spring*, 133.

23 Mishan, *Costs of Economic Growth*, 7. See also Mishan, "Economics of Disamenity."

24 "Progress to Unhappiness?," *Economist*, September 2, 1967, 793.

25 Kenneth E. Boulding, "Fun Games with the Gross National Product," in Helfrich, *Environmental Crisis*, 161.

26 Ayres and Kneese, "Production, Consumption, and Externalities," 283.

27 Ellul, *Technological Society*, 427.

28 Marcuse, *One-Dimensional Man*, xiii.

29 Marcuse, *One-Dimensional Man*, 255.

30 Quoted in Brick, *Transcending Capitalism*, 184.

31 Archibald MacLeish, "We Have Purpose . . . We All Know It," in *National Purpose*, 38; Jeffries, "'Quest for National Purpose' of 1960."

32 Quoted in Collins, *More*, 62–63.

33 Baudrillard, *Consumer Society*, 41; Yarrow, *Measuring America*, 169.

34 Schmelzer, *Hegemony of Growth*, 241; Alain Desrosières, "Bourdieu et les statisiciens: Une rencontre improbable et ses deux heritages," in Encrevé and Lagrave, *Travailler avec Bourdieu*, 209–18.

35 David Riesman, "Leisure and Work in Postindustrial Society," in Riesman, *"Abundance for What?" and Other Essays*, 182.

36 Robert A. Nisbet, "Introduction: The Study of Social Problems," in Merton and Nisbet, *Contemporary Social Problems*, 11.

37 Heyck, *Age of System*, 98–99.

38 Heilbroner, *Quest for Wealth*.

39 L. Cohen, *Consumer's Republic*, 194–289; Collins, *More*, 92–97; Weems, *Desegregating the Dollar*.

40 Martin Luther King Jr., "I Have a Dream," address delivered at the March on Washington for Jobs and Freedom, August 28, 1963, https://kinginstitute .stanford.edu/king-papers/documents/i-have-dream-address-delivered -march-washington-jobs-and-freedom. See also Martin Luther King Jr., "Address at the Conclusion of the Selma to Montgomery March," March 25, 1965, https://kinginstitute.stanford.edu/king-papers/documents/address -conclusion-selma-montgomery-march; Martin Luther King Jr., "Why Jesus Called a Man a Fool," sermon delivered at Mount Pisgah Missionary Baptist Church," August 27, 1967, https://kinginstitute.stanford.edu/king -papers/documents/why-jesus-called-man-fool-sermon-delivered-mount -pisgah-missionary-baptist.

41 *Toward a Social Report*, xi.

42 Friedan, *Feminine Mystique*, 37–39.

43 Betty Friedan, "I Say: Women Are People, Too!," *Good Housekeeping*, September 1960, 59–61, https://www.goodhousekeeping.com/life/career/ advice/a18890/1960-betty-friedan-article/, emphasis in original. On breadwinner liberalism, see Self, *All in the Family*, 17–46.

44 Boyle, *Tyranny of Numbers*, 179–80.

45 Robert F. Kennedy, speech at the University of Kansas, March 18, 1968, https://www.jfklibrary.org/Research/Research-Aids/Ready-Reference/ RFK-Speeches/Remarks-of-Robert-F-Kennedy-at-the-University-of -Kansas-March-18-1968.aspx.

46 Suri, *Power and Protest*, 164–94.

47 Wheatland, *Frankfurt School in Exile*, 301. As Quinn Slobodian has shown, West German students forged close connections with many Third World students as part of process in which young West German leftists identified with Third World revolutionary movements and struggles during the upheavals at home during the late 1960s. Slobodian, *Foreign Front*.

48 Schmelzer, *Hegemony of Growth*, 243; Morris-Suzuki, *History of Japanese Economic Thought*, 137–38.

49 Suri, *Power and Protest*, 212.

50 Michael Southern, "Uneasiness Underlies the Affluence," *Financial Times*, September 1, 1970, 11.

51 Dahrendorf quoted in Macekura, "Limits of Global Community," 495–98.

52 Caroline Bird, "The GNP: A Beast to Be Bridled?," *Think* 36, no. 3 (1970): 2, viewed in folder "Gross National Product and Accuracy of Statistics, 1965–1976," box 43, Oskar Morgenstern Papers, David M. Rubenstein Rare Book and Manuscript Library, Duke University.

53 Thompson, *Soviet Union under Brezhnev*, 76–80.

54 Ivanova, "Socialist Consumption and Brezhnev's Stagnation." For a longer study of Soviet economic reform attempts and the history of Soviet economic thought in the post-Brezhnev years, see Feygin, "Reforming the Cold War State."

55 K. Williams, *Prague Spring and Its Aftermath*, 25.

56 Quoted in Thompson, *Soviet Union under Brezhnev*, 141.

57 Suri, "Rise and Fall of an International Counterculture, 1960–1975," 50.

58 Zubok, *Failed Empire*, 180. On the importance of the "sixties" as a transformative period for young intellectuals in the USSR, see Dobson, "Post-Stalin Era," 918–19.

59 T. Brown, "'1968' East and West," 86.

60 Khrushchev quoted in Zubok, *Failed Empire*, 189; on East Germany, see T. Brown, "'1968' East and West," 86.

61 Teresa Bogucka, "Poland in 1968: 'The Freedom We Needed So Badly Was So Obvious Elsewhere,'" in Farik, *1968 Revisited*, 17, 19.

62 Suri, *Power and Protest*, 194–211.

63 Risch, "Soviet 'Flower Children.'"

64 Richta, *Civilization at the Crossroads*, 11–12.

65 Richta, *Civilization at the Crossroads*, 283, 85.

66 Nolan, *Transatlantic Century*, 269. On the connections and interactions between protest movements in Western and Eastern Europe, see also Klimke, Pekelder, and Scharloth, *Between Prague Spring and French May*.

67 Quoted in T. Brown, "'1968' East and West," 90.

68 Dudley Seers, "International Aid: The Next Steps," in *Problems of Foreign Aid*, 18.

69 Quoted in B. Ward, Runnalls, and D'Anjou, *Widening Gap*, 23.

70 Dudley Seers, "The Total Relationship," in Seers and Joy, *Development in a Divided World*, 340.

71 Dudley Seers, "The Meaning of Development," *Institute of Development*

Studies Communication, no. 4 (1969): 9, box 22, Dudley Seers Papers, Institute of Development Studies, Brighton, UK.

72   Hans Singer, "The New Poverty-Oriented Development Model and Its Implications," n.d., box 7, Hans Singer Papers, Institute of Development Studies, Brighton, UK.

73   Singer, "Notion of Human Investment," 4.

74   Singer, "New Poverty-Oriented Development Model and Its Implications." Singer also excavated the work of like-minded critics, such as Bert Hoselitz, who also questioned the relevance of GNP growth as a cure-all. Hans Singer, "Reflections of Sociological Aspects of Economic Growth Based on the Work of Bert Hoselitz," box 7, Singer Papers; Hoselitz, *Sociological Aspects of Economic Growth*.

75   Mkandawire, "Crisis in Economic Development Theory," 222.

76   Lewis, "Review of Economic Development," 12–16.

77   Ekbladh, *Great American Mission*, 246–48; Love, "Origins of Dependency Analysis"; B. N. Ghosh, *Dependency Theory Revisited*.

78   A. Hirschman, *Essays in Trespassing*, 21, 98–99.

79   Gilman, *Mandarins of the Future*, 203–40; Gilman, "Modernization Theory Never Dies," 144–46; Latham, *Right Kind of Revolution*, 157–67.

80   Myrdal, *Asian Drama*, 474, 18.

81   Quoted in Sen, *On Economic Inequality*, 16; Sen, *Collective Choice and Social Welfare*.

82   Rimmer, *Macromancy*, 16. Rimmer's critiques resonated with a growing number of neoclassical critiques of development economics and growth theory. See also P. Bauer, *Dissent on Development*; H. Johnson, "Word to the Third World."

83   Seers, "Birth, Life, and Death of Development Economics"; Albert O. Hirschman, "The Rise and Decline of Development Economics," in A. Hirschman, *Essays in Trespassing*, 1–24.

84   M. S. Jillani and Masooda Bano, "From 'Growth' to 'Growth with a Social Conscience': Haq as an Economic Planner in Pakistan," in K. Haq and Ponzio, *Pioneering the Human Development Revolution*, 18–23.

85   M. Haq, "System Is to Blame for the 22 Wealthy Families." For more on Haq's work, see Moyn, *Not Enough*, 127–45.

86   Mahbub ul Haq, "Employment in the 1970's: A New Perspective," May 1971, 6, "Haq, Mahbub ul—Articles and Speeches (1971–1977)," folder 1651847, Records of Office of External Affairs (WB/IBRD/IDA EXT), World Bank Group (WBG) Archives, Washington, DC.

87 "Papers and Proceedings of the Founding Conference," Institute of Development Studies, September 16–21, 1966, folder "Institute of Development Studies, 1966–1968," box S1, Gerald M. Maier Papers, David M. Rubenstein Rare Book and Manuscript Library, Duke University; *Ten Year Review and Annual Report 1976*.

88 "ILO Director-General Outlines World Employment Programme," May 16, 1969, WEP file number 1, ILO Archives; David A. Morse, "The Employment Problem in Developing Countries" in Robinson and Johnston, *Prospects for Employment Opportunities in the Nineteen Seventies*, 7–13.

89 Mahbub ul Haq, excerpt from speech, February 1972, WEP file number 159-22-3, ILO Archives.

90 "ILO to Aid National Employment Programme in Ceylon," May 19, 1970, Pioneer Project, Ceylon, 1970, Morse Cabinet Files Z 11/5/9/2, ILO Archives.

91 Richard Jolly, Dudley Seers, and Hans Singer, "The Pilot Missions under the World Employment Programme," in *Strategies for Employment Promotion*.

92 Richard Jolly, "Dudley Seers (1920–1983): His Contributions to Development Perspectives, Policy and Studies," in John Toye, ed. "Dudley Seers: His Work and Influence," *IDS Bulletin* 20, No. 3 (1989): 32–34; International Labour Office, *Employment, Incomes, and Equality*. Seers, Singer, and Jolly bolstered this research by supporting a growing volume of IDS-backed research around employment, poverty, and distributional concerns. *Ten Year Review and Annual Report 1976*, 34–55.

93 Hollis Chenery, interview transcript, January 27, 1983, World Bank Oral History Program, 5–6, https://oralhistory.worldbank.org/transcripts/transcript-oral-history-interview-hollis-b-chenery-held-january-27-1983-main-transcript; Chenery et al., *Redistribution with Growth*.

94 Nemchenok, "Dialogue of Power," 325.

95 M. Haq, "International Perspective on Basic Needs," 14.

96 Arndt, *Rise and Fall of Economic Growth*, 101.

97 Streeten et al., *First Things First*; Ghai, *Basic Needs Approach to Development*; see also Nemchenok, "Dialogue of Power," chapter 3.

98 Mahbub ul Haq, "The Crisis in Development Strategies," April 20, 1972, 4, "Haq, Mahbub ul—Articles and Speeches (1971–1977)," folder 1651847, Records of Office of External Affairs (WB/IBRD/IDA EXT), WBG Archives.

99 Nemchenok, "Dialogue of Power," 90–104; Corea quoted in M. Haq, "Crisis in Development Strategies," 95. See also Corea, "Aid and the Economy"; Corea, "Ceylon in the Sixties."

100 Clark, "Growthmanship."

101 Clark, "Growthmanship," 23. In 1963, Oskar Morgenstern published an updated version of his 1950 book on the problem of inaccuracy in economic analysis. "Statistics giving international comparisons of national incomes are among the most uncertain and unreliable statistics with which the public is being confronted." Morgenstern, *On the Accuracy of Economic Observations*, 282.

102 Clark, *Growthmanship*, 52–53.

103 Kuznets quoted in Bivar, "Kuznets, Frankenstein, and the GNP Monster."

104 Gubser, "Presentist Bias," 1803. The Kuznets essay was "Economic Growth and Income Inequality."

105 Kuznets, "Economic Growth and Income Inequality," 28.

106 Simon Kuznets, "Prize Lecture: Modern Economic Growth; Findings and Reflections," December 11, 1971, https://www.nobelprize.org/nobel_prizes/economic-sciences/laureates/1971/kuznets-lecture.html.

107 Mary S. Morgan, "Economics," in Porter and Ross, *Cambridge History of Science*, 7:294.

108 D. Rodgers, *Age of Fracture*, 63.

109 Peter Wagner, "Social Science and Social Planning during the Twentieth Century," in Porter and Ross, *Cambridge History of Science*, 7:605–6.

110 C. Jones, "The Delusion and Danger of Infinite Growth," *The New Republic*, October 1, 2019.

111 Boulding, "Economics of the Coming Spaceship Earth," 9–10.

112 Heyck, *Age of System*, 1–17.

113 Paul A. Samuelson, "Forward," in Mayumi and Gowdy, *Bioeconomics and Sustainability*, xiii.

114 Nicholas Georgescu-Roegen, "Process in Farming versus Process in Manufacturing: A Problem of Balanced Development," in Papi and Nunn, *Economic Problems of Agriculture in Industrial Societies*; Georgescu-Roegen, *Entropy Law and the Economic Process*; Gowdy and Mesner, "Evolution of Georgescu-Roegen's Bioeconomics," 147–48. On Georgescu-Roegen's intellectual trajectory and early life, see Kozo Mayumi and John M. Gowdy, "Introduction: Theory and Reality—The Life, Work and Thought of Nicholas Georgescu-Roegen," in Mayumi and Gowdy, *Bioeconomics and Sustainability*, 1–12.

115 Gowdy and Mesner, "Evolution of Georgescu-Roegen's Bioeconomics," 152.

116 Quoted in "Kenneth E. Boulding," in Oltmans, *On Growth*, 438–39. See also Boulding, "Shadow of the Stationary State."

117 Odum, *Environment, Power, and Society*.

118 Røpke, "Early History of Modern Ecological Economics," 299.

119 Merchant, *Death of Nature*.

120 Herman E. Daly, "The Stationary-State Economy: Toward a Political Economy of Biophysical Equilibrium and Moral Growth," in Daly, *Essays toward a Steady-State Economy*, 6/1–6/3.

121 Mill, *Principles of Political Economy*, 746–51; Herman E. Daly, "Introduction" in Daly, *Essays toward a Steady-State Economy*, 12–14. Daly used the phrase "stationary state" in some of his early publications before switching to "steady state." See Herman E. Daly, "Toward a Stationary-State Economy," in Harte and Socolow, *Patient Earth*, 226–44.

122 Daly, "Introduction," 20.

123 Daly, "In Defense of a Steady-State Economy," 945.

124 Daly, "Introduction," 25.

125 Daly, "Economics of the Steady State," 20.

126 Donella Meadows et al., *Limits to Growth*, 170–72.

127 Georgescu-Roegen, "Energy and Economic Myths," 368–69.

128 Kenneth E. Boulding to Nicholas Georgescu-Roegen, September 3, 1974, box 21, folder "Boulding, Kenneth," Nicholas Georgescu-Roegen Papers, David M. Rubenstein Rare Book and Manuscript Library, Duke University.

129 Herman Daly has argued that many important mainstream thinkers, such as Paul Samuelson, lauded Georgescu-Roegen's intellectual contributions, as did the "mafia" of growth economists at MIT (as Georgescu-Roegen referred to them while Samuelson and Robert Solow remained influential in the profession during the early 1970s). Herman E. Daly, "How Long Can Neoclassical Economists Ignore the Contributions of Georgescu-Roegen," in Mayumi and Gowdy, *Bioeconomics and Sustainability*, 13–16.

Chapter 4

1   Dennis Meadows, *Alternatives to Growth-I*, xviii.

2   Larry E. Ruff, "Limits to Growth '75 Conference," 3, November 19, 1975, Rockefeller Archives Center Virtual Vault, RAC.

3   Ruff, "Limits to Growth '75 Conference," 5.

4   Memo, "The Limits to Growth Conference," November 10, 1975, Central Intelligence Agency Electronic Reading Room, https://www.cia.gov/library/readingroom/docs/CIA-RDP80-00308A000100020009-7.pdf.

5   Statistics from Painter, *Oil and the American Century*, 216–17.

6   Yergin, *Prize*, 391.

7   Painter, "Oil and World Power," 167.

8   Dietrich, *Oil Revolution*, 28.

9   Painter, *Oil and the American Century*, 155.

10   Painter, *Oil and the American Century*, 156; Mitchell, "Economentality," 491–92.

11   J. R. McNeill and Peter Engelke, "Into the Anthropocene: People and Their Planet," in Iriye, *Global Interdependence*, 382–84.

12   McNeill, *Something New under the Sun*, 305.

13   Mitchell, "Economentality," 498.

14   McNeill, *Something New under the Sun*, 31.

15   One exajoule is equal to one quintillion (10^{18}) joules. Primary energy refers to energy not yet subjected to engineering processes, such as energy produced from raw fuels. Vaclav Smil, "Energy in the Twentieth Century," 23–24.

16   Eckes, *United States and the Global Struggle for Minerals*, 120–63. For an excellent analysis of the United States' global quest for resources, see Black, *Global Interior*, 117–244.

17   International Copper Study Group, *World Copper Factbook 2018*, 39.

18   World Steel Association, *World Steel in Figures 2018*, 6.

19   Jean Baptiste Fressoz and Christophe Bonneuil, "Growth Unlimited: The Idea of Infinite Growth from Fossil Capitalism to Green Capitalism," in Borowy and Schmelzer, *History of the Future of Economic Growth*, 60.

20   *World Trade Statistical Review 2017*, 100.

21   Thomas Robertson, "New Frontiers: World War II Technologies and the Opening of Tropical Environments to Development," in Macekura and Manela, *Development Century*, 107–29.

22   McCormick, *Global Environmental Movement*, 56–72.

23   Connelly, *Fatal Misconception*, 191.

24   Murphy, *Economization of Life*, 6–7.

25   Ehrlich *Population Bomb*, 170.

26   Quoted in Connelly, *Fatal Misconception*, 259.

27   Derek Hoff, "A Long Fuse," *Conversation*, July 10, 2018, https://theconversation.com/a-long-fuse-the-population-bomb-is-still-ticking-50-years-after-its-publication-96090.

28   Robertson, *Malthusian Moment*, 151.

29   Murphy, *Economization of Life*, 47–54.

30   Connelly, *Fatal Misconception*, 254–70.

31   Connelly, *Fatal Misconception*, 258–62; Matthew Connelly and Paul Ken-

nedy, "Must It Be the Rest against the West?," *Atlantic*, December 1994, https://www.theatlantic.com/past/docs/politics/immigrat/kennf.htm.

32 "Running Out of Everything . . . ," *Newsweek*, November 19, 1973, 117.

33 See, for instance, Beckerman, *In Defence of Growth*; L. Brown et al., "Are There Real Limits to Growth?"; Cole et al., *Thinking about the Future*; Dennis Meadows, *Alternatives to Growth-I.*

34 Olson and Landsberg, *No-Growth Society.*

35 "A Time of Learning to Live with Less," *Time*, December 3, 1973, 37, 38, 31, 29.

36 Norgaard, "Scarcity and Growth, 810.

37 Schmelzer, *Hegemony of Growth*, 247.

38 Sabin, *Bet*, 84–87.

39 Christian Parenti, "'The Limits to Growth': A Book That Launched a Movement," *Nation*, December 5, 2012, https://www.thenation.com/article/limits-growth-book-launched-movement/.

40 Seefried, "Towards *The Limits to Growth*?"

41 "Implications of Worldwide Population Growth for US Security and Overseas Interests," National Security Study Memorandum 200, December 10, 1974, https://decsearch.usaid.gov.

42 Andersson, *Future of the World*, 184–212.

43 "Growth Is Not a Four-Letter Word," *New York Times*, February 17, 1972, 37.

44 Simon quoted in Sabin, *Bet*, 80.

45 Kahn, Brown, and Martel, *Next 200 Years.*

46 See, for instance, Guy Streatfeild, "No Limit to the Growth Debate," *New Scientist* 57, no. 836 (March 8, 1973): 531–33; Mishan, *Economic Growth Debate.*

47 Sargent, *Superpower Transformed*, 41–130.

48 Statistics quoted in "Can Capitalism Survive?," *Time*, July 14, 1975, http://www.time.com/time/magazine/article/0,9171,917650,00.html.

49 Quoted in Schmelzer, *Hegemony of Growth*, 313.

50 Daly, "Steady-State Economics versus Growthmania," 150.

51 Daly, "In Defense of a Steady-State Economy," 952, 945.

52 Nicholas Georgescu-Roegen, "Bioeconomics: A New Look at the Nature of Economy Activity," draft manuscript, 1979, box 1, folder "Bioeconomics: A New Look at the Nature of Economy Activity, 1979," Georgescu-Roegen Papers.

53 Boulding, "Shadow of the Stationary State," 97–98.

54   Brick, *Transcending Capitalism*, 189–97; Bell, *Coming of Post-industrial Society*.

55   Brick, *Transcending Capitalism*, 199–200.

56   Meynaud, *Technocracy*.

57   Bell, *Coming of Post-industrial Society*; Winner, *Autonomous Technology*.

58   Brick, *Transcending Capitalism*, 152–218.

59   Quoted in "Ernest Mandel," in Oltmans, *On Growth*, 131–33.

60   Kidron, *Capitalism and Theory*, 19–23, 35.

61   Kidron, *Capitalism and Theory*, 85–86. The characterization of the Soviet growth obsession as evidence of "state capitalism" deviant from orthodox communism generated fierce debates among Marxist thinkers. See, for instance, M. C. Howard and King, "'State Capitalism' in the Soviet Union."

62   Baran, *Political Economy of Growth*, 37. In the early 1930s Baran studied at the Institute for Social Research in Frankfurt, where he began a lifelong friendship with Herbert Marcuse.

63   Baran and Sweezy, *Monopoly Capital*.

64   Galbraith, *Affluent Society*; Galbraith, *New Industrial State*.

65   Ellul, *Technological Society*, 154.

66   Riesman, "*Abundance for What?*," 306–7.

67   Geary, "Children of *The Lonely Crowd*," 621–22.

68   Marcuse, *The One-Dimensional Man*, 32.

69   Wheatland, *Frankfurt School in Exile*, 293.

70   Quoted in "Herbert Marcuse," in Oltmans, *On Growth*, 336–38.

71   Geary, "Children of *The Lonely Crowd*," 617–24.

72   Herbert Marcuse to Theodor Adorno, April 5, 1969, in Adorno and Marcuse, "Correspondence on the German Student Movement."

73   Quoted in "Noam Chomsky," in Oltmans, *On Growth*, 285, 290.

74   Quoted in "Aurelio Peccei," in Oltmans, *On Growth*, 479.

75   Feygin, "Reforming the Cold War State," 325–26.

76   Richta, "Scientific and Technological Revolution," 66.

77   Eglė Rindzevičiūtė, "Toward a Joint Future beyond the Iron Curtain: East-West Politics of Global Modelling," in Andersson and Rindzevičiūtė, *Struggle for the Long Term in Transnational Science and Politics*, 117–20.

78   John Noble Wilford, "Soviet Sees No Threat to Environment in Increasing Output under System," *New York Times*, March 30, 1972, 4.

79   D. Kelley, "Economic Growth and Environmental Quality in the USSR," 269.

80   Quoted in Abraham Brumberg, "Dissent in Russia," *Foreign Affairs* 52, no. 4 (July 1, 1974): 794.

81 Quoted in Thompson, *Soviet Union under Brezhnev*, 105.

82 Feygin, "Reforming the Cold War State," 324–57.

83 de Groot, "Golden Opportunity?"; de Groot, "Disruption."

84 Pearson, *Partners in Development*, 13, 17. On the broader context of World Bank policy during this period, see Sharma, *Robert McNamara's Other War*.

85 "The Columbia Declaration," in B. Ward, Runnalls, and D'Anjou, *Widening Gap*, 13. The declaration was drafted by Michael Bruno, Reginald Green, Mahbub ul Haq, Gerald K. Helleiner, Branko Horvat, Enrique Iglesias, Richard Jolly, and H. M. A. Onitri. See also Satterthwaite, *Barbara Ward*, 10–12.

86 Macekura, *Of Limits and Growth*, 91–120; Nemchenok, "Dialogue of Power," 55–56.

87 UN Document A/CONF.48/10/Annex I, "Report of a Panel of Experts Convened by the Secretary-General of the United Nations Conference on the Human Environment Held at Founex, Switzerland, 4–12 June 1971," 4, 19–20, 31; see also Nemchenok, "Dialogue of Power," 57–61. On claims of Haq's authorship, see Paul Streeten, "Foreword," in M. Haq, *Reflections on Human Development*, ix.

88 Macekura, *Of Limits and Growth*, 120–33.

89 Minutes of the Secretary of State's Staff Meeting, January 7, 1974, *FRUS, 1969–76*, vol. 35, National Security Policy, 1973–76, https://history.state.gov/historicaldocuments/frus1969–76v35/d29.

90 UN Document A/RES/S-6/3201, "Declaration on the Establishment of a New International Economic Order," May 1, 1974, http://www.un-documents.net/s6r3201.htm.

91 Charter of Economic Rights and Duties of States, Gen. Ass. Res. 3281 (XXIX), December 12, 1974, http://www.un-documents.net/a29r3281.htm.

92 Gilman, "New International Economic Order," 5–11.

93 McFarland, "New International Economic Order, 218–19, 220–28.

94 Andersson, "Future of the Western World, 143.

95 "Cocoyoc Declaration," 893, 899.

96 "Cocoyoc Declaration," 896–97.

97 Nemchenok, "Dialogue of Power," 155–59.

98 Tinbergen, *Reshaping the International Order*, 121.

99 Tinbergen, *Reshaping the International Order*, 140–87.

100 Getachew, *Worldmaking after Empire*, 145.

101 Memorandum of Conversation, May 26, 1975, *FRUS, 1969–1976*, vol. 31, Foreign Economic Policy, 1973–76, https://history.state.gov/historicaldocuments/frus1969–76v31/d294.

102 Gerald Ford, Remarks at the Conclusion of the Economic Summit Meeting at Rambouillet, France, November 17, 1975, https://www.presidency.ucsb.edu/node/257073.

103 On Carter's views of growth and their political consequences, see Collins, *More*, 156–65.

104 Artin, *Earth Talk*, 70.

105 M. Haq, "Limits to Growth," 8. Haq led a task force within the World Bank that produced a critical response to the *Limits to Growth* report. See *Report on the Limits to Growth: A Study by a Special Task Force of the World Bank*, September 1972, http://documents.worldbank.org/curated/en/313611468336648762/pdf/702220WP00Offi0owth00September01972.pdf.

106 Mahbub ul Haq, "Islamic Architecture and the Poor People of Islam," in Holod and Rastorfer, *Architecture and Community*, 41.

107 Senghor quoted in Oltmans, *On Growth II*, 107–8.

108 Quotes from Amilcar O. Herrera in Oltmans, *On Growth II*, 103, 104. The Bariloche Report appeared as *Catastrophe or New Society?* See also Andersson, "Future of the Western World," 131–32.

109 Kenneth Boulding to Al Hassler and Tom Artin, May 21, 1973, box 21, folder "Dai Dong Conference," Georgescu-Roegen Papers.

110 George Kennan, "To Prevent a World Wasteland: A Proposal," *Foreign Affairs* 48, no. 3 (April 1970): 408–11.

111 Getachew, *Worldmaking after Empire*, 154.

112 Artin, *Earth Talk*, 39.

113 Connelly, *Fatal Misconception*, chapters 8–9; Robertson, *Malthusian Moment*, 178–80.

114 Kenneth Boulding to Nicholas Georgescu-Roegen, September 3, 1974, box 21, folder "Boulding, Kenneth," Georgescu-Roegen Papers.

115 Daly, "Introduction," 10–12.

116 Singer, "New International Order," 546.

117 Mkandawire, "New International Economic Order," 77. The quote on the NIEO comes from Gilman, "New International Economic Order," 4.

118 Nemchenok, "Dialogue of Power," 129–31.

119 M. Haq, "International Perspective on Basic Needs," 13.

120 Kenneth Boulding to Al Hassler and Tom Artin, May 21, 1973, box 21, folder "Dai Dong Conference," Georgescu-Roegen Papers.

121 E. J. Mishan, "Ills, Bads, and Disamenities: The Wages of Growth," in Olson and Landsberg, *No-Growth Society*, 82.

122 Daly, "Stationary-State Economy," 170–73.

123 Nicholas Georgescu-Roegen, "The Steady State and Ecological Salvation: A Thermodynamic Analysis," 14, box 5, folder "The Steady State and Ecological Salvation," Georgescu-Roegen Papers.

124 Mishan, *Economic Growth Debate*, 12.

Chapter 5

1 Dudley Seers, "The World Context of Development," n.d., circa December 1973, box 6, Seers Papers.

2 Seers, "What Are We Trying to Measure?," 34.

3 Dudley Seers, "The Changing Definition and Measurement of Development," June 26, 1978, unpublished manuscript, box 8, Seers Papers.

4 Dudley Seers, "The Political Economy of National Accounting," in Cairncross and Puri, *Employment, Income Distribution and Development Strategy*, 196.

5 Fleury, "Drawing New Lines."

6 Jan Tinbergen, "First Progress Report," UNRISD, February 1965, United Nations Office at Geneva (UNOG) Registry Collection, Geneva, Switzerland, GX 10/2/2/77, box 1946, folder "United Nations Research Institute for Social Development." For more on UNRISD, see M. Ward, *Quantifying the World*, 144.

7 Drewnowski, *On Measuring and Planning the Quality of Life*, xi.

8 R. Bauer, *Social Indicators*.

9 Denis F. Johnston, "The Federal Effort in Developing Social Indicators and Social Reporting in the United States during the 1970s," in Bulmer, *Social Science Research and Government*, 287.

10 Solovey, "Senator Fred Harris's National Social Science Foundation Proposal," 77–78.

11 Julius Shiskin, Memorandum for Dr. Daniel P. Moynihan, Assistant to the President for Urban Affairs, September 25, 1969, folder "Garment, Leonard—1969–1970 n.d.," box I248, Daniel P. Moynihan Papers, Manuscript Division, Library of Congress; White House Press Conference transcript, July 15, 1970, folder, "Goals, National: Research 1970," box I284, Moynihan Papers; Solovey, "Senator Fred Harris's National Social Science Foundation Proposal," 77–78.

12 P. J. Loftus to Richard Stone, November 14, 1970, envelope 5/7/2, Stone Papers; "Report of the Expert Group on Welfare-Oriented Supplements to

the National Accounts and Balances and Other Measures of Levels of Living," UN Statistical Office, April 15, 1976, envelope 5/7/4, Stone Papers.

13   *1976 Progress Report on Phase II*, 11; Natalie Rogoff Ramsøy, "Social Indicators in the United States and Europe: Comments on Five Country Reports," in Van Dusen, *Social Indicators, 1973*, 41–62.

14   Rindzevičiūtė, "Struggle for the Soviet Future," 73; "Union of Soviet Socialist Republics—Standard of Living Indicators," in Economic Commission for Europe, *Approaches and Methods Used in Long-Term Social Planning and Policy-Making*, 118–28.

15   Hungarian Economic Planning Institute, "Main Tasks of the Long-Term Development of the Level of Living in Hungary in the Period 1970–1985, and a Simplified Model," in Economic Commission for Europe, *Approaches and Methods Used in Long-Term Social Planning and Policy-Making*, 105.

16   M. Ward, *Quantifying the World*, 153.

17   *Measuring Social Well-Being*, 5. UNRISD, the Russell Sage Foundation, and the World Bank also initiated similar research plans. Drewnowski, *Studies in the Measurement of Levels of Living and Welfare*; McGranahan, Richard-Proust, Sovani, and Subramanian, *Contents and Measurements of Socioeconomic Development*, 138; "Programme of Work for 1967–1968," July 1967, folder "United Nations Research Institute for Social Development," box 1946, UNOG Registry Collection, GX 10/2/2/77; Sheldon and Moore, *Indicators of Social Change*; Jain, *Size Distribution of Income*.

18   S. Chakravarty, "Guidelines for SSDS for Developing Countries," February 15, 1975, envelope 5/7/4, Stone Papers.

19   Hicks and Streeten "Indicators of Development," 570.

20   Parke and Seidman, "Social Indicators and Social Reporting," 2–3.

21   Rimmer, "'Basic Needs' and the Origins of the Development Ethos," 236.

22   See, for instance, *Quality of Life Concept*.

23   Hollie I. West, "'Quality of Life': Timely, Informative," *Washington Post*, December 30, 1974, C20.

24   Angus Campbell, "Quality of Life as a Psychological Phenomenon," in Strumpel, *Subjective Elements of Well-Being*, 11.

25   Richard D. James, "Measuring the Quality of Life," *Wall Street Journal*, May 18, 1972, 18.

26   "Defining the 'Quality of Life,'" *Guardian*, June 15, 1973, 19. See also *Measuring Social Well-Being*.

27   O'Connor, *Poverty Knowledge*, 183.

28   H. L. Watts, "The Poverty Datum Line in Three Cities and Four Towns in

South Africa in 1966," Institute for Social Research, University of Natal, Fact Paper No. 1 (1967), ii.

29 O'Connor, *Poverty Knowledge*, 184–85.

30 Sen, "Poverty"; Hicks and Streeten, "Indicators of Development," 568.

31 Hicks and Streeten, "Indicators of Development"; Nemchenok, "Dialogue of Power," 100–101.

32 Morris, *Measuring the Condition of the World's Poor*, 2.

33 Sartorius and Ruttan, "Source of the Basic Human Needs Mandate."

34 Morris, "Physical Quality of Life Index," 225.

35 Morris, *Measuring the Condition of the World's Poor*, 6.

36 "A New Index on the Quality of Life," *New York Times*, March 13, 1977, 125.

37 Dudley Seers, "Note on PQLI," n.d., unpublished manuscript, box 7, Seers Papers; Richard L. Strout, "Measuring Quality of Life—Not GNP," *Christian Science Monitor*, April 1, 1977, 35; Rimmer, review of *Measuring the Condition of the World's Poor*, by Morris David Morris.

38 Charles Yost, "A Third World Success Story," *Hartford Courant*, February 13, 1978, 14.

39 M. V. Kamath, "A New Yardstick of Progress: Limitations of Gross National Product," *Times of India*, April 1, 1977, 8.

40 J. K. Ghosh, Maiti, Rao, and Sinha, "Evolution of Statistics in India," 17–19.

41 Amartya Sen, "Poverty, Inequality and Unemployment: Some Conceptual Issues in Measurement" in Srinivasan and Bardhan, *Poverty and Income Distribution in India*, 67. On debates over poverty measurement in India during the 1970s, see M. N. Srinivas, "Village Studies, Participant Observation and Social Science Research in India," 1387–94; Bardhan, *Conversations between Economists and Anthropologists*; Byres, *Indian Economy*, 81–82.

42 "Notes on the Potential Use of the Physical Quality of Life Index in the Study of the Status of Women in India," May 21, 1979, 1, http://dec.usaid.gov.

43 Morris, "Physical Quality of Life Index," 233.

44 Sundaram, review of *Measuring the Conditions of India's Poor*, by M. David Morris and M. B. McAlpin, 303.

45 Vidwans, "Critique of Mukherjee's Index of Physical Quality of Life."

46 Larson and Wilford, "Physical Quality of Life Index," 584.

47 Kamath, "New Yardstick of Progress," 8.

48 Miles, *Social Indicators for Human Development*, 50.

49 Morris and McAlpin, *Measuring the Condition of India's Poor*, 88.

50 Morris, "Physical Quality of Life Index," 225.

51   Morris and McAlpin, *Measuring the Condition of India's Poor*, 88.

52   Miles, *Social Indicators for Human Development*, 48–54.

53   Griffin and Khan, "Poverty in the Third World, 303.

54   Jan Drewnowski, "Social Indicators and Welfare Measurement: Remarks on Methodology," in Baster, *Measuring Development*, 78.

55   Schmelzer, *Hegemony of Growth*, 307–8.

56   Crook, review of *Measuring the Condition of the World's Poor*," 333.

57   Rimmer, review of *Measuring the Condition of the World's Poor*, by Morris David Morris, 269; Habib, "Studying a Colonial Economy"; Roy, "Morris David Morris (1921–2011)," 29.

58   Singh, "'Basic Needs' Approach to Development vs. the New International Economic Order," 586. For similar critiques, see Sinha, Pearson, Kadekodi, and Gregory, *Income Distribution, Growth, and Basic Needs in India*, 19; Galtung, "New International Economic Order"; Haq, "An International Perspective on Basic Needs," 12–13; Sharma, "Between North and South."

59   Hart, "Informal Income Opportunities and Urban Employment in Ghana," 68.

60   Hart, "Informal Income Opportunities and Urban Employment in Ghana," 68–69.

61   The concept of "standing" comes from Peattie, "Idea in Good Currency," 855. On the history of unemployment and the global context for the ILO's work on informality during the 1970s, see Benanav, "Origins of Informality."

62   Benanav, "Origins of Informality," 107–9, 113–18.

63   WEP Information Sheet No. 29, April 4, 1972, WEP file number 159-3-227 (Kenya), Jacket 2, ILO Archives; Wilfred Jenks to Jomo Kenyatta, April 2, 1971, WEP file number 159-3-227 (Kenya), Jacket 2, ILO Archives.

64   "Basic Ideas for the High-Level Kenyan Mission," April 26, 1971, WEP file number 159-3-227 (Kenya), Jacket 1, ILO Archives.

65   The research team focused on many of the similar issues that Keith Hart had in Ghana, especially rural-urban migration and the "social conditions" of the urban poor. Hans Singer to George Lambert-Lamond, July 29, 1971, WEP file number 159-3-227 (Kenya), Jacket 1, ILO Archives.

66   International Labour Office, *Employment, Incomes, and Equality*, 5.

67   International Labour Office, *Employment, Incomes, and Equality*, 225.

68   Peattie, "Idea in Good Currency," 854.

69   International Labour Office, *Employment, Incomes, and Equality*, 21–22.

70   G. Rodgers, Swepston, Van Daele, and Lee, *International Labour Organization*, 186–204; Bangasser, "ILO and the Informal."

71 Manfred Bienefeld and Martin Godfrey, "Measuring Unemployment and the Informal Sector: Some Conceptual and Statistical Problems," *IDS Bulletin* 7, no. 3 (July 1975): 8.

72 See, for instance, Portes, Castells, and Benton, *Informal Economy*.

73 Blades, *Non-monetary (Subsistence) Activities*.

74 Clayton, "Kenya's Agriculture and the I.L.O. Employment Mission."

75 Leys, "Interpreting African Underemployment," 426.

76 Pigou, *Economics of Welfare*, 32.

77 Leghorn and Parker, *Woman's Worth*, 3.

78 Messac, "Outside the Economy," 563–64.

79 Self, *All in the Family*, 103–8; MacLean, *Freedom Is Not Enough*.

80 Leghorn and Parker, *Woman's Worth*, 169; "What's a Wife Worth?," in Leghorn and Warrior, *Houseworker's Handbook*, 17–18.

81 Oakley, *Sociology of Housework*, 93–94.

82 See, for instance, Reuben Gronau, "The Measurement of Output of the Non-market Sector: The Evaluation of Housewives' Time," in Moss, *Measurement of Economic and Social Performance*, 163–89.

83 Messac, "Outside the Economy," 556; "Introduction," in Federici and Austin, *Wages for Housework*, 17–19.

84 Federici, *Wages against Housework*, 8; see also "Theses on Wages for Housework (1974)," in Federici and Austin, *Wages for Housework*, 32–35.

85 Sarah Jaffe, "The Factory in the Family," *Nation*, March 14, 2018, https://www.thenation.com/article/wages-for-houseworks-radical-vision/.

86 Boserup, *Woman's Role in Economic Development*, 161–63.

87 Koczberski, "Women in Development"; Latham, *Right Kind of Revolution*, 174–75. See also Boris, *Making the Woman Worker*, 122–54.

88 Lourdes Benería, "Conceptualizing the Labour Force: The Underestimation of Women's Economic Activities," in Nelson, *African Women in the Development Process*, 11; Lourdes Benería, "Accounting for Women's Work," in Benería, *Women and Development*, 119–48; Shahrashoub Razavi and Carol Miller, "From WID to GAD: Conceptual Shifts in the Women and Development Discourse," Occasional Paper 1, February 1995, UNRISD, http://www.unrisd.org/unrisd/website/document.nsf/(httpPublications)/D9C3FCA78D3DB32E80256B67005B6AB5?OpenDocument.

89 Cited in Leghorn and Parker, *Woman's Worth*, 14.

90 Bhatt, *We Are Poor but So Many*, 9.

91 Bhatt, *We Are Poor but So Many*, 18–20.

92 Denning, "Wageless Life," 94–95.

93 Chen, Bonner, and Carré, "Organizing Informal Workers," 7–8.

94 "Introduction," in Federici and Austin, *Wages for Housework*, 27.

95 Barbara Ehrenreich, "Maid to Order," *Harper's Magazine*, April 1, 2000, 62.

96 Benería and Sen, "Class and Gender Inequalities," 158. See also Benería and Sen, "Accumulation, Reproduction.'" On the relationship between SEWA and the turn toward neoliberalism in international development, see Boris, *Making the Woman Worker*, 188–89.

97 Jaquette, "Women and Modernization Theory."

98 Nicholas Georgescu-Roegen to Kenneth Boulding, August 14, 1974, box 21, folder "Boulding, Kenneth," Georgescu-Roegen Papers.

99 Gross, "Reimagining Energy and Growth, 521.

100 Gross, "Reimagining Energy and Growth, 522–46.

101 On US energy policy, see McFarland, "Living in Never-Never Land"; Jacobs, *Panic at the Pump*.

102 Helm, *Energy, the State, and the Market*.

103 Hatch, *Politics and Nuclear Power*.

104 Daly, "Steady-State Economics versus Growthmania."

105 Daly, "On Economics as a Life Science."

106 Daly emphasized this in congressional testimony. US Senate, Subcommittee on Air and Water Pollution, Committee on Public Works, *The Impact of Growth on the Environment*, April 2–3, 1976, 93rd Cong., 1st sess., 1976, 5–6.

107 Norgaard, "Ecosystem Services." "It is a mark of our time, and a signal of the degree to which man is ecologically disconnected," concluded an US-based 1969 expert working group on environmental problems, that even "the benefits of nature need to be enumerated." *Man's Impact on the Global Environment*, 123.

108 Schumacher, *Small Is Beautiful*, 19.

109 Ehrlich and Mooney, "Extinction, Substitution, and Ecosystem Services"; Gómez-Baggethun, de Groot, Lomas, and Montes, "History of Ecosystem Services."

110 Sagoff, "Carrying Capacity and Ecological Economics," 610–11.

111 Westman, "How Much Are Nature's Services Worth?"

112 See, for instance, Orris C. Herfindahl and Allen V. Kneese, "Measuring Social and Economic Change: Benefits and Costs of Pollution," in Moss, *Measurement of Economic and Social Performance*, 509–31; Mishan, "Postwar Literature on Externalities."

113 Nordhaus and Tobin presented an early version of the MEW at a 1969 symposium of the American Association for the Advancement of Science but

published it first as William D. Nordhaus and James Tobin, "Is Growth Obsolete?," in *Economic Research*, 1–80.

114 NNW Measurement Committee, *Measuring Net National Welfare of Japan* (Tokyo: Printing Bureau Ministry of Finance, 1973), 16–20.

115 On the differences between Daly, Kneese, and Georgescu-Roegen and the relationship between the new "ecological economics" and older traditions of resource or environmental economics, see Røpke, "Early History of Modern Ecological Economics," 299–302.

116 Macekura, *Of Limits and Growth*, 244–57.

117 Macekura, *Of Limits and Growth*, 244–51.

118 Seers, "Total Relationship," 339–47.

119 M. Haq, "Negotiating the Future," 416.

120 Schmelzer, *Hegemony of Growth*, 309–12.

Chapter 6

1 Jimmy Carter, remarks at dedication ceremonies for the John F. Kennedy Library, October 20, 1979, https://www.presidency.ucsb.edu/node/248130.

2 Margaret Thatcher, speech to CNN World Economic Development Conference, September 19, 1992, https://www.margaretthatcher.org/document/108304.

3 Collins, *More*, 166–213.

4 George H. W. Bush, "Remarks to the Council of the Americas," May 22, 1990, http://www.presidency.ucsb.edu/ws/?pid=18508.

5 D. Rodgers, *Age of Fracture*, 44.

6 William J. Clinton, "Remarks to Future Leaders of Belarus in Minsk," January 15, 1994, http://www.presidency.ucsb.edu/ws/index.php?pid=50109.

7 On the 1980s as a "lost decade" of development, see Ekbladh, *Great American Mission*, 259; Mazower, *Governing the World*, 343–77.

8 George H. W. Bush, "Remarks following Discussions with Prime Minister Michael Manley of Jamaica," May 3, 1990, http://www.presidency.ucsb.edu/ws/?pid=18446.

9 Steven Pearlstein, "An Index of the Value of Goods, Services, and . . . Niceness?," *Washington Post*, May 19, 1993, F1; Daly, Cobb, and Cobb, *For the Common Good*, 401–56.

10 Clifford Cobb, Ted Halstead, and Jonathan Rowe, "If the GDP Is Up, Why Is America Down?," *Atlantic Monthly*, October 1995, 78.

11 *Human Development Report 1990*, 1.

12 On the genealogy and meaning of neoliberalism, see Slobodian, *Globalists*, 1–26; Mirowski, "Zero Hour of History?"

13 Krippner, *Capitalizing on Crisis*; Copley, "Why Were Capital Controls Abandoned?"; Sargent, *Superpower Transformed*, 190–97.

14 McCraw, *Prophets of Regulation*; Derthick and Quirk, *Politics of Deregulation*; Hammond and Knott, "Deregulatory Snowball," 3–5.

15 Daniel J. Sargent, "The United States and Globalization," in Ferguson, Maier, Manela, and Sargent, *Shock of the Global*, 61–68; R. Samuelson, *Great Inflation and Its Aftermath*, 105–38; on the defeat of inflation as a turning point, see Frieden, *Global Capitalism*, 374–76.

16 Giovanni Arrighi, "The World Economy and the Cold War," in Leffler and Westad, *Cambridge History of the Cold War*, 3:32–35.

17 Collins, *More*, 166–97.

18 Judt, *Postwar*, 542–43, 555–58.

19 Bernstein, *Perilous Progress*, 181–82.

20 Frieden, *Global Capitalism*, 398–99.

21 McCartin, *Collision Course*; Howell, *Trade Unions and the State*, 131–73; Judt, *Postwar*, 542.

22 Judt, *Postwar*, 701–84; Moravcsik, *Choice for Europe*; Frieden, *Global Capitalism*, 410–12.

23 Brands, *Making the Unipolar Moment*, 56.

24 Frieden, *Global Capitalism*, 416.

25 Panitch and Gindin, *Making of Global Capitalism*, 287.

26 Ruggie, "Multinationals as Global Institution," 321–25.

27 United Nations Conference on Trade and Development, *World Investment Report*.

28 Bernstein, *Perilous Progress*, 166.

29 Leffler, "Victory," 91–95.

30 Frieden, *Global Capitalism*, 380.

31 Bernstein, *Perilous Progress*, 159–61; D. Rodgers, *Age of Fracture*, 41–76, 86–87.

32 Mudge, *Leftism Reinvented*, 251–53, 283, 340–42.

33 Sandbach, "Rise and Fall of the *Limits to Growth* Debate"; Sabin, *Bet*, 131–80.

34 Yergin, *Prize*, 699–707; Garavini, *Rise and Fall of OPEC*, 301–60.

35 Sagoff, "Carrying Capacity and Ecological Economics," 611.

36 World Resources Institute, *World Resources, 1994–1995*, 5.

37 Nordhaus, Stavins, and Weitzman, "Lethal Model 2," 3–4.

38 Quoted in Yarrow, *Measuring America*, 183.

39 Fioramonti, *World after GDP*, 52–53; "What Is the Stability and Growth Pact?," *Guardian*, November 27, 2003, https://www.theguardian.com/world/2003/nov/27/qanda.business.

40 Schmelzer, *Hegemony of Growth*, 328.

41 Nemchenok, "Dialogue of Power," 209–43.

42 Arrighi, "World Economy and the Cold War," 3:34–35.

43 Eliana A. Cardoso and Albert Fishlow, "The Macroeconomics of the Brazilian External Debt" in Sachs, *Developing Country Debt and the World Economy*, 81–100; Connell and Dados, "Where in the World Does Neoliberalism Come From?," 122–24.

44 Pettinà and Kalinovsky, "From Countryside to Factory."

45 Unger, *International Development*, 145.

46 Alan M. Taylor, "The Global 1970s and the Echo of the Great Depression," in Ferguson, Maier, Manela, and Sargent, *Shock of the Global*, 103–10.

47 Jeffrey D. Sachs, "Introduction," in Sachs, *Developing Country Debt and the World Economy*, 6–17.

48 Krasner, *Structural Conflict*, 107.

49 Arestis, "Washington Consensus and Financial Liberalization," 252. On structural adjustment, see Kentikelenis and Babb, "Making of Neoliberal Globalization"; Reinsberg, Kentikelenis, Stubbs, and King, "World System and the Hollowing-Out of State Capacity"; Mohan, Brown, Milward, and Zack-Williams, *Structural Adjustment*; Barry Eichengreen, "The Globalization Wars: An Economist Reports from the Front Lines," *Foreign Affairs* 81, no. 4 (July–August 2002): 157–64; Teichman, *Politics of Freeing Markets In Latin America*; Babb, "Washington Consensus"; F. Stewart, *Adjustment and Poverty*; Arrighi, "World Economy and the Cold War," 3:36; Frieden, *Global Capitalism*, 374–76.

50 On the general trend of liberalization, see Simmons and Elkins, "Globalization of Liberalization"; McMichael, *Development and Social Change*, part 3; Toye, *Dilemmas of Development*; Ekbladh, *Great American Mission*, 257–74.

51 Armeane M. Choksi and Demetris Papageorgiou, "Economic Liberalization: What Have We Learned?," in Choksi and Papageorgiou, *Economic Liberalization in Developing Countries*, 1.

52 Brands, *Making the Unipolar Moment*, 201.

53 World Bank, *Accelerated Development in Sub-Saharan Africa*, 4; Allan, *Scientific Cosmology and International Orders*, 244–46.

54   Lal, *Poverty of "Development Economics."*

55   Mazower, *Governing the World*, 354.

56   Roland Dannreuther, "The Political Dimension: Authoritarianism and Democratization," in Fawcett and Sayigh, *Third World beyond the Cold War*, 38–39. On the neoliberal nature of the WTO, see Slobodian, *Globalists*, 218–62.

57   Frieden, *Global Capitalism*, 416–17.

58   Frieden, *Global Capitalism*, 462.

59   Berend, *Economic History of Twentieth-Century Europe*, 182–88; Mazower, *Dark Continent*, 371.

60   Bockman, *Markets in the Name of Socialism*, 157–224; Unger, *International Development*, 145–46; Ther, *Europe since 1989*, 43–44.

61   Blasi, Kroumova, and Kruse, *Kremlin Capitalism*; Burawoy, "Soviet Descent into Capitalism"; Stuckler, King, and McKee, "Mass Privatisation and the Post-Communist Mortality Crisis."

62   Judt, *Postwar*, 686–89.

63   Berend, *Economic History of Twentieth-Century Europe*, 186.

64   William J. Clinton, "Remarks to Future Russian Leaders in Moscow," September 1, 1998, http://www.presidency.ucsb.edu/ws/index.php?pid=54835.

65   Schmelzer, *Hegemony of Growth*, 328; Leffler, "Victory," 96–99.

66   Ther, *Europe since 1989*, 158.

67   Frieden, *Global Capitalism*, 425–26; Miller, *Struggle to Save the Soviet Economy*; Gerwitz, *Unlikely Partners*.

68   Allan, *Scientific Cosmology and International Orders*, 246–62.

69   On the origins and significance of "globalization" after Bretton Woods, see Sargent, *Superpower Transformed*, 229–310. For a survey of major policy changes, see also Zeiler, "Opening Doors in the World Economy," 326–61.

70   William J. Clinton, "Remarks at the World Trade Organization in Geneva, Switzerland," May 18, 1998, https://www.presidency.ucsb.edu/documents/remarks-the-world-trade-organization-geneva-switzerland.

71   Krippner, *Capitalizing on Crisis*, 33.

72   Panitch and Gindin, *Making of Global Capitalism*, 284–87.

73   M. Ward, *Quantifying the World*, 86.

74   Fioramonti, *World after GDP*, 52.

75   Cobb, Halstead, and Rowe, "If the GDP Is Up, Why Is America Down?," 68. See also Fioramonti, *World after GDP*, 51–53; Karabell, *Leading Indicators*, 159.

76   Karabell, *Leading Indicators*, 183.

77 Christophers, "Making Finance Productive."

78 Christophers, *Banking across Boundaries*, 161–80.

79 Shaikh and Tomak, *Measuring the Wealth of Nations*, 52–53.

80 Christophers, "Making Finance Productive," 113.

81 Mazzucato, *Value of Everything*, 245, 247.

82 Coyle, *GDP*, 88, 91.

83 Jerven, *Poor Numbers*.

84 See, for instance, Holz, "'Fast, Clear, and Accurate'"; Holz, "Quality of China's GDP Statistics"; Wallace, "Juking the Stats?"

85 Fioramonti, *Gross Domestic Problem*, 97.

86 Henderson, "What's Next in the Great Debate about Measuring Wealth and Progress?," 53–54.

87 M. Haq, *Reflections on Human Development*, 25.

88 Stanton, "Human Development Index," 8–10; Nussbaum and Sen, *Quality of Life*; Sen, *Commodities and Capabilities*.

89 Streeten, "Foreword," ix.

90 Richard Ponzio, "The Advent of the *Human Development Report*," in K. Haq and Ponzio, *Pioneering the Human Development Revolution*, 100.

91 Stanton, "Human Development Index," 15.

92 *Human Development Report 1990*, 1.

93 John Gittings, "New Indicator Puts Rich Countries under Microscope," *Guardian*, May 25, 1990.

94 Speich Chassé, "Roots of the Millennium Development Goals."

95 Srinivasan, "Human Development," 238–39.

96 Srinivasan, "Human Development," 240–41.

97 Ravallion, "Good and Bad Growth," 632–33.

98 Fioramonti, *Gross Domestic Problem*, 98.

99 Masood, *Great Invention*, 95–105.

100 The "criteria of sustainability and sufficiency are important guidelines, along with the principle of limited inequality and the goal of zero population growth. Moral and technical progress remain possible; only continued increase in the physical scale of the economy is ruled out," Daly wrote in 1986. Daly, "Toward a New Economic Model," 44.

101 For a fuller history of Daly, the ISEW, and the GPI, see Masood, *Great Invention*, 127–31; Fioramonti, *Gross Domestic Problem*, 88–91; Kubiszewski et al., "Beyond GDP."

102 Daly, Cobb, and Cobb, *For the Common Good*, 401–20.

103 Talbeth and Weisdorf, "Genuine Progress Indicator 2.0."

104 Robert Costanza, "Developing Ecological Economics at the Maryland International Institute for Ecological Economics," FA7321, reel 8981, Ford Foundation Archives, RAC; Røpke, "Early History of Modern Ecological Economics," 307.

105 L.T., "The Economist Explains: Ecological Economics," *Economist*, December 13, 2015, https://www.economist.com/the-economist-explains/2015/12/13/ecological-economics.

106 Sabin, *Bet*, 131–228; Sagoff, "Carrying Capacity and Ecological Economics," 618.

107 Nordhaus, Stavins, and Weitzman, "Lethal Model 2," 37–38.

108 Arrow et al. "Economic Growth."

109 Sagoff, "Carrying Capacity and Ecological Economics," 610.

110 Costanza et al., "Value of the World's Ecosystem Services," 259.

111 Sagoff, "Rise and Fall of Ecological Economics."

112 Masood, *Great Invention*, 134.

113 Norgaard, "Ecosystem Services."

114 Peter Passell, "Rebel Economists Add Ecological Cost to Prices of Progress," *New York Times*, November 27, 1990, https://www.nytimes.com/1990/11/27/science/rebel-economists-add-ecological-cost-to-price-of-progress.html.

115 Lawn, "Stock-Take of Green National Accounting Initiatives," 433.

116 Nordhaus and Kokkelenberg, *Nature's Numbers*, 3–9. On the UN supplemental accounts, see https://seea.un.org/content/seea-central-framework.

117 Davies, *Happiness Industry*, 146.

118 Richard Easterlin, "Does Economic Growth Improve the Human Lot? Some Empirical Evidence," in David and Reder, *Nations and Households in Economic Growth*, 121.

119 Richard Easterlin, "The Story of a Reluctant Economist," in Szenberg and Ramrattan, *Reflections of Eminent Economists*, 157.

120 Scitovsky, *Joyless Economy*; Scitovsky, *Human Desire and Economic Satisfaction*.

121 Masood, *Great Invention*, 107–14.

122 Patrick Collinson, "Overall UK Happiness Levels Given English Boost, ONS Says," *Guardian*, February 26, 2018, https://www.theguardian.com/world/2018/feb/26/overall-uk-happiness-level-given-boost-by-english-office-national-statistics-life-satisfaction-survey.

123 D'Acci, "Measuring Well-Being and Progress," 52–54.

124 Jackson Lears, "Get Happy!!," *Nation*, November 25, 2013, https://www
.thenation.com/article/get-happy-2/.

125 Davies, *Happiness Industry*, 274.

126 Quoted in Brands, *Making the Unipolar Moment*, 211.

127 George H. W. Bush, "Remarks to the Council of the Americas," May 22, 1990,
http://www.presidency.ucsb.edu/ws/?pid=18508.

128 John Gravois, "The de Soto Delusion," *Slate*, January 29, 2005, http://www
.slate.com/articles/news_and_politics/hey_wait_a_minute/2005/01/the
_de_soto_delusion.html.

129 Mitchell, "Work of Economics."

130 Mitchell, "Rethinking Economy," 1120. See also Gilbert, "On the Mystery of
Capital."

131 Waring, *If Women Counted*, 7.

132 Messac, "Outside the Economy," 567–68.

133 Murphy, *Economization of Life*, 113–24.

134 Hillary Rodham Clinton, "Investing in Sisterhood: An Agenda for the
World's Women," *Washington Post*, May 14, 1995, C1.

135 Messac, "Outside the Economy," 568.

136 Chen, Bonner, and Carré, "Organizing Informal Workers," 3–11.

137 WIEGO, "Informal Economy Debates: Dominant Schools of Thought,"
n.d., accessed June 20, 2018, http://www.wiego.org/sites/wiego.org/files/
resources/files/WIEGO_IE_Dominant_schools_of_thought.pdf.

138 The International Conference of Labour Statisticians, "Guidelines concerning a Statistical Definition of Informal Employment," 2003, http://
www.ilo.org/wcmsp5/groups/public/-dgreports/-stat/documents/
normativeinstrument/wcms_087622.pdf.

139 Murphy, *Economization of Life*, 105.

140 Felice, "Misty Grail."

141 Allan, *Scientific Cosmology and International Orders*, 262.

142 See note 4 of the introduction for a list of these recent works.

Conclusion

1 "Hans Rosling's 200 Countries, 200 Years, 4 Minutes—the Joy of Stats,"
BBC Four, November 26, 2010, https://www.youtube.com/watch?v=jbk
SRLYSojo.

2 See, for instance, Pinker, "Enlightenment Environmentalism."

3   Peter Thiel, Roberto Unger, and Cornel West, "American Democracy March 14, 2019 Lecture," March 18, 2019, https://www.youtube.com/watch ?reload=9&v=h2TrRWAkbr8.

4   Desrosières, *Politics of Large Numbers*; Mitchell, "Economentality"; Mitchell, *Rule of Experts*; Tooze, *Statistics and the German State*; Goswami, *Producing India*; Patriarca, *Numbers and Nationhood*; O'Bryan, *Growth Idea*; Collins, *More*; Yarrow, *Measuring America*; Speich Chassé, "Use of Global Abstractions"; Schmelzer, *Hegemony of Growth*.

5   On economists and public policy, see, for instance, D. Hirschman and Berman, "Do Economists Make Policies"; Fourcade, "Construction of a Global Profession."

6   Jerven, *Poor Numbers*; Jerven, *Economic Growth and Measurement Reconsidered*; Jerven, *Africa*.

7   Piketty and Saez, "Income Inequality in the United States, 1913–1998."

8   Atkinson and Piketty, *Top Incomes over the Twentieth Century*; Piketty and Saez, "Evolution of Top Incomes."

9   Piketty, *Capital in the Twenty-First Century*; Alvadredo, Chancel, Piketty, Saez, and Zucman, *World Inequality Report 2018*; F. Stewart, "Changing Perspectives on Inequality and Development." For a review of this recent literature, see Hager, "Varieties of Top Incomes?" See also Hickel, *Divide*.

10   D. Hirschman, "Inventing the Economy," 160.

11   Milanovic, *Global Inequality*. See also Lakner and Milanovic, "Global Income Distribution."

12   Zucman, *Hidden Wealth of Nations*, 3–4.

13   Ogle, "Archipelago Capitalism."

14   Financial Stability Board, *Global Shadow Banking Monitoring Report 2017*; Bank and Gabor, "Political Economy of Shadow Banking."

15   Adam Tooze, "Macroeconomics Predicted the Wrong Crisis," *Institute for New Economic Thinking*, September 10, 2018, https://www.ineteconomics .org/perspectives/blog/macroeconomics-predicted-the-wrong-crisis; Tooze, *Crashed*, 12–13.

16   Karabell, "Learning to Love Stagnation."

17   Gordon, *Rise and Fall of American Growth*, 605–52.

18   Tooze, *Crashed*, 456.

19   On recent debates over the future of economic growth, see also Timothy Shenk, "Apostles of Growth," *Nation*, November 5, 2014, https://www .thenation.com/article/apostles-growth/.

20   Macekura, *Of Limits and Growth*, 261–303.

21 Naomi Oreskes, "The Scientific Consensus on Climate Change: How Do We Know We're Not Wrong?," in Dimento and Doughman, *Climate Change*, 93; Chakrabarty, "Climate of History," 206–7.

22 Purdy, *After Nature*.

23 Duncan Clark, "Which Nations Are Most Responsible for Climate Change?," *Guardian*, April 21, 2001, https://www.theguardian.com/environment/2011/apr/21/countries-responsible-climate-change.

24 For a summary of the recent literature on this topic, see Islam and Winkel, "Climate Change and Social Inequality."

25 Boyd et al., "Typology of Loss and Damage Perspectives."

26 Alyssa Battistoni, "The Failure of Market Solutions and the Green New Deal—Pt 2," *Law and Political Economy Blog*, March 30, 2019, https://www.theguardian.com/environment/2011/apr/21/countries-responsible-climate-change.

27 The commission's report was published as Stiglitz, Sen, and Fitoussi, *Mismeasuring Our Lives*.

28 Jackson, *Prosperity without Growth*.

29 UNU-IHDP and UNEP, *Inclusive Wealth Report 2012*, xxiii.

30 International Institute for Sustainable Development, *Comprehensive Wealth in Canada 2018*, vi.

31 Charlotte Graham-McLay, "New Zealand's Next Liberal Milestone: A Budget Guided by 'Well-Being,'" *New York Times*, May 22, 2019, https://www.nytimes.com/2019/05/22/world/asia/new-zealand-wellbeing-budget.html.

32 Barbara Muraca and Matthias Schmelzer, "Sustainable Degrowth: Historical Roots of the Search for Alternative to Growth in Three Regions," in Borowy and Schmelzer, *History of the Future of Economic Growth*, 174–97; Demaria, Schneider, Sekulova, and Martinez-Alier, "What Is Degrowth?"

33 Demaria, Schneider, Sekulova, and Martinez-Alier, "What Is Degrowth?," 191; Kallis et al., "Research on Degrowth."

34 Kallis et al., "Research on Degrowth," 308.

35 Demaria, Schneider, Sekulova, and Martinez-Alier, "What Is Degrowth?," 195–201.

36 Gareth Dale, Manu V. Mathai, and Jose A. Puppim de Oliveira, "Introduction," in Dale, Mathai, and Puppim de Oliveira, *Green Growth*, 3–6; Bettina Bluemling and Sun-Jin Yun, "Giving Green Teeth to the Tiger? A Critique of 'Green Growth' in South Korea," in Dale, Mathai, and Puppim de Oliveira, *Green Growth*, 14–131; Ricardo Abramovay, "The Green Growth

Trap in Brazil," in Dale, Mathai, and Puppim de Oliveira, *Green Growth*, 150–65. For a representative think tank approach to green growth, see Pollin, Garrett-Peltier, Heintz, and Hendricks, "Green Growth."

37   Kallis et al., "Research on Degrowth," 296–300; Dale, Mathai, and Puppim de Oliveira, "Introduction," 14–19.

38   Giorgos Kallis, "A Green New Deal Must Not Be Tied to Economic Growth," *Truthout*, March 10, 2019, https://truthout.org/articles/a-green-new-deal -must-not-be-tied-to-economic-growth/. Within leftist circles, in particular, there has been a wide-ranging debate about the possibilities and limitations of green investment programs (such as the "Green New Deal") and whether they are compatible with a degrowth agenda (which remains an open question). For a sample of the debates surrounding green growth, see Benjamin Kunkel's interview in Daly, "Ecologies of Scale"; Robert Pollin, "De-growth vs. a Green New Deal"; Burton and Somerville, "Degrowth."

Bibliography

Archival Collections

Australia

Fryer Memorial Library, University of Queensland, St. Lucia

    Colin Clark Collection

France

Organisation for Economic Cooperation and Development (OECD) Library and Archives, Paris

    Council Minutes and Documents
    Development Assistance Committee
    Development Assistance Group
    Economic Policy Committee
    European Productivity Agency
    Executive Committee
    Manpower and Social Affairs Division

Switzerland

International Labour Organization Archives, Geneva

    File Series T
    David A. Morse Cabinet Files
    David A. Morse Correspondence
    World Employment Programme (WEP) Files

League of Nations Archives, Geneva

    Cotes des Series 180
    Cotes des Series 1227
    Cotes des Series 3911

United Nations Office in Geneva

UN Registry Collection

United Kingdom

British Library for Development Studies, Institute of Development Studies, University of Sussex, Brighton

Dudley Seers Papers
Hans Singer Papers

Department of Manuscripts and University Archives, King's College, Cambridge University, Cambridge

John Maynard Keynes Papers
Sir John Richard Nicholas Stone Papers

National Archives, Kew Gardens

Colonial Office Files (CO)
Her Majesty's Treasury Files (T)
Home Office Files (HO)
Ministry of Labour Files (LAB)

National Institute for Economic and Social Research Library and Archives, London

United States of America

Economists' Papers Archive, David M. Rubenstein Rare Book and Manuscript Library, Duke University, Durham, NC

Evsey Domar Papers
Nicholas Georgescu-Roegen Papers
Gerald M. Meier Papers
Oskar Morgenstern Papers
Robert M. Solow Papers

Hoover Institution Library and Archives, Stanford, CA

S. Herbert Frankel Papers
Ghana Central Bureau of Statistics

Library of Congress, Washington, DC

Daniel Patrick Moynihan Papers

Rockefeller Archive Center, Tarrytown, NY

Ford Foundation Archives
Rockefeller Foundation Records

Social Science Research Council Archives

United Nations Archives, New York City, NY

Committee on Contributions Archives
Statistical Division Archives
Statistical Office Archives

United States National Archives, College Park, MD

RG 43, Records of International Conferences, Commissions, and
   Expositions
RG 56, General Records of the Department of the Treasury
RG 59, Records of the Department of State
RG 469, Records of the US Foreign Assistance Agencies

World Bank Group, Washington, DC

Records of the Office of External Affairs
Records of President Robert S. McNamara
World Bank Oral History Program

Newspapers and Periodicals

Atlantic Monthly
Christian Science Monitor
Conversation
Economist
Hartford Courant
Financial Times
Foreign Affairs
Good Housekeeping
Guardian
Harper's Magazine
Institute of Development Studies (IDS) Bulletin
Institute for New Economic Thinking Blog
Law and Political Economy Blog
Nation
New Republic
New Scientist

Newsweek
New York Times
New York Times Magazine
Slate
Social Indicators Newsletter
Time
Times (London)
Times of India
Truthout
Wall Street Journal
Washington Post

Digital Repositories and Resources

American Presidency Project: https://www.presidency.ucsb.edu/
Congressional Record: https://www.congress.gov/congressional-record
John F. Kennedy Presidential Library: https://www.jfklibrary.org/archives
Martin Luther King Jr. Institute at Stanford University: https://
    kinginstitute.stanford.edu/
Nobel Prize Lectures: https://www.nobelprize.org/prizes
United Nations Research Institute for Social Development (UNRISD):
    http://www.unrisd.org/
United States Agency for International Development (USAID): https://dec
    .usaid.gov/
Woodrow Wilson International Center for Scholars Digital Archive: https://
    digitalarchive.wilsoncenter.org/
Youtube.com

Published Primary and Secondary Sources

1976 Progress Report on Phase II: Plan for Future Activities. Paris: Organisation for Economic Co-operation and Development, 1977.

Adorno, Theodor, and Herbert Marcuse. "Correspondence on the German Student Movement." *New Left Review* 1, no. 233 (January/February 1999): 123–36. https://newleftreview-org/I/233/theodor-adorno-herbert-marcuse-correspondence-on-the-german-student-movement.

Alacevich, Michele. "The World Bank and the Politics of Productivity: The Debate on Economic Growth, Poverty, and Living Standards in the 1950s." *Journal of Global History* 6, no. 1 (March 2011): 53–74.

Allan, Bentley B. "Paradigm and Nexus: Neoclassical Economics and the Growth Imperative in the World Bank, 1948–2000." *Review of International Political Economy* 26, no. 1 (2019): 183–206.

———. *Scientific Cosmology and International Orders*. New York: Cambridge University Press, 2018.

Alvadredo, Facundo, Lucas Chancel, Thomas Piketty, Emmanuel Saez, and Gabriel Zucman. *World Inequality Report 2018*. World Inequality Lab, 2018. https://wir2018.wid.world/.

Anderson, Stephen J. *Welfare Policy and Politics in Japan: Beyond the Developmental State*. New York: Paragon House, 1993.

Andersson, Jenny. "The Future of the Western World: The OECD and the Interfutures Project." *Journal of Global History* 14, no. 1 (2019): 126–44.

———. *The Future of the World: Futurology, Futurists, and the Struggle for the Post–Cold War Imagination*. Oxford: Oxford University Press, 2018.

Andersson, Jenny, and Eglė Rindzevičiūtė, eds. *The Struggle for the Long Term in Transnational Science and Politics: Forging the Future*. London: Routledge, 2015.

Arestis, Philip. "Washington Consensus and Financial Liberalization." *Journal of Post Keynesian Economics* 27, no. 2 (Winter 2004–5): 251–71.

Arndt, H. W. *Economic Development: The History of an Idea*. Chicago: University of Chicago Press, 1987.

———. *The Rise and Fall of Economic Growth: A Study in Contemporary Thought*. Melbourne: Longman Cheshire, 1978.

Arrow, Kenneth, et al. "Economic Growth, Carrying Capacity, and the Environment." *Science* 268 (April 28, 1995): 520–21.

Artin, Tom. *Earth Talk: Independent Voices on the Environment*. New York: Grossman, 1973.

Atkinson, Anthony, and Thomas Piketty. *Top Incomes over the Twentieth Century*. Oxford: Oxford University Press, 2006.

Ayres, Robert U., and Allen V. Kneese. "Production, Consumption, and Externalities." *American Economic Review* 59, no. 3 (June 1969): 282–96.

Babb, Sarah. "The Washington Consensus as Policy Paradigm: Its Origins, Trajectory, and Likely Successor." *Review of International Political Economy* 20, no. 2 (2013): 268–97.

Bangasser, Paul E. "The ILO and the Informal Sector: An Institutional History." Employment Paper 2000/9. Geneva: International Labour Organization, 2000.

Bank, Cornel, and Daniela Gabor. "The Political Economy of Shadow Banking." *Review of International Political Economy* 23, no. 6 (2016): 901–14.

Baran, Paul. *The Political Economy of Growth*. New York: Monthly Review Press, 1957.

Baran, Paul, and Paul M. Sweezy. *Monopoly Capital: An Essay on the American Economic and Social Order*. New York: Monthly Review Press, 1966.

Bardhan, Pranab, ed. *Conversations between Economists and Anthropologists: Methodological Issues in Measuring Economic Change in Rural India*. Delhi: Oxford University Press, 1989.

Barnett, Enid. *The Keynesian Arithmetic in War-Time Canada: The Development of the National Accounts, 1939–1945*. Kingston, ON: Harbinger House, 1998.

Barnett, Vincent. *The History of Russian Economic Thought*. London: Routledge, 2005.

Baster, Nancy, ed. *Measuring Development: The Role and Adequacy of Development Indicators*. London: Frank Cass, 1972.

Baudrillard, Jean. *The Consumer Society: Myths and Structures*. London: Sage, 1998.

Bauer, Peter T. *Dissent on Development*. London: Weidenfeld and Nicolson, 1971.

Bauer, Raymond A., ed. *Social Indicators*. Cambridge, MA: MIT Press, 1966.

Bayly, C. A. *The Birth of the Modern World: Global Connections and Comparisons*. Malden, MA: Blackwell, 2004.

Beckerman, Wilfred. *In Defence of Growth*. London: Jonathan Cape, 1974.

Bell, Daniel. *The Coming of Post-industrial Society: A Venture in Social Forecasting*. New York: Basic Books, 1973.

Benanav, Aaron. "The Origins of Informality: The ILO at the Limit of the Concept of Unemployment." *Journal of Global History* 14 no. 1 (2019): 107–25.

Benería, Lourdes, ed. *Women and Development: The Sexual Division of Labor in Rural Societies*. New York: Praeger, 1982.

Benería, Lourdes, and Gita Sen. "Accumulation, Reproduction, and 'Women's Role in Economic Development': Boserup Revisited." *Signs* 7, no. 2 (Winter 1981): 279–98.

———. "Class and Gender Inequalities and Women's Role in Economic Development: Theoretical and Practical Implications." *Feminist Studies* 8, no. 1 (Spring 1982): 157–76.

Benham, Frederic. "The Estimation of National Product in Underdeveloped Countries." *Bulletin de L'Institut International de Statistique* 33, no. 3 (December 1951): 7–12.

Berend, Ivan T. *An Economic History of Twentieth-Century Europe: Economic Regimes from Laissez-Faire to Globalization.* Cambridge: Cambridge University Press, 2006.

Berkowitz, Edward, and Kim McQuaid. "Welfare Reform in the 1950s." *Social Service Review* 54, no. 1 (March 1980): 45–58.

Bernstein, Michael A. "Numerable Knowledge and Its Discontents." *Reviews in American History* 18, no. 2 (June 1990): 151–64.

———. *A Perilous Progress: Economists and Public Purpose in Twentieth-Century America.* Princeton, NJ: Princeton University Press, 2001.

Berolzheimer, Alan R. "A Nation of Consumers: Mass Consumption, Middle-Class Standards of Living, and American National Identity, 1910–1950." PhD diss., University of Virginia, 1996.

Bhatt, Ela R. *We Are Poor but So Many: The Story of Self-Employed Women in India.* Oxford: Oxford University Press, 2006.

Bivar, Venus. "Kuznets, Frankenstein, and the GNP Monster." Paper presented at the American Society for Environmental History Annual Conference, Riverside, CA, March 17, 2018.

Black, Megan. *The Global Interior: Mineral Frontiers and American Power.* Cambridge, MA: Harvard University Press, 2018.

Blades, Derek W. *Non-monetary (Subsistence) Activities in the National Accounts of Developing Countries.* Paris: Development Centre of the Organisation for Economic Co-operation and Development, 1975.

Blasi, Joseph, Maya Kroumova, and Douglas Kruse. *Kremlin Capitalism: Privatizing the Russian Economy.* Ithaca, NY: Cornell University Press, 1997.

Bockman, Johanna. *Markets in the Name of Socialism: The Left-Wing Origins of Neoliberalism.* Stanford, CA: Stanford University Press, 2011.

Boianovsky, Mauro, and Kevin D. Hoover. "In the Kingdom of Solovia: The Rise of Growth Economics at MIT, 1956–1970." Annual supplement, *History of Political Economy* 46 (2014): 198–228.

Booker, H. S. Review of *The Measurement of Colonial National Incomes*, by Phyllis Deane. *Economica* 15, no. 60 (November 1948): 316–20.

Boris, Eileen. *Making the Woman Worker: Precarious Labor and the Fight for Global Standards, 1919–2019*. New York: Oxford University Press, 2019.

Borowy, Iris, and Matthias Schmelzer, eds. *History of the Future of Economic Growth: Historical Roots of Current Debates on Sustainable Degrowth*. London: Routledge, 2017.

Boserup, Ester. *Woman's Role in Economic Development*. London: George Allen and Unwin, 1970.

Bouk, Dan. *How Our Days Became Numbered: Risk and the Rise of the Statistical Individual*. Chicago: University of Chicago Press, 2015.

Boulding, Kenneth E. "The Shadow of the Stationary State." *Daedalus* 102, no. 4 (Fall 1973): 89–101.

Boumans, Marcel. *How Economists Model the World into Numbers*. London: Routledge, 2005.

Boyd, Emily, Rachel A. James, Richard G. Jones, Hannah R. Young, and Friederike E. L. Otto. "A Typology of Loss and Damage Perspectives." *Nature Climate Change* 7 (2017): 723–29.

Boyle, David. *The Tyranny of Numbers: Why Counting Can't Make Us Happy*. London: HarperCollins, 2000.

Brands, Hal. *Making the Unipolar Moment: US Foreign Policy and the Rise of the Post–Cold War Order*. Ithaca, NY: Cornell University Press, 2016.

Brick, Howard. *Transcending Capitalism: Visions of a New Society in Modern American Thought*. Ithaca, NY: Cornell University Press, 2006.

Brown, Lowell S., Leonardo Castillejo, H. F. Jones, T. W. B. Kiblle, and M. Rowan-Robinson. "Are There Real Limits to Growth? A Reply to Beckerman." *Oxford Economic Papers* 25, no. 3 (November 1973): 455–60.

Brown, Timothy S. "'1968' East and West: Divided Germany as a Case Study in Transnational History." *American Historical Review* 114, no. 1 (February 2009): 69–96.

Bulmer, Martin, ed. *Social Science Research and Government: Comparative Essays on Britain and the United States*. Cambridge: Cambridge University Press, 1987.

Bulmer, Martin, Kevin Bales, and Kathryn Kish Sklar, eds. *The Social Survey in Historical Perspective, 1880–1940*. Cambridge: Cambridge University Press, 1991.

Burawoy, Michael. "The Soviet Descent into Capitalism." *American Journal of Sociology* 102, no. 5 (March 1997): 1430–44.

Burton, Mark, and Peter Somerville. "Degrowth: A Defence." *New Left Review* 115 (January–February 2019): 95–104.

Byres, Terence J., ed. *The Indian Economy: Major Debates since Independence.* Delhi: Oxford University Press, 1998.

Cairncross, Alec, and Mohinder Puri, eds. *Employment, Income Distribution and Development Strategy: Problems of the Developing Countries.* New York: Holmes and Meier, 1976.

Caldwell, Curt. *NSC 68 and the Political Economy of the Early Cold War.* Cambridge: Cambridge University Press, 2011.

Calhoun, Craig, ed. *Sociology in America: A History.* Chicago: University of Chicago Press, 2007.

Carson, Carol. The History of the United States Income and Product Accounts: The Development of an Analytical Tool." PhD diss., George Washington University, 1971.

Carson, Rachel. *Silent Spring.* Boston: Houghton Mifflin, 1962.

Case, Anne, and Angus Deaton. "Rising Morbidity and Mortality in Midlife among White Non-Hispanic Americans in the 21st Century." *Proceedings of the National Academy of Sciences of the United States of America* 112, no. 49 (2015): 15078–83.

Catastrophe or New Society? A Latin American World Model. Ottawa: International Development Research Center, 1976.

Cebul, Brent. *Illusions of Progress: Business, Poverty, and Liberalism in the American Century.* Philadelphia: University of Pennsylvania Press, forthcoming.

Chakrabarty, Dipesh. "The Climate of History: Four Theses." *Critical Inquiry* 35 (Winter 2009): 197–222.

Chandler, Alfred D., Jr. *Scale and Scope: The Dynamics of Industrial Capitalism.* Cambridge, MA: Harvard University Press, 1990.

Chen, Martha, Chris Bonner, and Françoise Carré. "Organizing Informal Workers: Benefits, Challenges and Successes." 2015 UN Development Programme Human Development Report Office Background Paper. http://hdr.undp.org/sites/default/files/chen_hdr_2015_final.pdf.

Chenery, Hollis, Montek S. Ahluwalia, C. L. G. Bell, John H. Duloy, and Richard Jolly, eds. *Redistribution with Growth.* New York: Oxford University Press, 1974.

Choksi, Armeane M., and Demetris Papageorgiou, eds. *Economic Liberalization in Developing Countries.* New York: Oxford University Press, 1986.

Christophers, Brett. *Banking across Boundaries: Placing Finance in Capitalism.* New York: John Wiley and Sons, 2013.

———. "Making Finance Productive." *Economy and Society* 40, no. 1 (2011): 112–40.

Clark, Colin. *Growthmanship: A Study in the Mythology of Investment.* London: Institute of Economic Affairs, 1961.

———. "Review." *International Affairs* 25, no. 1 (January 1949): 80–81.

Clavin, Patricia. *Securing the World Economy: The Reinvention of the League of Nations, 1920–1946.* Oxford: Oxford University Press, 2013.

Clayton, Eric S. "Kenya's Agriculture and the I.L.O. Employment Mission—Six Years After." *Journal of Modern African Studies* 16, no. 2 (June 1978): 311–18.

"The Cocoyoc Declaration." *International Organization* 29, no. 3 (Summer 1975): 893–901.

Coffin, Judith G. "A 'Standard' of Living? European Perspectives on Class and Consumption in the Early Twentieth Century." *International Labor and Working-Class History* 55 (Spring 1999): 6–26.

Cohen, Daniel. *The Infinite Desire for Growth.* Translated by Jane Marie Todd. Princeton, NJ: Princeton University Press, 2018.

Cohen, Lizabeth. *A Consumer's Republic: The Politics of Mass Consumption in Postwar America.* New York: Vintage Books, 2003.

Cole, H. S. D., Christopher Freeman, Marie Jahoda, and K. L. R. Pavitt. *Thinking about the Future: Critique of "Limits to Growth."* Sussex: University of Sussex Press, 1973.

Collins, Robert M. *More: The Politics of Economic Growth in Postwar America.* New York: Oxford University Press, 2000.

Connell, Raewyn, and Nour Dados. "Where in the World Does Neoliberalism Come From? The Market Agenda in Southern Perspective." *Theory and Society* 43, no. 2 (March 2014): 117–38.

Connelly, Matthew. *Fatal Misconception: The Struggle to Control World Population.* Cambridge, MA: Harvard University Press, 2008.

Cook, Eli. *The Pricing of Progress: Economic Indicators and the Capitalization of American Life.* Cambridge, MA: Harvard University Press, 2017.

Cooper, Frederick. *Citizenship between Empire and Nation: Remaking France and French Africa, 1945–1960.* Princeton, NJ: Princeton University Press, 2014.

Copley, Jack. "Why Were Capital Controls Abandoned? The Case of Britain's Abolition of Exchange Controls, 1977–1979." *British Journal of Politics and International Relations* 21, no. 2 (May 2019): 403–20.

Corea, Gamani. "Aid and the Economy." *Marga Quarterly Journal* 1, no. 1 (1971): 19–54.

———. "Ceylon in the Sixties." *Marga Quarterly Journal* 1, no. 2 (1971): 1–30.

Costanza, Robert, et al. "The Value of the World's Ecosystem Services and Natural Capital." *Nature* 387 (May 1997): 253–60.

Cottrell, Allin F., and W. P. Cockshott. "Calculation, Complexity and Planning: The Socialist Calculation Debate Once Again." *Review of Political Economy* 5, no. 1 (1993): 73–122.

Coyle, Diane. *GDP: A Brief but Affectionate History.* Princeton, NJ: Princeton University Press, 2014.

Crook, N. R. Review of *Measuring the Condition of the World's Poor: The Physical Quality of Life Index*, by Morris David Morris. *Third World Planning Review* 3, no. 3 (August 1981): 332–33.

Crosby, Alfred W. *The Measure of Reality: Quantification and Western Society, 1250–1600.* Cambridge: Cambridge University Press, 1997.

Cubitt, Geoffrey, ed. *Imagining Nations.* Manchester: Manchester University Press, 1998.

Cullather, Nick. "Development? It's History." *Diplomatic History*, 24 no. 4 (Fall 2000): 641–53.

———. "The Foreign Policy of the Calorie." *American Historical Review* 112, no. 2 (April 2007): 337–64.

———. *The Hungry World: America's Cold War Battle against Poverty in Asia.* Cambridge, MA: Harvard University Press, 2013.

———. "The Third Race." *Diplomatic History* 33, no. 3 (June 2009): 507–12.

D'Acci, Luca. "Measuring Well-Being and Progress." *Social Indicators Research* 104, no. 1 (October 2011): 47–65.

Dale, Gareth. "The Growth Paradigm: A Critique." *International Socialism* 134 (2012): 55–88.

Dale, Gareth, Manu V. Mathai, and Jose A. Puppim de Oliveira, eds. *Green Growth: Ideology Political Economy, and the Alternatives.* London: Zed Books, 2016.

Daly, Herman E. "Ecologies of Scale." Interview by Benjamin Kunkel. *New Left Review* 109 (January–February 2018): 80–104.

———. "The Economics of the Steady State." *American Economic Review* 64, no. 2 (May 1974): 15–21.

———, ed. *Essays toward a Steady-State Economy.* Cuernavaca, Mexico: Centro Intercultural de Documentación, 1971.

———. "In Defense of a Steady-State Economy." *American Agricultural Economics* 54, no. 5 (1972): 945–54.

———. "On Economics as a Life Science." *Journal of Political Economy* 76, no. 3 (May–June 1968): 392–406.

———. "Steady-State Economics versus Growthmania: A Critique of the Orthodox Conceptions of Growth, Wants, Scarcity, and Efficiency." *Policy Sciences* 5, no. 2 (June 1974): 149–67.

———. "Toward a New Economic Model." *Bulletin of the Atomic Scientists* 42, no. 4 (April 1986): 42–44.

———, ed. *Toward a Steady-State Economy*. San Francisco: W. H. Freeman, 1973.

Daly, Herman E., and John B. Cobb Jr. with contributions by Clifford W. Cobb. *For the Common Good: Redirecting the Economy toward Community, the Environment, and a Sustainable Future*. Boston: Beacon, 1989.

David, Paul A., and Melvin W. Reder, eds. *Nations and Households in Economic Growth: Essays in Honor of Moses Abramovitz*. New York: Academic, 1974.

Davie, Grace. *Poverty Knowledge in South Africa: A Social History of the Human Science, 1855–2005*. New York: Cambridge University Press, 2015.

Davies, William. *The Happiness Industry: How the Government and Big Business Sold Us Well-Being*. London: Verso, 2015.

Deane, Phyllis. *Colonial Social Accounting*. Cambridge: Cambridge University Press, 1953.

———. *The Measurement of Colonial National Incomes*. Cambridge: Cambridge University Press, 1948.

———. "Measuring National Income in Colonial Territories." *Studies in Income and Wealth* 8, no. 6 (1946): 154–68.

Deaton, Angus. "John Richard Nicholas Stone: 1913–1991." *Proceedings of the British Academy* 82 (1993): 475–92.

De Grazia, Victoria. *Irresistible Empire: America's Advance through Twentieth-Century Europe*. Cambridge, MA: Belknap Press of Harvard University Press, 2005.

de Groot, Michael. "Disruption: Economic Globalization and the End of the Cold War." PhD diss., University of Virginia, 2018.

———. "A Golden Opportunity? The Soviet Union, CMEA, and the Energy Crisis of the 1970s." *Journal of Cold War Studies* (forthcoming).

Demaria, Federico, François Schneider, Filka Sekulova, and Joan Martinez-Alier. "What Is Degrowth? From an Activist Slogan to a Social Movement." *Environmental Values* 22 (2013): 191–215.

Denning, Michael. "Wageless Life." *New Left Review* 66 (November–December 2010): 79–97.

Deringer, William. *Calculated Values: Finance, Politics, and the Quantitative Age.* Cambridge, MA: Harvard University Press, 2018.

Derthick, Martha, and Paul J. Quirk. *The Politics of Deregulation.* Washington, DC: Brookings Institution Press, 1985.

Desrosières, Alain. *The Politics of Large Numbers: A History of Statistical Reasoning.* Translated by Camille Naish. Cambridge, MA: Harvard University Press, 1998.

Dietrich, Christopher R. W. *Oil Revolution: Anticolonial Elites, Sovereign Rights, and the Economic Culture of Decolonization.* Cambridge: Cambridge University Press, 2017.

Dimento, Joseph F. C., and Pamela Doughman, eds. *Climate Change: What It Means for Us, Our Children, and Our Grandchildren.* Cambridge, MA: MIT Press, 2007.

Dobson, Miriam. "The Post-Stalin Era: De-Stalinization, Daily Life, and Dissent." *Kritika: Explorations in Russian and Eurasian History* 12, no. 4 (Fall 2011): 905–24.

Dodge, J. Richards. "The Standard of Living in the United States." *Science* 16, no. 396 (September 5, 1890): 131–33.

Domar, Evsey E. *Essays in the Theory of Economic Growth.* New York: Oxford University Press, 1957.

Dosman, Edgar J. *The Life and Times of Raúl Prebisch, 1901–1986.* Montreal: McGill–Queen's University Press, 2008.

Drewnowski, Jan. *On Measuring and Planning the Quality of Life.* The Hague: Mouton, 1974.

——. *Studies in the Measurement of Levels of Living and Welfare.* Geneva: United Nations Research Institute for Social Development, 1970.

Duncan, Joseph W., and William C. Shelton. *Revolution in United States Government Statistics, 1926–1976.* Washington, DC: Government Printing Office, 1978.

Eckes, Alfred E., Jr. *The United States and the Global Struggle for Minerals.* Austin: University of Texas Press, 1979.

Economic Commission for Europe. *Approaches and Methods Used in Long-Term Social Planning and Policy-Making.* New York: United Nations, 1973.

Economic Research: Retrospect and Prospect. Vol. 5, *Economic Growth.* New York: National Bureau of Economic Research, 1972.

An Economic Survey of the Colonial Empire. London: His Majesty's Stationery Office, 1934.

Ehrlich, Paul R. *The Population Bomb*. New York: Ballantine Books, 1968.

Ehrlich, Paul R., and Harold A. Mooney. "Extinction, Substitution, and Ecosystem Services." *BioScience* 33, no. 4 (1983): 248–54.

Ekbladh, David. *The Great American Mission: Modernization and the Construction of an American World Order*. Princeton, NJ: Princeton University Press, 2010.

Ellul, Jacques. *The Technological Society*. Translated by John Wilkinson. New York: Alfred A. Knopf, 1964.

Encrevé, Pierre, and Rose Mary Lagrave, eds. *Travailler avec Bourdieu*. Paris: Flammarion, 2003.

Engerman, David C. "Bernath Lecture: American Knowledge and Global Power." *Diplomatic History* 31, no. 4 (September 2007): 599–622.

———. *Know Your Enemy: The Rise and Fall of America's Soviet Experts*. New York: Oxford University Press, 2009.

———. *The Price of Aid: The Economic Cold War in India*. Cambridge, MA: Harvard University Press, 2018.

———. "The Price of Success: Economic Sovietology, Development, and the Costs of Interdisciplinarity." Annual supplement, *History of Political Economy* 42 (2010): 234–60.

Farik, Nora, ed. *1968 Revisited: 40 Years of Protest Movements*. Brussels: Heinrich Böll Foundation EU Regional Office, 2008.

Fawcett, Louise, and Yezid Sayigh. *The Third World beyond the Cold War: Continuity and Change*. Oxford: Oxford University Press, 1999.

Federici, Silvia. *Wages against Housework*. Bristol, UK: Falling Wall Press, 1975.

Federici, Silvia, and Arlen Austin. *Wages for Housework: The New York Committee 1972–1977; History, Theory, Documents*. Brooklyn, NY: Autonomedia, 2017.

Felice, Emanuele. "The Misty Grail: The Search for a Comprehensive Measure of Development and the Reasons for GDP Primacy." *Development and Change* 47, no. 5 (2016): 967–94.

Ferguson, Niall, Charles S. Maier, Erez Manela, and Daniel J. Sargent, eds. *The Shock of the Global: The 1970s in Perspective*. Cambridge, MA: Belknap Press of Harvard University Press, 2010.

Feygin, Yakov. "Reforming the Cold War State: Economic Thought, Internationalization, and the Politics of Soviet Reform, 1955–1985." PhD diss., University of Pennsylvania, 2017.

Financial Stability Board. *Global Shadow Banking Monitoring Report 2017.* Basel: FSB, March 2018.

Fioramonti, Lorenzo. *Gross Domestic Problem: The Politics behind the World's Most Powerful Number.* London: Zed Books, 2013.

———. *The World after GDP: Economics, Politics, and International Relations in the Post-growth Era.* Cambridge, UK: Polity, 2017.

Fleury, Jean-Baptiste. "Drawing New Lines: Economists and Other Social Scientists on Society in the 1960s." Annual supplement, *History of Political Economy* 42 (2010): 315–42.

Flora, Peter, ed. *Growth to Limits: The Western European Welfare States since World War II.* Vol. 4. Berlin: Walter de Gruyet, 1987.

Forclaz, Amalia Ribi. "Agriculture, American Expertise, and the Quest for Global Data: Leon Estabrook and the First World Agricultural Census of 1930." *Journal of Global History* 11, no. 1 (2016): 44–65.

Fourcade, Marion. "Cents and Sensibility: Economic Valuation and the Nature of 'Nature.'" *American Journal of Sociology* 116, no. 6 (May 2011): 1721–77.

———. "The Construction of a Global Profession: The Transnationalization of Economics." *American Journal of Sociology* 112, no. 1 (2006): 145–94.

———. *Economists and Societies: Discipline and Profession in the United States, Britain, and France, 1890s to 1990s.* Princeton, NJ: Princeton University Press, 2009.

Frankel, S. Herbert. *Capital Investment in Africa: Its Course and Effects.* London: Oxford University Press, 1938.

———. *The Economic Impact of Under-developed Societies: Essays on International Investment and Social Change.* Oxford: Basil Blackwell, 1953.

———. Review of *The Measurement of Colonial National Incomes,* by Phyllis Deane. *Economic Journal* 59, no. 236 (December 1949): 593–95.

———. "United Nations Primer for Development." *Quarterly Journal of Economics* 66, no. 3 (August 1952): 301–26.

Friedan, Betty. *The Feminine Mystique.* New York: Dell, 1963.

Frieden, Jeffry A. *Global Capitalism: Its Fall and Rise in the Twentieth Century.* New York: W. W. Norton, 2006.

Furukawa, Kojun. *Social Welfare in Japan: Principles and Applications.* Melbourne: Trans Pacific Press, 2008.

Galbraith, John Kenneth. *The Affluent Society.* Boston: Houghton Mifflin, 1958.

———. *The New Industrial State.* Boston: Houghton Mifflin, 1967.

Galtung, Johan. "The New International Economic Order and the Basic Needs Approach." *Alternatives: Global, Local, Political* 4, no. 4 (1979): 455–76.

Gann, L. H. *A History of Northern Rhodesia: Early Days to 1953*. London: Chatto and Windus, 1964.

Garavini, Giuliano. *The Rise and Fall of OPEC in the Twentieth Century*. Oxford: Oxford University Press, 2019.

Geary, Daniel. "Children of *The Lonely Crowd*: David Riesman, the Young Radicals, and the Splitting of Liberalism in the 1960s." *Modern Intellectual History* 10, no. 3 (2013): 603–33.

Georgescu-Roegen, Nicholas. "Energy and Economic Myths." *Southern Economic Journal* 41, no. 3 (January 1975): 347–81.

———. *Energy and Economic Myths: Institutional and Analytical Economic Essays*. New York: Pergamon, 1976.

———. *The Entropy Law and the Economic Process*. Cambridge, MA: Harvard University Press, 1971.

Gerwitz, Julian. *Unlikely Partners: Chinese Reformers, Western Economists, and the Making of Global China*. Cambridge, MA: Harvard University Press, 2017.

Getachew, Adom. *Worldmaking after Empire: The Rise and Fall of Self-Determination*. Princeton, NJ: Princeton University Press, 2019.

Geyer, Michael, and Adam Tooze, eds. *The Cambridge History of World War II*. Cambridge: Cambridge University Press, 2015.

Ghai, Dharam P., A. R. Kahn, E. L. H. Lee, and T. Alfthan. *The Basic Needs Approach to Development: Some Issues regarding Concepts and Methodology*. Geneva: International Labour Office, 1977.

Ghosh, Arunabh. "Making It Count: Statistics and State-Society Relations in the Early People's Republic of China, 1949–1959." PhD diss., Columbia University, 2014.

Ghosh, B. N. *Dependency Theory Revisited*. Burlington, VT: Ashgate, 2001.

Ghosh, J. K., P. Maiti, T. J. Rao, and B. K Sinha. "Evolution of Statistics in India." *International Statistical Review* 67, no. 1 (April 1999): 13–34.

Giffen, Robert. "The Importance of General Statistical Ideas." *Journal of the Royal Statistical Society* 64, no. 3 (September 1901): 444–61.

Gilbert, Alan. "On the Mystery of Capital and the Myths of Hernando de Soto: What Difference Does Legal Title Make?" *International Development Planning Review* 24, no. 1 (2002): 1–19.

Gilman, Nils. *Mandarins of the Future: Modernization Theory in Cold War America*. Baltimore: Johns Hopkins University Press, 2003.

———. "Modernization Theory Never Dies." Annual supplement, *History of Political Economy* 50 (December 2018): 133–51.

———. "The New International Economic Order: A Reintroduction." *Humanity* 6, no. 1 (Spring 2015): 1–16.

Glickman, Lawrence. "Inventing the 'American Standard of Living': Gender, Race, and Working-Class Identity, 1880–1925." *Labor History* 34, no. 2 (1993): 221–35.

Gómez-Baggethun, Erik, Rudolf de Groot, Pedro L. Lomas, and Carlos Montes. "The History of Ecosystem Services in Economic Theory and Practice: From Early Notions to Markets and Payment Schemes." *Ecological Economics* 69, no. 6 (2010): 1209–18.

Gordon, Robert J. *The Rise and Fall of American Growth: The US Standard of Living since the Civil War*. Princeton, NJ: Princeton University Press, 2016.

Esping-Andersen, Gøsta. *The Three Worlds of Welfare Capitalism*. Princeton, NJ: Princeton University Press, 1990.

Goswami, Manu. *Producing India: From Colonial Economy to National Space*. Chicago: University of Chicago Press, 2004.

Gottlieb, Robert. *Forcing the Spring: The Transformation of the American Environmental Movement*. Washington, DC: Island, 2005.

Gould, Arthur. *Capitalist Welfare Systems: A Comparison of Japan, Britain, and Sweden*. London: Longman Group UK, 1993.

Gowdy, John, and Susan Mesner. "The Evolution of Georgescu-Roegen's Bioeconomics." *Review of Social Economy* 56, no. 2 (Summer 1998): 136–58.

Griffin, Keith, and Azizur Rahman Khan. "Poverty in the Third World: Ugly Facts and Fancy Models." *World Development* 6, no. 3 (1978): 295–304.

Gross, Stephen G. "Reimagining Energy and Growth: Decoupling and the Rise of a New Energy Paradigm in West Germany, 1973–1986." *Central European History* 50, no. 4 (2017): 514–46.

Grossman, Gregory. *Soviet Statistics of Physical Output of Industrial Commodities: Their Compilation and Quality*. Princeton, NJ: Princeton University Press, 1960.

Grove, Richard. *Green Imperialism: Colonial Expansion, Tropical Island Edens, and the Origins of Environmentalism, 1600–1860*. Cambridge: Cambridge University Press, 1996.

Gubser, Michael. "The Presentist Bias: Ahistoricism, Equity, and International Development in the 1970s." *Journal of Development Studies* 48, no. 12 (2012): 1799–812.

Gutmann, Peter M., ed. *Economic Growth: An American Problem*. Englewood Cliffs, NJ: Prentice-Hall, 1964.

Habib, Irfan. "Studying a Colonial Economy—without Perceiving Colonialism." *Modern Asian Studies* 19, no. 3 (1985): 355–81.

Hager, Sandy Brian. "Varieties of Top Incomes?" *Socio-economic Review* (2018): 1–24.

Hall, N. F. *Preliminary Investigation into Measures of a National or International Character for Raising the Standard of Living.* Geneva: League of Nations, 1938.

Hammond, Thomas H., and Jack H. Knott. "The Deregulatory Snowball: Explaining Deregulation in the Financial Industry." *Journal of Politics* 50, no. 1 (February 1988): 3–30.

Haq, Khadija, and Richard Ponzio, eds. *Pioneering the Human Development Revolution: An Intellectual Biography of Mahbub ul Haq.* New Delhi: Oxford University Press, 2008.

Haq, Mahbub ul. "An International Perspective on Basic Needs." *Finance and Development* 17, no. 3 (September 1980): 11–14.

———. "The Limits to Growth: A Critique." *Finance and Development* 9, no. 4 (December 1972): 2–8.

———. "Negotiating the Future." *Foreign Affairs* 59, no. 2 (Winter 1980): 398–417.

———. *The Poverty Curtain: Choices for the Third World.* New York: Columbia University Press, 1976.

———. *Reflections on Human Development.* New York: Oxford University Press, 1995.

Hardin, Garrett. "Tragedy of the Commons." *Science* 162, no. 3859 (1968): 1243–48.

Hareven, Tamara K., and Maris A. Vinovskis, eds. *Family and Population in Nineteenth-Century America.* Princeton, NJ: Princeton University Press, 1978.

Hart, Keith. "Informal Income Opportunities and Urban Employment in Ghana." *Journal of Modern African Studies* 11, no. 1 (March 1973): 61–89.

Harte, John, and Robert H. Socolow, eds. *Patient Earth.* New York: Holt, Rinehart, and Winston, 1971.

Hatch, Michael. *Politics and Nuclear Power: Energy Policy in Western Europe.* Lexington: University of Kentucky Press, 1986.

Heilbroner, Robert L. *The Quest for Wealth: A Study of Acquisitive Man.* New York: Simon and Schuster, 1956.

Helfrich, Harold W., ed. *The Environmental Crisis: Man's Struggle to Live with Himself.* New Haven, CT: Yale University Press, 1970.

Helleiner, Eric. "The Development Mandate of International Institutions: Where Did It Come From?" *Studies in Comparative International Development* 44, no. 3 (September 2009): 189–211.

Helm, Dieter. *Energy, the State, and the Market: British Energy Policy since 1979.* Oxford: Oxford University Press, 2010.

Henderson, Hazel. "What's Next in the Great Debate about Measuring Wealth and Progress?" *Challenge* 39, no. 6 (1996): 50–56.

Herrera, Yoshiko M. *Mirrors of the Economy: National Accounts and International Norms in Russia and Beyond.* Ithaca, NY: Cornell University Press, 2010.

Hexter, Maurice B. "Implications of a Standard of Living." *American Journal of Sociology* 22, no. 2 (September 1916): 212–25.

Heyck, Hunter. *Age of System: Understanding the Development of Modern Social Science.* Baltimore: Johns Hopkins University Press, 2015.

Hickel, Jason. *The Divide: Global Inequality from Conquest to Free Markets.* New York: W. W. Norton, 2018.

Hicks, Norman, and Paul Streeten. "Indicators of Development: The Search for a Basic Needs Yardstick." *World Development* 7, no. 6 (1979): 567–80.

Higgs, Kerryn. *Collision Course: Endless Growth on a Finite Planet.* Cambridge, MA: MIT Press, 2014.

Hirschman, Albert O. *Essays in Trespassing: Economics to Politics and Beyond.* Cambridge: Cambridge University Press, 1981.

Hirschman, Daniel. "Inventing the Economy, or: How We Learned to Stop Worrying and Love the GDP." PhD diss., University of Michigan, 2016.

Hirschman, Daniel, and Elizabeth Popp Berman. "Do Economists Make Policies? On the Political Effects of Economics." *Socio-economic Review* 12 (2014): 779–811.

Hobsbawm, E. J. "The Standard of Living during the Industrial Revolution: A Discussion." *Economic History Review* 16, no. 1 (1963): 119–34.

Hodge, Joseph Morgan. *Triumph of the Expert: Agrarian Doctrines of Development and the Legacies of British Colonialism.* Athens: Ohio University Press, 2007.

———. "Writing the History of Development (Part 1: The First Wave)." *Humanity: An International Journal of Human Rights, Humanitarianism, and Development* 6, no. 3 (2015): 429–63.

———. "Writing the History of Development (Part 2: Longer, Deeper, Wider)." *Humanity: An International Journal of Human Rights, Humanitarianism, and Development* 7, no. 1 (2016): 125–74.

Hoekstra, Rutger. *Replacing GDP by 2030: Towards a Common Language for the Well-Being and Sustainability Community*. Cambridge: Cambridge University Press, 2019.

Holod, Renata, and Darl Rastorfer, eds. *Architecture and Community*. New York: Aperture, 1983.

Holz, Carsten A. "'Fast, Clear, and Accurate': How Reliable Are Chinese Output and Economic Growth Statistics?" *China Quarterly* 173 (March 2003): 122–63.

———. "The Quality of China's GDP Statistics." *China Economic Review* 30 (2014): 309–38.

Hoselitz, Bert F. *The Sociological Aspects of Economic Growth*. Glencoe: Free Press, 1960.

Howard, Christopher. *The Hidden Welfare State: Tax Expenditures and Social Policy in the United States*. Princeton, NJ: Princeton University Press, 1997.

Howard, M. C., and J. E. King. "'State Capitalism' in the Soviet Union." *History of Economics Review* 34, no. 1 (2001): 110–26.

Howell, Chris. *Trade Unions and the State: The Construction of Industrial Relations Institutions in Britain, 1890–2000*. Princeton, NJ: Princeton University Press, 2009.

Hudson, Peter James. *Bankers and Empire: How Wall Street Colonized the Caribbean*. Chicago: University of Chicago Press, 2016.

Human Development Report 1990. New York: Oxford University Press, 1990.

Iandolo, Alessandro. "The Rise and Fall of the 'Soviet Model of Development' in West Africa, 1957–1964." *Cold War History* 12, no. 4 (2012): 683–704.

Igo, Sarah E. *The Averaged American: Surveys, Citizens, and the Making of a Mass Public*. Cambridge, MA: Harvard University Press, 2007.

International Bank for Reconstruction and Development (IBRD). *The Basis of a Development Program for Colombia: Report of a Mission*. Washington, DC: International Bank for Reconstruction and Development, 1950.

International Copper Study Group. *The World Copper Factbook 2018*. Lisbon: ICSG, 2018.

International Institute for Sustainable Development. *Comprehensive Wealth in Canada 2018—Measuring What Matters in the Long Term*. Winnipeg: IISD, 2018. https://www.iisd.org/sites/default/files/publications/comprehensive-wealth-canada-2018.pdf.

International Labour Office. *Economic Stability in the Post-war World, Part II: The Conditions of Prosperity after the Transition from War to Peace*. Geneva: League of Nations, 1945.

———. *Employment, Incomes, and Equality: A Strategy for Increasing Productive Employment in Kenya*. Geneva: ILO, 1972.

———. *The International Labour Organisation: The First Decade*. London: George Allen and Unwin, 1931.

———. *The Workers Standard of Life in Countries with Depreciated Currency*. Geneva: ILO, 1925.

———. *The Worker's Standard of Living*. Geneva: ILO, 1938.

Iriye, Akira, ed. *Global Interdependence: The World after 1945*. Cambridge, MA: Harvard University Press, 2014.

Irwin, Ryan. "Some Parts Sooner, Some Later, and Finally All." *H-Diplo State of the Field Essay* 142 (October 2016): 1–25. https://networks.h-net.org/system/files/contributed-files/e142_0.pdf.

Islam, S. Nazrul, and John Winkel. "Climate Change and Social Inequality." UN Department of Social and Economic Affairs Working Paper No. 152, October 2017. http://www.un.org/esa/desa/papers/2017/wp152_2017.pdf.

Ittmann, Karl, Dennis D. Cordell, and Gregory H. Maddox, eds. *The Demographics of Empire: The Colonial Order and the Creation of Knowledge*. Athens: Ohio University Press, 2010.

Ivanova, Anna. "Socialist Consumption and Brezhnev's Stagnation: A Reappraisal of Late Communist Everyday Life." *Kritika: Explorations in Russian and Eurasian History* 17, no. 3 (Summer 2016): 665–78.

Jackson, Tim. *Prosperity without Growth*. London: Routledge, 2009.

Jacobs, Meg. *Panic at the Pump: The Energy Crisis and the Transformation of American Politics in the 1970s*. New York: Hill and Wang, 2016.

Jain, S. *Size Distribution of Income: A Compilation of Data*. Washington, DC: World Bank, 1975.

Jaquette, Jane S. "Women and Modernization Theory: A Decade of Feminist Criticism." *World Politics* 34, no. 2 (January 1982): 267–84.

Jarrett, H., ed. *Environmental Quality in a Growing Economy*. Baltimore: Johns Hopkins University Press, 1966.

Jeffries, John W. "The 'Quest for National Purpose' of 1960." *American Quarterly* 30, no. 4 (Autumn 1978): 451–70.

Jerven, Morten. *Africa: Why Economists Got It Wrong*. London: Zed Books, 2015.

———. *Economic Growth and Measurement Reconsidered in Botswana, Kenya, Tanzania, and Zambia, 1965–1995*. Oxford: Oxford University Press, 2014.

———. *Poor Numbers: How We Are Misled by African Development Statistics and What to Do about It*. Ithaca, NY: Cornell University Press, 2013.

———. "Users and Producers of African Income: Measuring the Progress of African Economies." *African Affairs* 110, no. 439 (April 2011): 169–90.

Johnson, Harry. "A Word to the Third World: A Western Economist's Frank Advice." *Encounter* 37 (October 1971): 3–10.

Johnson, Simon, and Peter Temin. "The Macroeconomics of NEP." *Economic History Review* 46, no. 4 (1993): 750–67.

Jones, William O. "Colonial Social Accounting." *Journal of the American Statistical Association* 50, no. 271 (September 1955): 665–76.

Jonsson, Fredrik Albritton. "The Origins of Cornucopianism: A Preliminary Genealogy." *Critical History Studies* 1, no. 1 (Spring 2014): 151–68.

Judt, Tony. *Postwar: A History of Europe since 1945*. New York: Penguin, 2005.

Jundt, Thomas. "Dueling Visions for the Postwar World: The UN and UNESCO 1949 Conferences on Resources and Nature, and the Origins of Environmentalism." *Journal of American History* 101, no. 1 (June 2014): 44–70.

Kahn, Herman, William Brown, and Leon Martel. *The Next 200 Years: A Scenario for America and the World*. New York: Morrow, 1976.

Kallis, Giorgos, Vasilis Kostakis, Steffen Lange, Barbara Muraca, Susan Paulson, and Matthias Schmelzer. "Research on Degrowth." *Annual Review of Environment and Resources* 43 (2018): 291–316.

Kapur, Devesh, John P. Lewis, and Richard Webb, eds. *The World Bank: Its First Half Century*. Washington, DC: Brookings Institution Press, 1997.

Karabell, Zachary. *The Leading Indicators: A Short History of the Numbers That Rule Our World*. New York: Simon and Schuster, 2014.

———. "Learning to Love Stagnation." *Foreign Affairs* 95, no. 2 (March/April 2016): 47–53.

Katznelson, Ira. *When Affirmative Action Was White: An Untold History of Racial Inequality in Twentieth-Century America*. New York: W. W. Norton, 2005.

Keasbey, Lindley M. "The Economic State." *Political Science Quarterly* 8, no. 4 (December 1893): 601–24.

Kelley, Donald R. "Economic Growth and Environmental Quality in the USSR: Soviet Reaction to the 'Limits of Growth.'" *Revue Canadienne des Slavistes* 18 (September 1976): 266–83.

Kelley, Judith G., and Beth A. Simmons. "Politics by Number: Indicators as Social Pressure in International Relations." *American Journal of Political Science* 59, no. 1 (January 2015): 55–70.

Kemp, Janet. *Housing Conditions in Baltimore*. Baltimore: Federated Charities, 1907.

Kentikelenis, Alexander E., and Sarah Babb. "The Making of Neoliberal Globalization: Norm Substitution and the Politics of Clandestine Institutional Change." *American Journal of Sociology* 124, no. 6 (2019): 1720–62.

Kessler-Harris, Alice. *In Pursuit of Equity: Women, Men, and the Quest for Economic Citizenship in 20th Century America*. New York: Oxford University Press, 2002.

Kidron, Michael. *Capitalism and Theory*. London: Pluto, 1974.

Klimke, Martin, Jacco Pekelder, and Joachim Scharloth, eds. *Between Prague Spring and French May: Opposition and Revolt in Europe, 1960–1980*. New York: Berghahn Books, 2011.

Koczberski, Gina. "Women in Development: A Critical Analysis." *Third World Quarterly* 19, no. 3 (September 1998): 395–409.

Kott, Sandrine, and Joelle Droux, eds. *Globalizing Social Rights: The International Labour Organization, 1940–1970*. Geneva: International Labour Office, 2012.

Kramer, Paul A. *The Blood of Government: Race, Empire, the United States, and the Philippines*. Chapel Hill: University of North Carolina Press, 2006.

Krasner, Stephen. *Structural Conflict: The Third World against Global Liberalism*. Berkeley: University of California Press, 1985.

Krippner, Greta. *Capitalizing on Crisis: The Political Origins of the Rise of Finance*. Cambridge, MA: Harvard University Press, 2011.

Kubiszewski, Ida, Robert Costanza, Carol Franco, Philip Lawn, John Talberth, Tim Jackson, and Camille Aylmer. "Beyond GDP: Measuring and Achieving Genuine Global Progress." *Ecological Economics* 93 (2013): 57–68.

Kuznets, Simon. "Economic Growth and Income Inequality." *American Economic Review* 45, no. 1 (March 1955): 1–28.

Lakner, Christoph, and Branko Milanovic. "Global Income Distribution: From the Fall of the Berlin Wall to the Great Recession." *World Bank Economic Review* 30, no. 2 (2016): 203–32.

Lal, Deepak. *The Poverty of "Development Economics."* London: Institute for Economic Affairs, 1983.

Larson, David A., and Walton T. Wilford. "The Physical Quality of Life Index: A Useful Social Indicator?" *World Development* 7, no. 6 (1979): 581–84.

Latham, Michael E. *The Right Kind of Revolution: Modernization, Development, and US Foreign Policy from the Cold War to the Present*. Ithaca, NY: Cornell University Press, 2011.

Latouche, Serge. *Farewell to Growth*. Translated by David Macey. Cambridge, UK: Polity, 2009.

Lawn, Philip. "A Stock-Take of Green National Accounting Initiatives." *Social Indicators Research* 80, no. 2 (January 2007): 427–60.

Leffler, Melvyn P. *For the Soul of Mankind: The United States, the Soviet Union, and the Cold War*. New York: Hill and Wang, 2007.

Leffler, Melvyn P., and Odd Arne Westad, eds. *The Cambridge History of the Cold War*. Cambridge: Cambridge University Press, 2010.

Lehmann, David. "Dudley Seers (1920–1983)." *Bulletin of Latin American Research* 2, no. 2 (May 1983): 1–2.

Leghorn, Lisa, and Katherine Parker. *Woman's Worth: Sexual Economics and the World of Women*. Boston: Routledge and Kegan Paul, 1981.

Leghorn, Lisa, and Betsy Warrior. *Houseworker's Handbook*. Cambridge, MA: Woman's Center, 1974.

Leopold, Aldo. *A Sand County Almanac: With Essays on Conservation from Round River*. 1949. New York: Ballantine Books, 1966.

Lepenies, Philipp. *The Power of a Single Number: A Political History of GDP*. Translated by Jeremy Gaines. New York: Columbia University Press, 2016.

Levy, Jonathan. *Freaks of Fortune: The Emerging World of Capitalism and Risk in America*. Cambridge, MA: Harvard University Press, 2012.

Lewis, W. Arthur. "A Review of Economic Development." *American Economic Review* 55, no. 2 (1965): 1–16.

———. *The Theory of Economic Growth*. London: Allen and Unwin, 1955.

Leys, Colin. "Interpreting African Underemployment: Reflections on the ILO Report on Employment, Incomes and Equality in Kenya." *African Affairs* 72, no. 289 (October 1973): 419–29.

Lichtenstein, Nelson. *State of the Union: A Century of American Labor*. Princeton, NJ: Princeton University Press, 2003.

Love, Joseph L. "The Origins of Dependency Analysis." *Journal of Latin American Studies* 22, no. 1 (February 1990): 143–68.

Lundestad, Geir, ed. *International Relations since the End of the Cold War*. Oxford: Oxford University Press, 2013.

Macekura, Stephen. "Dudley Seers, the Institute for Development Studies, and the Fracturing of International Development Thought in the 1960s and the 1970s." *History of Political Economy* 52, no. 1 (February 2020): 47–75.

———. *Of Limits and Growth: The Rise of Global Sustainable Development in the Twentieth Century*. New York: Cambridge University Press, 2015.

———. "The Limits of Global Community: The Nixon Administration and Global Environmental Politics." *Cold War History* 11, no. 4 (2011): 489–518.

———. "The Point Four Program and International Development Policy." *Political Science Quarterly* 128, no. 1 (Spring 2013): 127–60.

Macekura, Stephen, and Erez Manela, eds. *The Development Century: A Global History*. New York: Cambridge University Press, 2018.

MacLean, Nancy. *Freedom Is Not Enough: The Opening of the American Workplace*. Cambridge, MA: Harvard University Press, 2006.

Maier, Charles S. "The Politics of Productivity: Foundations of American International Economic Policy after World War II." *International Organization* 31, no. 4 (1977): 607–33.

———. *Recasting Bourgeois Europe: Stabilization in France, Germany, and Italy in the Decade after World War I*. Princeton, NJ: Princeton University Press, 1988.

Man's Impact on the Global Environment: Report of the Study of Critical Environmental Problems (SCEP). Cambridge, MA: MIT Press, 1970.

Marcuse, Herbert. *One-Dimensional Man: Studies in the Ideology of Advanced Industrial Society*. Boston: Beacon, 1964.

Markoff, John, and Veronica Montecinos. "The Ubiquitous Rise of Economists." *Journal of Public Policy* 13, no. 1 (January–March 1993): 37–68.

Masood, Ehsan. *The Great Invention: The Story of GDP and the Making (and Unmaking) of the Modern World*. New York: Pegasus Books, 2016.

Mayumi, Kozo, and John M. Gowdy, eds. *Bioeconomics and Sustainability: Essays in Honor of Nicholas Georgescu-Roegen*. Cheltenham, UK: Edward Elgar, 1999.

Mazower, Mark. *Dark Continent: Europe's Twentieth Century*. London: Penguin, 1998.

———. *Governing the World: The History of an Idea*. New York: Penguin, 2012.

Mazzucato, Mariana. *The Value of Everything: Making and Taking in the Global Economy*. London: Allen Lane, 2018.

Mboya, Tom. *The Challenge of Nationhood: A Collection of Speeches and Writings by Tom Mboya*. New York: Praeger, 1970.

McCartin, Joseph A. *Collision Course: Ronald Reagan, the Air Traffic Controllers, and the Strike That Changed America*. New York: Oxford University Press, 2011.

———. *Labor's Great War: The Struggle for Industrial Democracy and the Origins of Modern American Labor Relations, 1912–1921*. Chapel Hill: University of North Carolina Press, 1997.

McCormick, John. *The Global Environmental Movement*. 2nd ed. Chichester: John Wiley and Sons, 1995.

McCraw, Thomas. *Prophets of Regulation*. Cambridge, MA: Belknap Press of Harvard University Press, 1984.

McFarland, Victor. "Living in Never-Never Land: The United States, Saudi Arabia, and Oil in the 1970s." PhD diss., Yale University, 2014.

———. "The New International Economic Order, Interdependence, and Globalization." *Humanity* 6, no. 1 (Spring 2015): 217–33.

McGranahan, D. V., C. Richard-Proust, N. V. Sovani, and M. Subramanian. *Contents and Measurements of Socioeconomic Development*. New York: Praeger, 1972.

McMichael, Philip. *Development and Social Change: A Global Perspective*. Thousand Oaks, CA: Pine Forge, 1996.

McNeill, J. R. *Something New under the Sun: An Environmental History of the Twentieth-Century World*. New York: W. W. Norton, 2000.

McVety, Amanda Kay. *Enlightened Aid: US Development as Foreign Policy in Ethiopia*. New York: Oxford University Press, 2012.

Meadows, Dennis L., ed. *Alternatives to Growth-I: A Search for Sustainable Futures*. Cambridge: Ballinger, 1975.

Meadows, Donella H., Dennis L. Meadows, Jørgen Randers, and William W. Behrens III. *The Limits to Growth*. New York: Universe Books, 1972.

Measurement of National Income and the Construction of National Accounts: Report of the Sub-committee on National Income Statistics of the League of Nations Committee of Statistical Experts. Geneva: United Nations, 1947.

Measures for the Economic Development of Under-developed Countries. New York: United Nations, 1951.

Measuring Social Well-Being: A Progress Report on the Development of Social Indicators. Paris: OECD, 1976.

Menand, Louis. *The Metaphysical Club: A Story of Ideas in America*. New York: Farrar, Straus and Giroux, 2001.

Merchant, Carolyn. *The Death of Nature: Women, Ecology, and the Scientific Revolution*. New York: HarperCollins, 1980.

Merton, Robert K., and Robert A. Nisbet. *Contemporary Social Problems*. 2nd ed. New York: Harcourt, Brace, and World, 1966.

Messac, Luke. "Outside the Economy: Women's Work and Feminist Economics in the Construction of National Income Accounting." *Journal of Imperial and Commonwealth History* 46, no. 3 (2018): 552–78.

Mettler, Suzanne. *The Submerged State: How Invisible Government Policies Undermine American Democracy*. Chicago: University of Chicago Press, 2011.

Meynaud, Jean. *Technocracy*. Translated by Paul Barnes. New York: Free Press, 1964.

Milanovic, Branko. *Global Inequality: A New Approach for the Age of Innovation*. Cambridge, MA: Harvard University Press, 2016.

Miles, Ian. *Social Indicators for Human Development*. New York: St. Martin's, 1985.

Mill, John Stuart. *Principles of Political Economy with Some of Their Applications to Social Philosophy*. London: Longmans, Green, 1926.

Miller, Chris. *The Struggle to Save the Soviet Economy: Mikhail Gorbachev and the Collapse of the Soviet Union*. Chapel Hill: University of North Carolina Press, 2016.

Milward, Alan S. *The European Rescue of the Nation-State*. London: Routledge, 2000.

———. *War, Economy, and Society, 1939–1945*. Berkeley: University of California Press, 1979.

Mirowski, Philip. *More Heat Than Light: Economics as Social Physics, Physics as Nature's Economics*. New York: Cambridge University Press, 1989.

———. "The Zero Hour of History? Is Neoliberalism Some Sort of 'Mode of Production'?" *Development and Change* 47, no. 3 (2016): 586–97.

Mishan, Ezra J. *The Costs of Economic Growth*. New York: Staples, 1967.

———. *The Economic Growth Debate: An Assessment*. London: George Allen and Unwin, 1977.

———. "The Economics of Disamenity." *Natural Resources Journal* 14, no. 1 (January 1974): 55–86.

———. "The Postwar Literature on Externalities: An Interpretative Essay." *Journal of Economic Literature* 9, no. 1 (March 1971): 1–28.

Mitchell, Timothy. "Econometality: How the Future Entered Government." *Critical Inquiry*, no. 40 (Summer 2014): 479–507.

———. "Rethinking Economy." *Geoforum* 39 (2008): 1116–21.

———. *Rule of Experts: Egypt, Techno-politics, Modernity*. Berkeley: University of California Press, 2002.

———. "The Work of Economics: How a Discipline Makes Its World." *European Journal of Sociology* 46 (2005): 297–320.

Mitra-Kahn, Benjamin. "Redefining the Economy: How the 'Economy' Was Invented in 1620, and Has Been Redefined Ever Since." PhD diss., City University London, 2011.

Mkandawire, Thandika. "The Crisis in Economic Development Theory." *Africa Development* 15, no. 3/4 (1990): 209–30.

———. "The New International Economic Order, Basic Needs Strategies and the Future of Africa." *Afrique et Développement* 5, no. 3 (1980): 68–89.

Mohan, Giles, Ed Brown, Bob Milward, and Alfred B. Zack-Williams. *Structural Adjustment: Theory, Practice, and Impacts.* London: Routledge, 2000.

Moon, Suzanne. *Technology and Ethical Idealism: A History of Development in the Netherlands East Indies.* Leiden: CNWS, 2007.

Moravcsik, Andrew. *The Choice for Europe: Social Purpose and State Power from Messina to Maastricht.* Ithaca, NY: Cornell University Press, 1998.

Morgenstern, Oskar. *On the Accuracy of Economic Observations.* 2nd ed. Princeton, NJ: Princeton University Press, 1963.

Morris, Morris David. *Measuring the Condition of the World's Poor: The Physical Quality of Life Index.* New York: Pergamon, 1979.

———. "A Physical Quality of Life Index." *Urban Ecology* 3, no. 3 (1978): 225–40.

Morris, Morris David, and Michelle B. McAlpin. *Measuring the Condition of India's Poor: The Physical Quality of Life Index.* New Delhi: Promilla, 1982.

Morris-Suzuki, Tessa. *A History of Japanese Economic Thought.* London: Routledge, 1989.

Moses, Bernard. "The Economic Situation in Japan." *Journal of Political Economy* 6, no. 2 (March 1898): 168–96.

Moskowitz, Marina. *Standard of Living: The Measure of the Middle Class in Modern America.* Baltimore: Johns Hopkins University Press, 2004.

Moss, Milton, ed. *The Measurement of Economic and Social Performance.* New York: National Bureau of Economic Research, 1973.

Moyn, Samuel. *Not Enough: Human Rights in an Unequal World.* Cambridge, MA: Belknap Press of Harvard University Press, 2018.

Mudge, Stephanie L. *Leftism Reinvented: Western Parties from Socialism to Neoliberalism.* Cambridge, MA: Harvard University Press, 2018.

Murphy, Michelle. *The Economization of Life.* Durham, NC: Duke University Press, 2017.

Myrdal, Gunnar. *Asian Drama: An Inquiry into the Poverty of Nations.* New York: Twentieth Century Fund, 1968.

The National Purpose. New York: Holt, Rinehart, and Winston, 1960.

Nelson, Nicki, ed. *African Women in the Development Process.* London: Frank Cass, 1981.

Nemchenok, Victor V. "A Dialogue of Power: Development, Global Civil Society, and the Third World Challenge to International Order, 1969–1981." PhD diss., University of Virginia, 2013.

NNW Measurement Committee. *Measuring Net National Welfare of Japan.* Tokyo: Printing Bureau Ministry of Finance, 1973.

Nolan, Mary. *The Transatlantic Century: Europe and America, 1890–2010.* Cambridge: Cambridge University Press, 2012.

Nordhaus, William D., Robert N. Stavins, and Martin L. Weitzman. "Lethal Model 2: The Limits to Growth Revisited." *Brookings Papers on Economy Activity* 2 (1992): 1–59.

Nordhaus, William D., and Edward C. Kokkelenberg, eds. *Nature's Numbers: Expanding the National Economic Accounts to Include the Environment.* Washington, DC: National Academy Press, 1999.

Norgaard, Richard B. "Ecosystem Services: From Eye-Opening Metaphor to Complexity Blinder." *Ecological Economics* 69, no. 6 (2010): 1219–27.

———. "Scarcity and Growth: How Does It Look Today?" *American Journal of Agricultural Economics* 57, no. 5 (1975): 810–14.

Nussbaum, Martha C., and Amartya Sen, eds. *The Quality of Life.* Oxford: Oxford University Press, 1993.

Nutter, G. Warren, ed. *Growth of Industrial Production in the Soviet Union.* Princeton, NJ: Princeton University Press, 1962.

Oakley, Ann. *The Sociology of Housework.* London: Martin Robertson, 1974.

O'Bryan, Scott. *The Growth Idea: Purpose and Prosperity in Postwar Japan.* Honolulu: University of Hawaii Press, 2009.

O'Connor, Alice. *Poverty Knowledge: Social Science, Social Policy, and the Poor in Twentieth-Century US History.* Princeton, NJ: Princeton University Press, 2001.

Odum, Howard T. *Environment, Power, and Society.* New York: John Wiley and Sons, 1971.

Ogle, Vanessa. "Archipelago Capitalism: Tax Havens, Offshore Money, and the State, 1950s–1970s." *American Historical Review* 122, no. 5 (December 2017): 1431–58.

Okigbo, Pius N. C. *Nigerian National Accounts, 1950–57.* Enugu: Government Printer, 1962.

Olson, Mancur, and Hans H. Landsberg, eds. *The No-Growth Society.* New York: W. W. Norton, 1973.

Oltmans, Willem L., ed. *On Growth.* New York: Capricorn Books, 1974.

———. *On Growth II*. New York: Capricorn Books, 1975.

Oshima, Harry T. "National Income Statistics of Underdeveloped Countries." *Journal of the American Statistical Association* 52, no. 278 (June 1957): 162–74.

———. "Reinterpreting Japan's Postwar Growth." *Economic Development and Cultural Change* 31, no. 1 (October 1982): 1–43.

Packard, Vance. *The Waste Makers*. New York: David McKay, 1960.

Painter, David. *Oil and the American Century: The Political Economy of US Foreign Oil Policy, 1941–1954*. Baltimore: Johns Hopkins University Press, 1986.

———. "Oil and World Power." *Diplomatic History* 17, no. 1 (Winter 1993): 159–70.

Panitch, Leo, and Sam Gindin. *The Making of Global Capitalism: The Political Economy of American Empire*. London: Verso Books, 2013.

Papi, U., and C. Nunn, eds. *Economic Problems of Agriculture in Industrial Societies*. London: MacMillan, 1965.

Parke, Robert, and David Seidman. "Social Indicators and Social Reporting." *Annals of the American Academy of Political and Social Science* 435 (1978): 1–22.

Patel, Kiran Klaus. *The New Deal: A Global History*. Princeton, NJ: Princeton University Press, 2016.

Patriarca, Silvana. *Numbers and Nationhood: Writing Statistics in Nineteenth-Century Italy*. Cambridge: Cambridge University Press, 1996.

Patterson, James T. *America's Struggle against Poverty in the Twentieth Century*. Cambridge, MA: Harvard University Press, 2000.

Peacock, Alan T., and Douglas G. M. Dosser. *The National Income of Tanganyika*. London: Her Majesty's Stationery Office, 1958.

Pearce, Kimber Charles. *Rostow, Kennedy, and the Rhetoric of Foreign Aid*. East Lansing: Michigan State University Press, 2001.

Pearson, Lester B. *Partners in Development: Report of the Commission on International Development*. New York: Praeger, 1969.

Peattie, Lisa. "An Idea in Good Currency and How It Grew: The Informal Sector." *World Development* 15, no. 7 (1987): 851–60.

Petersen, Neal H., John P. Glennon, David W. Mabon, Ralph R. Goodwin, and William Z. Slany, eds. *Foreign Relations of the United States, 1950, National Security Affairs: Foreign Economic Policy*. Washington, DC: Government Printing Office, 1977.

Pettinà, Vanni, and Artemy M. Kalinovsky. "From Countryside to Factory: Industrialisation, Social Mobility, and Neoliberalism in Soviet Central Asia and Mexico." *Journal fuer Entwicklungspolitik* 33, no. 3 (2018): 91–118.

Phelps, Edmund. "The Golden Rule of Accumulation: A Fable for Growthmen." *American Economic Review* 51, no. 4 (September 1961): 638–43.

Philipsen, Dirk. *The Little Big Number: How GDP Came to Rule the World and What to Do about It.* Princeton, NJ: Princeton University Press, 2015.

Pigou, Arthur. *Economics of Welfare.* London: Macmillan, 1920.

Piketty, Thomas. *Capital in the Twenty-First Century.* Cambridge, MA: Harvard University Press, 2014.

Piketty, Thomas, and Emmanuel Saez. "Income Inequality in the United States, 1913–1998." *Quarterly Journal of Economics* 68, no. 1 (February 2003): 1–39.

———. "The Evolution of Top Incomes: A Historical and International Perspective." NBER Working Paper 11955, 2006.

Piketty, Thomas, Emmanuel Saez, Gabriel Zucman. "Distributional National Accounts: Methods and Estimates for the United States." *Quarterly Journal of Economics* 133, no. 2 (2018): 553–609.

Pilling, David. *The Growth Delusion: Wealth, Poverty, and the Well-Being of Nations.* New York: Tim Duggan Books, 2018.

Pinker, Steven. "Enlightenment Environmentalism: The Case for Ecomodernism." *Breakthrough Journal*, no. 8 (Winter 2018): 29–41. https://thebreakthrough.org/index.php/journal/past-issues/no.-8-winter-2018/enlightenment-environmentalism.

Pollin, Robert. "De-growth vs. a Green New Deal." *New Left Review* 112 (July–August 2018): 5–25.

Pollin, Robert, Heidi Garrett-Peltier, James Heintz, and Bracken Hendricks. "Green Growth: A US Program for Controlling Climate Change and Expanding Job Opportunities." Washington, DC: Center for American Progress and Political Economy Research Institute, 2014. https://www.americanprogress.org/issues/green/reports/2014/09/18/96404/green-growth/.

Pope, Clayne L. "The Changing View of the Standard-of-Living Question in the United States." *American Economic Review* 83, no. 2 (May 1993): 331–36.

Porter, Theodore M. *The Rise of Statistical Thinking, 1820–1920.* Princeton, NJ: Princeton University Press, 1986.

———. *Trust in Numbers: The Pursuit of Objectivity in Science and Public Life.* Princeton, NJ: Princeton University Press, 1995.

Porter, Theodore M., and Dorothy Ross, eds. *The Cambridge History of Science.* Cambridge: Cambridge University Press, 2003.

Portes, Alejandro, Manuel Castells, and Lauren A. Benton, eds. *The Informal Economy: Studies in Advanced and Less Developed Countries.* Baltimore: Johns Hopkins University Press, 1989.

Prest, A. R., and I. G. Stewart. *The National Income of Nigeria: 1950–1951*. London: Her Majesty's Stationery Office, 1953.

Problems of Foreign Aid: A Conference Report. Dar es Salaam: Printpak Tanzania, 1965.

Prospects for Employment Opportunities in the Nineteen Seventies. London: Her Majesty's Stationery Office, 1971.

Psalidopoulos, Michalis, ed. *The Canon in the History of Economics: Critical Essays*. London: Routledge, 2002.

Purdey, Stephen J. *Economic Growth, the Environment, and International Relations: The Growth Paradigm*. London: Routledge, 2009.

Purdy, Jedediah. *After Nature: A Politics for the Anthropocene*. Cambridge, MA: Harvard University Press, 2015.

The Quality of Life Concept: A Potential New Tool for Decision-Makers. Washington, DC: Environmental Protection Agency, 1973.

Rao, C. H. Hanumantha, and P. C. Joshi, eds. *Reflection on Economic Development and Social Change: Essays in Honour of Professor V. K. R. V. Rao*. New Delhi: Allied, 1979.

Rao, S. L., ed. *The Partial Memoirs of V. K. R. V. Rao*. New Delhi: Oxford University Press, 2002.

Rao, V. K. R. V. "Some Reflections on the Comparability of Real National Income of Industrialized and Under-developed Countries." *Review of Income and Wealth* 3 (1953): 178–210.

Rauchway, Eric. "The High Cost of Living in the Progressives' Economy." *Journal of American History* 88, no. 3 (December 2001): 898–924.

Ravallion, Martin. "Good and Bad Growth: The Human Development Reports." *World Development* 25, no. 5 (1997): 631–38.

Recent Economic Changes in the United States. Vols. 1 and 2. Cambridge, MA: National Bureau of Economic Research, 1929.

Reinsberg, B., A. Kentikelenis, T. Stubbs, and L. King. "The World System and the Hollowing-Out of State Capacity: How Structural Adjustment Programs Impact Bureaucratic Quality in Developing Countries." *American Journal of Sociology* 124, no. 4 (2019): 1222–57.

Report on International Definition and Measurement of Standards and Levels of Living. New York: United Nations, 1954.

Richta, Radovan. *Civilization at the Crossroads: Social and Human Implications of the Scientific and Technological Revolution*. Translated by Marian Slingova. Prague: International Arts and Sciences, 1969.

———. "The Scientific and Technological Revolution." *Australian Left Review* 1, no. 7 (1967): 54–67.

Riesman, David. *"Abundance for What?" and Other Essays.* Garden City, NY: Doubleday, 1964.

Riley, Charlotte Lydia. "Monstrous Predatory Vampires and Beneficent Fairy-Godmothers: British Post-war Colonial Development in Africa." PhD diss., University College London, 2013.

Riley, T. J. Review of *The Standard of Living in New York City,* by Robert Coit Chapin. *American Journal of Sociology* 15, no. 2 (October 1909): 268–74.

Rimmer, Douglas. "'Basic Needs' and the Origins of the Development Ethos." *Journal of the Developing Areas* 15, no. 2 (1981): 215–38.

———. *Macromancy: The Ideology of "Development Economics."* Tonbridge, UK: Tonbridge Printers, 1973.

———. Review of *Measuring the Condition of the World's Poor: The Physical Quality of Life Index,* by Morris David Morris. *Journal of the Developing Areas* 17, no. 2 (January 1983): 268–69.

Rindzevičiūtė, Eglė. "A Struggle for the Soviet Future: The Birth of Scientific Forecasting in the Soviet Union." *Slavic Review* 75, no. 1 (Spring 2016): 52–76.

Risch, William Jay. "Soviet 'Flower Children': Hippies and the Youth Counter-culture in 1970s L'viv." *Journal of Contemporary History* 40, no. 3 (July 2005): 565–84.

Rist, Gilbert. *The History of Development: From Western Origins to Global Faith.* 3rd ed. Translated by Patrick Camiller. New York: Zed Books, 2008.

Rivas, Darlene. *Missionary Capitalist: Nelson Rockefeller in Venezuela.* Chapel Hill: University of North Carolina Press, 2002.

Robertson, Thomas. *The Malthusian Moment: Global Population Growth and the Birth of American Environmentalism.* New Brunswick, NJ: Rutgers University Press, 2012.

Robinson, Ronald, and Peter Johnston, eds. *Prospects for Employment Opportunities in the Nineteen Seventies.* London: Her Majesty's Stationery Office, 1971.

Rodgers, Daniel T. *Age of Fracture.* Cambridge, MA: Belknap Press of Harvard University Press, 2011.

Rodgers, Gerry, Lee Swepston, Jasmien Van Daele, and Eddy Lee. *The International Labour Organization and the Quest for Social Justice, 1919–2009.* International Labour Organization: Geneva, 2009.

Røpke, Inge. "The Early History of Modern Ecological Economics." *Ecological Economics* 50 (2004): 293–314.

Rose, Lisle A., and Neal H. Petersen, eds. *Foreign Relations of the United States, 1952–1954, National Security Affairs.* Vol. 2, part 1. Washington, DC: Government Printing Office, 1984.

Rosenberg, Emily S., ed. *A World Connecting, 1870–1945.* Cambridge, MA: Belknap Press of Harvard University Press, 2012.

Rosenstein-Rodan, P. N. "Problems of Industrialization of Eastern and Southeastern Europe." *Economic Journal* 53, no. 210/211 (June–September 1943): 202–11.

Rosenthal, Caitlin C. "From Memory to Mastery: Accounting for Control in America: 1750–1880." *Enterprise and Society* 14, no. 4 (December 2013): 732–48.

Rostow, W. W. *The Stages of Economic Growth: A Non-Communist Manifesto.* Cambridge: Cambridge University Press, 1960.

Roy, Tirthankar. "Morris David Morris (1921–2011)." *Economic and Political Weekly* 46, no. 13 (March 26–April 1, 2011): 27–30.

Ruggie, John Gerard. "Multinationals as Global Institution: Power, Authority, and Relative Autonomy." *Regulation and Governance* 12, no. 3 (September 2018): 317–33.

Sabin, Paul. *The Bet: Paul Ehrlich, Julian Simon, and Our Gamble over the Earth's Future.* New Haven, CT: Yale University Press, 2013.

Sachs, Jeffrey D., ed. *Developing Country Debt and the World Economy.* Chicago: University of Chicago Press, 1989.

Sackley, Nicole. "Passage to Modernity: American Social Scientists, India, and the Pursuit of Development, 1945–1961." PhD diss., Princeton University, 2004.

Sagoff, Mark. "Carrying Capacity and Ecological Economics." *BioScience* 45, no. 9 (October 1995): 610–20.

———. "The Rise and Fall of Ecological Economics." *Breakthrough Journal* 2 (2011): 43–56. https://thebreakthrough.org/index.php/journal/past-issues/issue-2/the-rise-and-fall-of-ecological-economics/#body47.

Samuelson, Robert J. *The Great Inflation and Its Aftermath: The Past and Future of American Affluence.* New York: Random House, 2008.

Sanchez-Sibony, Oscar. "Economic Growth in the Governance of the Cold War Divide: Mikoyan's Encounter with Japan, Summer 1961." *Journal of Cold War Studies* 20, no. 2 (Spring 2018): 129–54.

Sandbach, Francis. "The Rise and Fall of the *Limits to Growth* Debate." *Social Studies of Science* 8 (1978): 495–520.

Sargent, Daniel J. "The Cold War and the International Political Economy in the 1970s." *Cold War History* 13, no. 3 (2013): 393–425.

———. *A Superpower Transformed: The Remaking of American Foreign Relations in the 1970s.* New York: Oxford University Press, 2015.

Sartorius, Rolf H., and Vernon W. Ruttan. "The Source of the Basic Human Needs Mandate." *Journal of Developing Areas* 23, no. 3 (1989): 332–37.

Satterthwaite, David. *Barbara Ward and the Origins of Sustainable Development.* London: IIED, 2006.

Schmelzer, Matthias. "The Growth Paradigm: History, Hegemony, and the Contested Making of Economic Growthmanship." *Ecological Economics* 118 (2015): 262–71.

———. *The Hegemony of Growth: The Making and Remaking of the Economic Growth Paradigm and the OECD, 1948 to 2010.* Cambridge: Cambridge University Press, 2016.

Schoijet, Mauricio. "Limits to Growth and the Rise of Catastrophism." *Environmental History* 4, no. 4 (October 1999): 515–30.

Schor, Paul. *Counting Americans: How the US Census Classified the Nation.* Translated by Lys Ann Weiss. New York: Oxford University Press, 2017.

Schumacher, E. F. *Small Is Beautiful: Economics as If People Mattered.* New York: Harper and Row, 1973.

Scitovsky, Tibor. *Human Desire and Economic Satisfaction: Essays on the Frontiers of Economics.* Brighton, UK: Wheatsheaf Books, 1986.

———. *The Joyless Economy: An Inquiry into Human Satisfaction and Consumer Dissatisfaction.* New York: Oxford University Press, 1976.

Scott, James C. *Against the Grain: A Deep History of the Earliest States.* New Haven, CT: Yale University Press, 2017.

———. *Seeing Like a State: How Certain Schemes to Improve the Human Condition Have Failed.* New Haven, CT: Yale University Press, 1998.

Seefried, Elke. "Towards *The Limits to Growth*? The Book and Its Reception in West Germany and Britain, 1972–1973." *German Historical Institute London Bulletin* 33, no. 1 (May 2011): 3–37.

Seers, Dudley. "The Birth, Life, and Death of Development Economics." *Development and Change* 10 (1979): 707–19.

———. "The Limitations of the Special Case." *Bulletin of the Institute of Economics and Statistics, Oxford* 25, no. 2 (1963): 77–98.

———. "The Role of National Income Estimates in the Statistical Policy of an Underdeveloped Area." *Review of Economic Studies* 10 (1952–53): 159–68.

———. "Why Visiting Economists Fail." *Journal of Political Economy* 70, no. 4 (1962): 325–38.

Seers, Dudley, and Leonard Joy, eds. *Development in a Divided World*. Harmondsworth, UK: Penguin Books, 1970.

Seers, Dudley, and C. R. Ross. *Report on the Financial and Physical Problems of Development in the Gold Coast*. Accra: Office of the Government Statistician, 1952.

Self, Robert O. *All in the Family: The Realignment of American Democracy since the 1960s*. New York: Hill and Wang, 2012.

Sen, Amartya. *Collective Choice and Social Welfare*. San Francisco: Holden-Day, 1970.

———. *Commodities and Capabilities*. New York: Oxford University Press, 1999.

———. *On Economic Inequality*. Oxford: Clarendon, 1973.

———. "Poverty: An Ordinal Approach to Measurement." *Econometrica* 44, no. 2 (March 1976): 219–31.

Shaikh, Anwar, and Ahnet Tomak. *Measuring the Wealth of Nations: The Political Economy of National Accounts*. Cambridge: Cambridge University Press, 1994.

Sharma, Patrick Allan. "Between North and South: The World Bank and the New International Economic Order." *Humanity* 6, no. 1 (2015): 189–200.

———. *Robert McNamara's Other War: The World Bank and International Development*. Philadelphia: University of Pennsylvania Press, 2017.

Sheldon, Eleanor Bernert, and Wilbert E. Moore, eds. *Indicators of Social Change: Concepts and Measurements*. New York: Russell Sage Foundation, 1968.

Shenk, Timothy. "Inventing the American Economy." PhD diss., Columbia University, 2016.

Simmons, Beth A., and Zachary Elkins. "The Globalization of Liberalization: Policy Diffusion in the International Political Economy." *American Political Science Review* 98, no. 1 (2004): 171–89.

Simpson, Brad. "Indonesia's 'Accelerated Modernization' and the Global Discourse of Development." *Diplomatic History* 33, no. 3 (2009): 467–86.

Singer, H. W. "The New International Order: An Overview." *Journal of Modern African Studies* 16, no. 4 (December 1978): 539–48.

———. "The Notion of Human Investment." *Review of Social Economy* 24, no. 1 (1966): 1–20.

Singh, Ajit. "The 'Basic Needs' Approach to Development vs. the New International Economic Order: The Significance of Third World Industrialization." *World Development* 7, no. 6 (June 1979): 585–606.

Sinha, R., Peter Pearson, Gopal Kadekodi, and Mary Gregory. *Income Distribution, Growth, and Basic Needs in India.* London: Croom Helm, 1979.

Slobodian, Quinn. *Foreign Front: Third World Politics in Sixties West Germany.* Durham, NC: Duke University Press, 2012.

———. *Globalists: The End of Empire and the Birth of Neoliberalism.* Cambridge, MA: Harvard University Press, 2018.

Smil, Vaclav. "Energy in the Twentieth Century: Resources, Conversion, Costs, Uses, and Consequences." *Annual Review of Energy and the Environment* 25 (2000): 21–51.

———. *Energy Transitions: Global and National Perspectives.* 2nd ed. Santa Barbara, CA: Praeger, 2017.

Soll, Jacob. *The Reckoning: Financial Accountability and the Rise and Fall of Nations.* New York: Basic Books, 2014.

Solovey, Mark. "Senator Fred Harris's National Social Science Foundation Proposal: Reconsidering Federal Science Policy, Natural Science–Social Science Relations, and American Liberalism during the 1960s." *ISIS* 103, no. 1 (2012): 54–82.

Speich, Daniel. "Travelling with the GDP through Early Development Economics' History." Working Papers on the Nature of Evidence: How Well Do Facts Travel? No. 33/2008, London School of Economics, Department of Economic History, September 2008.

Speich Chassé, Daniel. "The Roots of the Millennium Development Goals: A Framework for Studying the History of Global Statistics." *Historical Social Research / Historische Sozialforschung* 41, no. 2 (2016): 218–37.

———. "The Use of Global Abstractions: National Income Accounting in the Period of Imperial Decline." *Journal of Global History* 6, no. 1 (2011): 7–28.

Spulber, Nicolas. *Foundations of Soviet Strategy for Economic Growth: Selected Soviet Essays, 1924–1930.* Bloomington: Indiana University Press, 1964.

Srinivas, M. N. "Village Studies, Participant Observation and Social Science Research in India." *Economic and Political Weekly* 10, no. 33/35 (August 1975): 1387–94.

Srinivasan, T. N. "Human Development: A New Paradigm or Reinvention of the Wheel?" *American Economic Review* 84, no. 2 (May 1994): 238–43.

Srinivasan, T. N., and P. K. Bardhan. *Poverty and Income Distribution in India.* Calcutta: Statistical Publishing Society, 1974.

Stanton, Elizabeth A. "Human Development Index: A History." Working Paper No. 127, Political Economy Research Institute, University of Massachusetts Amherst, 2007.

Stapleford, Thomas A. *The Cost of Living in America: A Political History of Economic Statistics, 1880–2000*. Cambridge: Cambridge University Press, 2009.

———. "Defining a 'Living Wage' in America: Transformations in Union Wage Theories, 1870–1930." *Labor History* 49, no. 1 (2008): 1–22.

Staples, Amy L. S. *The Birth of Development: How the World Bank, Food and Agriculture Organization, and the World Health Organization Changed the World, 1945–1965*. Kent, OH: Kent State University Press, 2006.

Steinmetz, George, ed. *The Politics of Method in the Human Sciences: Positivism and Its Epistemological Others*. Durham, NC: Duke University Press, 2005.

Stewart, Frances. *Adjustment and Poverty: Options and Choices*. London: Routledge, 1995.

———. "Changing Perspectives on Inequality and Development." *Studies in Comparative International Development* 51 (2016): 60–80.

Stiglitz, Joseph E., Amartya Sen, and Jean Paul Fitoussi. *Mismeasuring Our Lives: Why GDP Doesn't Add Up*. New York: New Press, 2010.

Strategies for Employment Promotion. Geneva: International Labour Organization, 1973.

Streeten, Paul, Shahid Javed Burki, Mahbub ul Haq, Norman Hicks, and Frances Stewart. *First Things First: Meeting Basic Human Needs in the Developing Countries*. New York: Oxford University Press, 1981.

Strumpel, Burkhard, ed. *Subjective Elements of Well-Being*. Paris: OECD, 1972.

Stuckler, David, Lawrence King, and Martin McKee. "Mass Privatisation and the Post-Communist Mortality Crisis: A Cross-National Analysis." *Lancet* 373, no. 9661 (2009): 399–407.

Studenski, Paul. *The Income of Nations: Theory, Measurement, and Analysis; Past and Present*. New York: New York University Press, 1958.

Sundaram, K. Review of *Measuring the Conditions of India's Poor*, by M. David Morris and M. B. McAlpin. *Indian Economic Review* 18, no. 2 (July–December 1983): 300–305.

Suri, Jeremi. *Power and Protest: Global Revolution and the Rise of Détente*. Cambridge, MA: Harvard University Press, 2003.

———. "The Rise and Fall of an International Counterculture, 1960–1975." *American Historical Review* 114, no. 1 (February 2009): 45–68.

A System of National Accounts and Supporting Tables: Report Prepared by a Group of National Income Experts Appointed by the Secretary-General. New York: United Nations, 1953.

Szenberg, Michael, and Lall Ramrattan, eds. *Reflections of Eminent Economists.* Cheltenham, UK: Edward Elgar, 2004.

Talbeth, John, and Michael Weisdorf. "Genuine Progress Indicator 2.0: Pilot Accounts for the US, Maryland, and City of Baltimore 2012–2014." *Ecological Economics* 142 (2017): 1–11.

Teichman, Judith A. *The Politics of Freeing Markets in Latin America: Chile, Argentina, and Mexico.* Chapel Hill: University of North Carolina Press, 2001.

Ten Year Review and Annual Report 1976. Brighton: Institute of Development Studies, 1977.

Ther, Philipp. *Europe since 1989: A History.* Translated by Charlotte Hughes-Kreutzmüller. Princeton, NJ: Princeton University Press, 2016.

Thompson, William J. *The Soviet Union under Brezhnev.* London: Routledge, 2003.

Tignor, Robert L. *W. Arthur Lewis and the Birth of Development Economics.* Princeton, NJ: Princeton University Press, 2006.

Tilley, Helen. *Africa as a Living Laboratory: Empire, Development, and the Problem of Scientific Knowledge.* Chicago: University of Chicago Press, 2011.

Tinbergen, Jan. *Reshaping the International Order: A Report to the Club of Rome.* New York: E. P. Dutton, 1976.

Tobin, William A. "Studying Society: The Making of 'Recent Social Trends in the United States, 1929–1933." *Theory and Society* 24, no. 4 (August 1995): 537–65.

Tooze, J. Adam. *Crashed: How a Decade of Financial Crises Changed the World.* New York: Viking, 2018.

———. *Statistics and the German State, 1900–1945: The Making of Modern Economic Knowledge.* Cambridge: Cambridge University Press, 2001.

———. "Trouble with Numbers: Statistics, Politics, and History in the Construction of Weimar's Trade Balance, 1918–1924." *American Historical Review* 113, no. 3 (June 2008): 678–700.

Toward a Social Report. Washington, DC: Government Printing Office, 1969.

Toye, John. *Dilemmas of Development: Reflection on the Counter-revolution in Development Theory and Practice.* London: Basil Blackwell, 1987.

Toye, John, and Richard Toye. "The Origins and Interpretation of the Prebisch-Singer Thesis." *History of Political Economy* 35, no. 3 (2003): 437–67.

Unger, Corinna R. *International Development: A Postwar History*. London: Bloomsbury Academic, 2018.

United Nations Conference on Trade and Development. *World Investment Report: Transnational Corporations as Engines of Growth*. New York: United Nations Centre on Transnational Corporations, 1992.

United Nations University International Human Dimensions Programme and United Nations Environment Programme. *Inclusive Wealth Report 2012: Measuring Progress towards Sustainability*. Cambridge: Cambridge University Press, 2012. http://f.cl.ly/items/2C2y022A2j1s472s0T1I/IWR%20Lo -Res.pdf.

van Beusekom, Monica. *Negotiating Development: African Farmers and Colonial Experts at the Office du Niger, 1920–1960*. Oxford: Oxford University Press, 2002.

Van Dusen, Roxann A., ed. *Social Indicators, 1973: A Review Symposium*. Washington, DC: Social Science Research Council, 1974.

Van Hook, James C. *Rebuilding Germany: The Creation of the Social Market Economy, 1945–1957*. Cambridge: Cambridge University Press, 2004.

Vidwans, S. M. "A Critique of Mukherjee's Index of Physical Quality of Life." *Social Indicators Research* 17 (1985): 127–46.

Wallace, Jeremy L. "Juking the Stats? Authoritarian Information Problems in China." *British Journal of Political Science* 46, no. 1 (January 2016): 11–29.

Ward, Barbara, J. D. Runnalls, and Lenore D'Anjou, eds. *The Widening Gap: Development in the 1970s*. New York: Columbia University Press, 1971.

Ward, Michael. *Quantifying the World: UN Ideas and Statistics*. Bloomington: Indiana University Press, 2004.

Waring, Marilyn. *If Women Counted: A New Feminist Economics*. New York: Harper and Row, 1988.

Weems, Robert E. *Desegregating the Dollar: African-American Consumerism in the Twentieth Century*. New York: New York University Press, 1998.

Weller, Christian E., and Angela Hanks. "The Widening Racial Wealth Gap in the United States after the Great Recession." *Forum for Social Economics* 47, no. 2 (2018): 237–52.

Westad, Odd Arne. *The Cold War: A World History*. New York: Basic Books, 2017.

———. *The Global Cold War*. Cambridge: Cambridge University Press, 2005.

Westman, Walter A. "How Much Are Nature's Services Worth?" *Science* 197, no. 4307 (September 2, 1977): 960–64.

Wheatland, Thomas. *The Frankfurt School in Exile*. Minneapolis: University of Minnesota Press, 2009.

Wiles, Peter. "Growth versus Choice." *Economic Journal* 66, no. 262 (June 1956): 244–55.

Williams, Faith M., and Carle C. Zimmerman. *Studies of Family Living in the United States and Other Countries: An Analysis of Material and Method.* Washington, DC: US Department of Agriculture, 1935.

Williams, Kieran. *The Prague Spring and Its Aftermath: Czechoslovak Politics, 1968–1970.* Cambridge: Cambridge University Press, 1997.

Williams, Raymond. *Keywords: A Vocabulary of Culture and Society.* London: Croom Helm, 1976.

Winner, Langdon. *Autonomous Technology: Technics-Out-of-Control.* Cambridge, MA: MIT Press, 1977.

World Bank. *Accelerated Development in Sub-Saharan Africa: An Agenda for Action.* Washington, DC: World Bank, 1981.

World Resources Institute. *World Resources, 1994–1995.* New York: Oxford University Press, 1994.

World Steel Association. *World Steel in Figures 2018.* Brussels: World Steel Association, 2018.

World Trade Organization. *World Trade Statistical Review 2017.* Geneva: World Trade Organization, 2018.

Wrigley, Chris, ed. *Challenges of Labour: Central and Western Europe, 1917–1920.* London: Routledge, 1993.

Yarrow, Andrew L. *Measuring America: How Economic Growth Came to Define American Greatness in the Late Twentieth Century.* Amherst: University of Massachusetts Press, 2010.

Yergin, Daniel. *The Prize: The Epic Quest for Oil, Money, and Power.* New York: Free Press, 2008.

Young, Alden. *Transforming Sudan: Decolonization, Economic Development, and State Formation.* New York: Cambridge University Press, 2018.

Zachariah, Benjamin. *Developing India: An Intellectual and Social History, c. 1930–50.* New Delhi: Oxford University Press, 2005.

Zubok, Vladislav. *A Failed Empire: The Soviet Union in the Cold War from Stalin to Gorbachev.* Chapel Hill: University of North Carolina Press, 2007.

Zucman, Gabriel. *The Hidden Wealth of Nations.* Chicago: University of Chicago Press, 2015.

Index

Page numbers in italics refer to figures.

foreign capital, 50–51

fossil fuels, 4, 8, 76, 107–9, 159–60.
 See also climate change

France, 14–15, 29–30, 33, 44, 64, 116,
 132, 142, 202

Franchini, G., 92

Frank, Andre Gunder, 91

Frankel, Sally Herbert, 52–56, 71,
 91, 175

Frankfurt School, 81

free trade, 32, 56, 166, 176

French Institute of Sociology, 23

French physiocrats, 16

Friedan, Betty, 83–84

Friedman, Milton, 70, 97

Frisch, Ragnar, 70

Fundación Bariloche, 133

Galbraith, John Kenneth, 82, 118, 120

Gallup polling company, 189

gender, 1, 6, 49, 65, 83–84, 138–39,
 147, 150–59, 191. *See also* sexism;
 women's labor

General Agreement on Tariffs and
 Trade (GATT), 37, 170, 175–76

Genuine Progress Indicator (GPI),
 167, 186

George Mason University, 171

Georgescu-Roegen, Nicholas, 2, 98,
 100–101, 117–18, 136, 159–61, 195–
 97, 204, 237n129, 249n115

Germany, 15, 29, 39, 202

Getachew, Adom, 131

Ghana, 54, 56, 62, 68, 150–51

Giffen, Sir Robert, 17

glasnost, 177

globalization, 12–13, 28–31, 37, 63–
 70, 115, 122, 130, 164, 179–83, 200

Global South, 7, 106, 173–76, 191,
 203. *See also* North-South conflicts

GNP growth: benefits of, 135;
 embrace of, 44, 59; pursuit of, 110

Gold Coast, 54, 56, 62

gold standard, 37, 116

Good Housekeeping, 84

Gorbachev, Mikhail, 87, 177

Gordon, Robert, 201

Goswami, Manu, 198

Grant, James, 146

Great Depression, 3, 25–33, 38, 40,
 96, 199

Great Leap Forward, 66

great-power politics, 38

great recession of 2007–9, 9, 168, 197

green GDP estimates, 188

Green New Deal, 258n38

Griffin, Keith, 149

Gronau, Reuben, 155

gross domestic product (GDP), 160,
 168, 180, 184–85, 188, 195, 203–6,
 213n3

gross national happiness, 189

gross national product (GNP): and
 the Cold War, 67; creation of, 6,
 33–39, 55, 96, 162, 180, 221n101;
 critiques of, 85, 101, 137, 167–68,
 186, 206; dominance of, 1–2, 5, 39,
 42, 62, 68, 70, 82, 93, 195, 223n4,
 236n101; and GDP, 213n3; as a
 narrative, 70; and overall economic health, 35; and population, 112; and sovereignty, 59; and
 trickle-down effects, 58. *See also*
 growth paradigm

Group of 7 (G-7), 129, 169

Group of 77 (G-77), 128–29